MURDEROUS WOMEN

PAUL HESLOP

MURDEROUS WOMEN

FROM SARAH DAZLEY TO RUTH ELLIS

The History Press

'Truth will come to light; murder cannot be hid long.'

William Shakespeare, *The Merchant of Venice*

First published 2009

The History Press
The Mill, Brimscombe Port
Stroud, Gloucestershire, GL5 2QG
www.thehistorypress.co.uk

British Library Cataloguing in Publication Data.
A catalogue record for this book is available from the British Library.

ISBN 978 0 7509 5081 7
Typesetting and origination by The History Press
Printed in Great Britain

Contents

Foreword

As a former colleague and personal friend of Paul Heslop for forty years, there is no one better qualified to focus on the subject of murderous women.

A few years ago I accompanied Paul to the former home of multiple killer Mary Anne Cotton in West Auckland, when he was researching the case for a television documentary. He identified the house from old photographs, and knocked at the door. The current occupant had scant knowledge of the house's history (maybe just as well). However, immediately on entry Paul began to immerse himself into the atmosphere of this simple, small terraced dwelling, wondering what thoughts would have flickered through Mary Anne Cotton's mind when she looked out of the front window as she viewed the tranquillity of village life beyond the nightmares within.

In an age where 'cold case' examination of old crimes has become the genre of modern times, with forensic advances accelerating, we still need the questioning minds of 'detectives' such as Paul to disentangle the tight knots of justice.

His ability to professionally and thoroughly evaluate events through critical research unravels both the history and mystery of each case, which are presented in an absorbing way. His verdicts at the termination of each chapter are, on occasions, controversial, but they spring from a wealth of investigative experience and common sense.

The evidence is presented to the reader in Paul's unique style, which captures some of the essence I felt in the house where Mary Anne Cotton murdered her stepson. *Murderous Women* is an illuminating read, and, given that the original verdicts are recorded as fact, can we really be certain that justice has been served in every case 'without a scintilla of doubt'?

Arthur McKenzie, 2009

Arthur McKenzie was a career detective with Northumbria Police, whose service included investigating corruption in Hong Kong. Over the past thirty years he has become an established author, playwright, television scriptwriter, radio pundit and journalist. His stage plays include *The Boilerhunters*, which also featured on BBC Radio Four's *Saturday Night Theatre*, *Man in a Bottle*, *My Son's on the Force*, *Pickets and Pigs* and *Cuddy's Miles*. His television credits include *The Bill*, *Harry*, *Casualty*, *Spender* and *Wycliffe*, as well as many documentaries.

Acknowledgements

The author wishes to thank staff at the County Archives and Record Offices at: Bedford, Dumfries, Lincoln, Durham, Taunton, Reading, Hertford, Barnsley, and Airdrie; the Mitchell Library, Glasgow; the Central Resources Library, Hatfield; the British Newspaper Library, Colindale. Also Ken Wells, curator at Thames Valley Police Museum, for permission to use the images in the Amelia Dyer case.

Please note that in exceptional circumstances some images may have been reproduced without sanction of the original publisher, but only after exhausting all means of identifying them.

Finally, please note that the names of counties appear as they were known before the Local Government reforms in 1974 and 1975.

About the Author

Paul Heslop is a retired police officer with over thirty years' service with Northumbria Police and Hertfordshire Constabulary. He learned basic policing skills on the streets of Newcastle upon Tyne, when contact with the public was vital, and street supervision by sergeants and inspectors was the rule. He became a 'career detective', serving in CID and Regional Crime Squads in both forces, the latter including the investigation into serious crime in London and the Home Counties. He retired in 1995. Since then his writing career includes features for regional newspapers and magazines on subjects including, health and safety, country walking, local history and true crime. His published works also include *Cumbria Murders* (Sutton Publishing, 2007). He lives in Cumbria with his wife, Kate.

A Public Execution in Kent, 1867

She had told her sister the day before the crime that she would do it. 'The child shall not go back to her father's house. I will take her out into the fields and put her into a ditch and drown her.' The child was her stepdaughter, 11-year-old Louise, her husband's 'bastard', as she described her. On Saturday 25 August 1867, when visiting her parents at New Romney, she had taken Louise for a walk on the Kent marshes, a place of 'shallow and stagnant ditches, varying in depth and sometimes furnished with sluices'. It was getting dark when they left, and at ten o'clock she returned without the child.

'Where is Louise?' her mother asked.

'Oh, mother,' she replied, 'two horses frightened us into a ditch. I went in after her and tried to get her out.' Her husband saw her skirts were wet. Neither he nor her mother was satisfied with her story, and the police were called.

She told Constable Aspinall, 'You will find the child just above Cobb's Bridge.'

The policeman searched and found Louise. She was lying in a ditch, in fourteen inches of water. A child of four or five could have scrambled out, yet death was due to drowning. At the Spring Assizes at Maidstone the following March, the jury took just twelve minutes to return a guilty verdict. Justice Byles told her, 'You have been convicted of the murder of this poor child. The sentence is that you be taken to the place from whence you came, and from thence to a place of execution, and there hanged by the neck until you are dead. And may the Lord have mercy on your soul.'

In the condemned cell in Maidstone Gaol, Frances Kidder confessed to the crime, but denied it was premeditated. On the day of reckoning, 2 April 1868, she walked with a firm step to the scaffold. Steady hands helped her to the drop, where she was supported by two warders, the proceedings watched by a crowd of 2,000 or so. The scaffold was draped with a black cloth, so that when she fell nothing would be seen of her except her head. Before the cap was put over her face she smiled and said, 'Lord Jesus, forgive me.' When Calcraft pulled the bolt, she struggled before life ceased.

The *Maidstone and Kentish Journal* reported that the crowd was 'particularly orderly', with little of the 'coarseness and brutal joking' that too often prevailed at executions. Frances Kidder, aged 25, was the last woman to be publicly hanged in Britain.

1

A Denial of Guilt

Sarah Dazley, Bedfordshire, 1843

'In consequence of various rumours being spread that the deceased had come to an unfair death, the coroner for Bedfordshire, Ezra Eagles Esq., has ordered the body to be disinterred.' So reported the *Bedford Mercury and Huntingdon Express* concerning the death of William Dazley. 'The most conclusive evidence has been obtained,' reported the newspaper, 'about which we are requested not to give any clue until the inquest has found a verdict, as justice might be perverted by premature publicity and the supposed guilty party having absconded.'

It was almost five months, since 3 November 1842 to be precise, that William Dazley was buried in the churchyard at Wrestlingworth. And now they were digging him up. But the residents of Wrestlingworth were far from mystified as to the 'conclusive evidence', and they knew perfectly well who the 'supposed guilty party' was: the deceased's flirtatious wife, Sarah.

On 27 March 1843, William Dazley's exhumed remains were placed in the aisle of Wrestlingworth Parish Church, the coffin lid was removed and the body, 'in a fair state of preservation', was formally identified. Two surgeons, Isaac Hurst and George Dixon Hedley, then commenced a port-mortem examination. They removed the whole of the alimentary canal – both the throat and the intestines – which they placed into a stone jar and sent to Bedford Infirmary for analysis. The inquest, held at the Chequers Inn, was then adjourned pending the result.

But what had alerted the authorities to possible foul play? Rumours that Dazley's wife, Sarah, had poisoned him, had reached the ears of the local policeman, PC Forester. PC Forester had told the chairman of the Quarter Sessions, Francis Pym, who in turn had instructed the coroner to hold the inquest. Rumours also reached the ears of Sarah herself, who fled, taking the road to London with a man called Samuel Stebbing.

The fleeing Sarah went to the house of one of her brothers, Edward Reynolds. He wrote to another brother, John, at Potton near Wrestlingworth, saying, 'Sarah has arrived safe and well'. John Reynolds must have been an upstanding citizen, for he told the police. Superintendent Blunden of Biggleswade was dispatched to London, and detained Sarah at her brother's house.

'I know they said I murdered my husband,' said Sarah, 'but they can't prove I bought the poison, or gave him anything but what I bought of the doctor. They say the last thing I gave him was out of a teacup, but that is not true, for I gave him some pills. If you had not come for me I should have given myself up, for I am sorry I done it.' Those last six words seem damning, but it would be a surprise if Sarah ever admitted she uttered them.

In the meantime, the coroner was told that analysis of William Dazley's alimentary canal had revealed white arsenic 'in considerable quantity'.

Sarah Dazley had to be taken back to Wrestlingworth, but first she had to appear before the Lord Mayor of London, suspected by now of having murdered two husbands and her own child. Sarah, speaking with assuredness, readily admitted her identity, saying the moment she had heard there were suspicions she had resolved to return to Bedfordshire to clear her character.

'How long were you married to your first husband?' the Lord Mayor asked.

'Six years.'

'Your second husband?'

'Two years and nineteen days.'

'How old was your child when it died?'

'Ten months.'

'Why did you run away when the inquest was summoned?'

'I did not run away. I came to London to look for a situation, because the parish refused to do anything for me.'

His lordship informed Sarah he had been told she was to be married again, that banns had been read, but cancelled. 'No, no such thing,' she lied (they had been read by the Revd Twiss on 5 February).

Inspector Woodroffe, presenting the case, declared his lordship's information was correct, saying that, as Mrs Dazley and the person she was going to marry were going to church, a man who was acquainted with the husband-to-be had said, 'You are not going to marry that she-devil who has already murdered two husbands and her child.'

The husband-to-be, George Waldock, promptly withdrew the banns. There can be little wonder that the Lord Mayor believed Dazley had a case to answer, and she was given over to the custody of Superintendent Blunden. En route to Wrestlingworth they stayed overnight at the Spread Eagle Inn, Biggleswade. Two women residents at the Spread Eagle, Mary Ann Knibbs and Fanny Simmons, were instructed by Blunden to sleep with her that night. Their testimonies, concerning what she allegedly told them, would weigh heavily against her at her trial.

The following day the inquest into the death of William Dazley was resumed. Sarah Dazley was present and 'much affected', her assuredness having deserted her.

Elizabeth Dazley, William Dazley's mother, told the court that her son had taken ill one Sunday the previous October and had died the following Sunday.

Ann Mead, a 14-year-old orphan, had lived in Wrestlingworth with the Dazleys until she became ill on the Wednesday before William Dazley died. Ann said she had seen Sarah making three pills on the Tuesday. She made them in a blue saucer and wrapped them in a piece of newspaper. Sarah asked William to take the pills, but he would not. After Sarah had gone out, Ann tied to persuade him, believing they would make him better. She swallowed one herself, saying, 'See me take one.' William Dazley, presumably reassured, then swallowed one of the pills. After about quarter of an hour Ann became ill. She was sick, suffering from aching in her chest and throat and was ill for the next three days until she left the house, never to return. Dazley became more ill than he had been before.

Mary Carver, a local woman, had gone with Sarah to the house of Mr Sandel, the local doctor, that Wednesday morning. Sarah asked Sandel to give her a few pills, as her husband would not take his medicine. Sandel said he would send him three resting pills, which he put into a box. On the way home Mrs Carver saw Sarah throw the pills into a ditch, and take three others from her pocket and put them into the box, saying they would do her husband 'more good'. Mary Carver witnessed the painful wretchings of both Ann Mead and William Dazley. Ann Mead was fortunate to survive.

On 23 October, Sandel was called by a tearful Sarah to the Dazley household. He found William to be 'under severe sickness', complaining of irritation to stomach and bowels. He prescribed a saline medicine to allay irritation. The following Tuesday he called again and prescribed further treatment, after which he seemed to get better. Then, suddenly, he learned that Dazley was dead. Sandel was so surprised he asked Sarah for permission to carry out a post-mortem examination on her late husband, but both she and William's mother refused. When asked by a member of the inquest jury about prescribing pills for William Dazley, Sandel said he did not recall prescribing pills (except the resting pills, made of opium), but he had prescribed powder, and he explained precisely what it was. He was adamant the powder was not white in colour.

One wonders about Sarah Dazley's feelings when, at the inquest, she heard the gruesome details of the post-mortem examination on her late husband, given by the surgeon, George Dixon Hedley.

From the stomach, 2½ ounces of 'dirty brown fluid' was poured into a glass and a white powder subsided at the bottom. More white powder was found in the gullet and intestines. In the lower part of the small intestine the surgeon found roundworms, 'fresh and un-decomposed'. He boiled some of the particles of white powder in distilled water. One portion of the resulting liquid was 'introduced' into a glass vessel called a Marsh's Apparatus, with distilled water, sulphuric acid and a piece of zinc, and the gas formed by this was set on fire. A piece of plate glass was held over the flame, upon which a ring of metallic arsenic was deposited. More experiments followed, all tests combining to prove the white powder to be arsenic.

'Are you of opinion enough to cause death?' the coroner asked.

'Certainly,' Hedley replied. 'I have no doubt the deceased died from the effect of arsenic. I also believe the extraordinary preservation of the internal parts of the body has resulted from arsenic.' He might have added, 'sufficiently enough for worms to thrive five months after the body was buried.' The inquest jury decided that 'William Dazley died from the effects of arsenic administered to him with a guilty knowledge by Sarah Dazley'. That amounted to wilful murder, said the coroner. Sarah was taken to Bedford Gaol to await trial. It was a place she was familiar with, having visited her father there when she was a little girl.

Sarah Dazley was born Sarah Reynolds at Potton, Bedfordshire, about 1815. Her father, Philip, was the village barber and rat catcher. He worked hard for a living, but nonetheless fell into debt, even squandering the small fortune left to him by his father. He ended up in Bedford Gaol where he contracted consumption. He died in 1824.

In 1835, Sarah, aged 19, married Simeon Mead of nearby Tadlow, Cambridgeshire. The couple went to live in Wrestlingworth. They had a son, Jonas. The marriage lasted only five years, for Simeon died on 10 June 1840, aged only 24. That October, Sarah married William Dazley. The following month, her son, little Jonas Mead, was dead; he was just nine months old. Father and son had died barely six months apart.

In July 1842, when Sarah was married to William Dazley, she had visited the house of George Waldock, a 'rustic labourer'.

'How do you like married life?' Waldock asked her.

'Very well,' replied Sarah, adding that she had a good husband, but thought he would soon be in the churchyard.

'Why so?' asked Waldock.

'I can't help thinking so,' she replied.

In February 1843, four months after William Dazley's death, Elizabeth Dazley, his mother, visited Simeon Mead's mother, and they spoke of the loss of their sons. Mrs Dazley said she had 'no doubt' that both had been poisoned by her daughter-in-law. Mrs Mead was aghast.

'Poisoned?' she exclaimed, 'do you think so?'

'Yes,' replied Mrs Dazley, 'I know Sarah gave your son some quicksilver (mercury) among some sliced onion.' Mrs Mead knew her son was partial to sliced onion, so this unexpected revelation would have struck a cord. She might have wondered why Mrs Dazley had not said so before.

With William Dazley's untimely death attributed to poisoning by arsenic, it was hardly surprising that the coroner ordered the exhumation of the bodies of Simeon and Jonas Mead. On 20 April 1843, there was an inquest into their deaths.

Keziah Mead, Simeon's mother, spoke of her son complaining about being ill. He was unwell for two weeks, then became worse on the Sunday before he died, when he complained about his throat. Betsy Mead, his sister, said her brother had complained about his chest, and said that there was white froth running from his mouth. Betsy had frequently heard Sarah say that she wished he were dead. They quarrelled frequently, and she had heard Sarah say, 'Damn you, I wish you had never come near me.' Hannah Darts said she had been with Simeon the night before he died, when he complained about his throat and mouth and was in great pain; Elizabeth Dazley (William's mother) said that Simeon had complained of pains in his throat and mouth. She said she had seen Simeon and Sarah quarrelling over a shilling; he had wanted it and had knocked her down and taken it. She had later heard Sarah declare, 'Damn him, I'll poison him but what I'll get rid of him.'

Noah Darts, a carpenter, had made the coffins for both father and son. He said they had been buried in the same churchyard at Tadlow, in separate graves. He was able to identify Simeon Mead's coffin, upon which he had affixed a plate bearing the inscription 'S.M. aged 24'. No one could identify Simeon Mead's body, of which only the skeleton remained. It was not possible to establish whether or not he had been poisoned.

The inquest was then opened into the death of 9 month old Jonas. Betsy Mead, the child's aunt, said Jonas was not a sickly child. She had heard his mother, Sarah, say to him, 'I wish you were dead,' several times, but had thought nothing of it. Keziah, Jonas's grandmother, saw nothing amiss with him save for a bad cough. Elizabeth Dazley said Sarah was 'a brute of a mother who never washed the child or kept it clean'.

Sarah Morley saw Jonas just before he died. Sarah had brought him to her cottage, saying he was 'very ill', and she was off to Potton to see if she could get anything for him from the doctor. Leaving the little boy with Mrs Morley, Sarah returned two hours later with three powders, saying she had to give one to Jonas when she got home. The child was 'wonderfully ill', said Mrs Morley. Sarah took the child home, and returned one and a half hours later when she said Jonas was 'dead and laid out'. If the testimony of witnesses was not damning enough, the result of the post-mortem examination most certainly was, as George Hedley explained.

Jonas's body, though decomposed, was nevertheless in a 'state of preservation suitable for examination'. Hedley found metallic arsenic in the belly, enough to kill. Having heard the evidence on father and son, Simeon and Jonas Mead, the jury's verdict on the former was that he died on 10 June 1840, after 'an illness', and that Jonas had 'died from arsenic administered to him with guilty knowledge by his mother, Sarah Dazley'. Hearing the verdict on the death of Jonas, the crowd outside was reportedly showing 'strong feelings' against Mrs Dazley. It was hardly surprising.

Sarah Dazley stood trial at Bedford Assizes that July. Judge Baron Alderson presided. The courtroom was packed to 'an almost suffocating degree'. Dazley was indicted with murdering both her husbands and Jonas Mead, her son, but the charge of murdering Simeon Mead was 'ignored', and that of Jonas set aside. She was tried for the murder of William Dazley only, which she denied. The prosecution would have little difficulty in proving William Dazley was murdered; it would be another matter to prove that the person responsible was his wife.

Mr Prendergast, prosecuting counsel, said Dazley's wife attended William during his illness. No medicine was given to him but by her, he said, and she was in possession of arsenic when his illness commenced, on Sunday 23 October 1842. Elizabeth Dazley gave a full account of her visits to the Dazley household during her son's week-long illness. She had visited him every day. On the Sunday she heard him complain of a pain in the stomach. On Monday morning he was vomiting, and he was sick again on Tuesday. Wednesday morning he appeared a little better, but was vomiting again later that same day, when he appeared worse. He complained of pain in the bowels and she laid a bran poultice on his stomach. He complained of heat in the throat and she put three leeches on it. 'They drew, and he bled profusely.' She remained with her son all night Wednesday. William vomited into a pot, which she emptied into some straw in the front yard. The consequences of this were as damning as the testimony of any witness. Ebenezer Gurry, a neighbour, kept a pig in the yard. It was a healthy pig, about ten weeks old. On the morning after Mrs Dazley emptied the pot in the yard, he found the pig dead, 'swelled like a bladder'.

On Thursday morning William Dazley was more cheerful, although still vomiting; on Friday morning he was the same. On Saturday, about two o'clock, he got out of bed for an hour and by six o'clock he was talking quite cheerfully. But at one o'clock on the Sunday morning, when his mother visited, she found him in severe pain. He died at half past six. This was the harrowing account of a mother who attended her dying son for a whole week as his intestines succumbed to the effects of arsenic. There was no hospital, no close treatment by doctors, only the scant attention by the local surgeon who had no hope of saving his patient.

Mary Carver, who saw Sarah Dazley take three of Sandel's pills from their box and throw them into a ditch, told the court that she saw Dazley replace them with three pills of her own, which she took from a piece of newspaper she carried in her pocket, saying they would 'do him the most good'.

William Sandel, the surgeon, said he found Dazley complaining of pain in the stomach, sickness and retching. He thought it was a common irritation of the stomach and that he should have saline composed of carbonate of soda and tartaric acid for effervescing. He later sent an aperient (laxative) powder, and found Dazley better by the Wednesday, but the following Monday he heard he was dead. Sandel did not keep arsenic, and he never prescribed any white powder. He never suspected William Dazley had been poisoned.

William Dazley's two brothers were with him throughout his last night and when he died. John Dazley sat up with him, and saw Sarah put some white powder into a cup, along with some water, which she stirred with a spoon. 'She took it from a paper at the bedside,' he said, telling her husband to drink it, and that he would soon be 'better or worse'. William drank it down, then vomited and complained of pain. Mr O'Malley, defending, asked him about the light. 'It was candle-light,' said John Dazley, 'and the candle was half burnt out.' It stood on the table where the white powder was, about 2ft from the bed. The light was on the same side she stood at, so he could see the cup.

Gilbert Dazley, the other brother, saw Sarah with white powder, which 'she took from her bosom'. The powder was wrapped in paper. She told her husband if it 'operated right' he would soon be better, if it 'operated wrong' he would soon be dead. Mr Sandel had said so. She put the powder into a teacup and poured water from a teapot into it. Her husband was unwilling to drink it at first, but eventually did so. He began retching and went to his room about 4 a.m. and stayed there until he died.

Mr J. Burnham, a chemist, knew Sarah Dazley as someone who 'had been in the habit' of coming back and forward as a customer. He recalled selling her one pennyworth of arsenic 'in the fall of last year'. She told him she had wanted to poison some rats and mice.

The testimonies of the two women who slept with Sarah at the Spread Eagle Inn, Biggleswade, were now given. Mary Ann Knibbs and Fanny Simmons confirmed they were asked to sleep with Sarah 'by the constable' (Superintendent Blunden). Their testimonies were conveniently identical. 'Get into bed and I'll tell you all about it,' Sarah was alleged to have told them. They said Sarah told them that her husband had taken ill and that, at the request of his mother, she had gone to the doctor's. She hadn't thrown any pills away, as Mary Carver had said.

Simmons told Sarah it was reported that she had said that she would have 'seven husbands in seven years'. Sarah had replied, 'I did not say so. I said I would have seven husbands in ten years'. According to the women, she added, 'No one knows where I bought the poison. No one saw me give it to him.' Damning indeed – if she said so.

George Dixon Hedley reiterated the findings of his post-mortem examination, giving specifics: 'We found at least a drachm of arsenic in the body.' This was more than enough to kill. 'Arsenic is not readily thrown out when vomiting,' he explained, which accounts for it remaining in William Dazley's insides, even when he was being sick. He would not have expected Dazley to live two or three days 'after the contents of the bowels had escaped into the cavity'.

Sarah Dazley had no right to testify in her own defence. The law then presumed that anyone charged with a crime would say anything to secure acquittal and could not therefore be relied upon to tell the truth. No witness was called on her behalf. Instead, Mr O'Malley, her counsel, rose and told the jury that the case against Dazley was one built of prejudice. There had been rumours, he said, that had circulated 'far and wide'. Stories had been told about the crime, presuming she was guilty. Justice could only be done by juries acting contrary to prejudices.

'Expressions Mrs Dazley had used had been raked together, considerably coloured and presented to the jury as material evidence to prove her guilt,' he said. Her conduct was of the highest character, and there was no circumstance of her married life showing any malice or evil disposition towards her husband. It might be assumed they were a loving couple. Referring to their quarrelling, he asked, 'Where are the wives who would not sometimes in the lightness of their hearts indulge in frivolities?' He meant, of course, that all married couples quarrelled, and sometimes said 'I wish you were dead', without meaning it.

Could the jury believe the prisoner guilty? O'Malley asked. William Dazley is taken ill one Sunday. He dies the next. Does the prisoner seek opportunity to poison him? She sends for his relations and friends. For what? To witness her guilt? She sends for the doctor, who would have been most capable of discovering poison. She sends for him twice again, and goes once herself. Would a guilty person have done so? Crime seeks seclusion, but she sought to make it public. He drew attention to the administration of powder and pills, pointing out that others were always present.

William Dazley died by taking arsenic. But did his wife have arsenic in her possession? Mr Burnham, the chemist, said he sold her arsenic. Yet there was no entry of the sale. As to the two brothers who sat by candlelight, could they really have seen the colour of the powder they saw Sarah administer? There was a discrepancy: one swore the powder was lying at the bedside, the other that she took it from her bosom. And suppose arsenic was in the house. It was not improbable that in the hurry and confusion of the moment, she might have picked it up by mistake, and poisoned her husband by accident. What motive was there? It had not been shown that there was an attachment to any other man. As to her refusal to allow Mr Sandel to examine her husband's body, it was natural for any wife to refuse consent. Dazley's mother had refused too.

The judge told the jury, 'The questions to consider were: Did William Dazley die from the effects of poison administered to him by someone? And was the poison wilfully administered?' Mr Sandel had no arsenic in his shop, so he could not have made the mistake of giving it to Mrs Dazley. As to there being no record of the purchase of arsenic, would every 'one pennyworth' sold be recorded? Several people said powder had been given by Mrs Dazley to her husband, even if there were discrepancies in their evidence. He added, 'You must look for the truth, dreading not the consequences.' In other words, the jury must not take into account the fate of Mrs Dazley if they should find her guilty; their verdict was all that mattered. After only half an hour they returned a guilty verdict.

An 'awful silence' prevailed as the judge fixed his eyes on the woman in the dock. The silence continued for some time, so that the clerk thought the judge must somehow have missed the verdict. Finally, his lordship spoke. 'Sarah Dazley, you have been tried and found guilty of a most atrocious crime, the murder of your husband. I regret ...' Then he was overcome, and remained silent awhile with his face in his hands before continuing, 'I regret that the murder of your husband is not the only murder you have been guilty of. I allude to this to soften your hard and impenitent heart ...' Sarah Dazley now broke down and wept. 'To murder the man you love and cherish is a crime truly appalling,' said his lordship, 'but to lay your murderous hand on your own helpless babe, to take away the life of your only child is a crime we have no language to express. Though your guilt is great and your time is short, there is everything to encourage you to fall at the footstool of your offended Maker and plead for pardon. It now only remains for me to pass the awful sentence of the law upon you, Sarah Dazley, that you be taken from this place to the gaol whence you came, and that you be hanged by the neck until you be dead, and that your body be buried within the precincts of the gaol. And may God have mercy upon your soul.'

Sarah Dazley, overcome as she was, exclaimed simply, 'I am not guilty!'

Post-Trial

It was common for convicted persons who had been sentenced to death, who had earlier denied their crime, to confess before execution. Sarah Dazley was convicted of murdering her second husband, suspected but not tried of murdering her first as well as their baby, and accused by the judge of murdering the latter. But she never confessed to anything. Instead, she hoped for a reprieve, based on her apparent belief that 'hanging was not so frequent as formerly'. She cited a case where, she said, a woman called Johnson, convicted of murdering her children some years before at Cambridge, was pardoned even as she ascended the gallows. If she thought she might yet escape the noose, based on these grounds, it was little wonder she never confessed.

Far from showing repentance, Dazley made a statement in which she accused her husband, William, of murdering her child, Jonas, and that he took the arsenic himself through remorse, or maybe to cause her suffering by being falsely charged with his murder and hanged. If she really believed that, why didn't she urge her defence to say so at her trial?

The executioner arrived from London, 'a person dressed in a suit of black, recognised as the fearful extinguisher of criminal life'. One newspaper reported:

> We never saw Bedford in such a state of excitement. On no occasion have so many women been visible in the streets. Carriages of all descriptions, from a gentleman's to a chimney sweep's cart, are arriving, pouring in new population, amongst whom is an immense proportion of the abandoned of both sexes on the lookout for a subject to victimise.

Public hangings were about more than witnessing the dispensation of justice. They were also an excuse for a shindig, a get-together of the masses, a reason to drink and sing and pick pockets. They were, in truth, a shameful episode in history. People invented ballads about the condemned, and the crowds sang along, fuelled by alcohol as the day wore on and long after the accused had hanged. Of Dazley's execution, the *Northamptonshire Mercury* reported that 'Vagabonds of both sexes were bawling out the last dying speech and confession of the woman of three murders, when in truth she did not acknowledge one.'

There were conflicting accounts of the execution of Sarah Dazley. In one:

> The procession appeared on the top of the gaol porch at twelve o'clock. The chaplain read prayers, in which the prisoner fervently joined. At the conclusion she was asked if she had anything to confess. 'No,' she replied, 'if I confess to the crime I shall die with a lie in my mouth.' She ascended the ladder to the drop, where the executioner placed a man's nightcap over her head and face, then the rope about her neck, which he fastened to the beam above. Then the bolts were drawn. A shriek from the crowd burst forth as the culprit fell, her arms pinioned and her hands clasped. She heaved her bosom heavily several times, her body quivered and she again heaved her bosom, more feebly than before and hung dead till one o'clock when her body was taken down and carried into the gaol ...

In another account, Dazley, when asked if she had anything to confess, replied, simply, 'I have nothing to say.' After the service was read she shook hands with the minister and gaoler and said, 'God bless you,' before ascending to the platform, saying, 'Lord have mercy on my soul,' which she continued to repeat during preparations by the executioner and until the bolts were drawn and she was 'launched into eternity'.

Whichever account is correct, there would be no doubt that many would be shocked at the hanging of someone who had not confessed. A confession justified an execution; no confession left that ray of doubt. Twelve thousand people watched Sarah Dazley hang. After the deed they drank their fill, and sang verses allegedly written by Dazley herself, in reality penned by a local printer. A public hanging was a day of profit for many, but surely a day of loss for decency and justice itself.

Author's Verdict

There can be no doubt that William Dazley and little Jonas Mead were murdered by means of arsenic poisoning. But was the culprit Sarah Dazley? There was no evidence that it was she who poisoned Jonas; no person saw her administer anything to him. Nor was there any proof that she administered poison to her first husband, Simeon Mead, nor indeed that he was poisoned at all. But she poisoned

William, at least her relatives and neighbours would have said so, for the evidence of 'rumour' had her convicted before she was even arrested, let alone tried.

There is much cause to believe that a jury sitting somewhere other than in Bedfordshire should have heard this case; twelve men good and true who had never heard of Sarah Dazley and the gossip that abounded in the village community of Wrestlingworth and nearby. Then she might have had a more impartial hearing by people who could have drawn their own conclusions, taken from the evidence rather than what they heard on the grapevine.

That said, there was much to condemn her. Throwing away pills and substituting them with her own; administering white powder, even in front of witnesses; her readiness to marry before her late husbands were scarcely cold in their graves; fleeing to London when she heard of the impending disinterment and forthcoming inquest into the death of her second husband. Buying arsenic was commonplace then, so its purchase at the chemist's was not that significant, except that it proved she had it.

Her counsel said, 'It had not been shown that there was an attachment to any other man.' Any other man? There was always another man. If she killed Simeon Mead, was it because he knocked her down, or because she was fed up with one husband and wanted another? If she killed Jonas, was it because he was in the way so soon after she acquired another husband? Did she kill William Dazley because she was fed up with him, and killing had become easy? George Waldock may count himself to be a lucky fellow indeed, for he would surely have been next.

2

Premeditated Murder

Maria Manning, Bermondsey, London, 1849

Patrick O'Connor, an Irishman, was a customs officer. He lived at Greenwood Street, Mile End, and his life was routinely spent between his lodgings, his place of work at London Docks and visiting the house of Frederick and Maria Manning at 3 Miniver Place, Bermondsey. He was a popular chap, and when he apparently disappeared, not having been seen since Thursday 9 August, some of his workmates made it their business to enquire about his welfare. There was one obvious place to start their enquiries, and on Sunday 12 August, William Keating and David Graham came knocking on the Mannings' door.

Keating and Graham knew O'Connor had planned to visit the Mannings on the Thursday, as at about 4.45 p.m. that day, they had chanced upon him at the end of London Bridge and he had showed them an invitation from Mrs Manning to dine with them that very evening. O'Connor had walked off in the direction of Miniver Place and had not been seen or heard of since.

When Mrs Manning opened the door, Keating asked her if O'Connor had dined with her that Thursday evening. He had not, she replied. He asked her if she had been to his lodgings since then. She had called at his lodgings that evening, she said, to enquire after his health, as he had been at her house on the *Wednesday* evening when he had not been well. That was strange, remarked Keating, as he had seen Mr O'Connor at the end of London Bridge on the Thursday, going towards her house. Could they speak to Mr Manning, they asked? Alas, no, she said, as her husband was out, possibly 'gone to church'.

The next day, William Flynn, another customs officer, called at 3 Miniver Place, in company with a plain clothes policeman, PC James Burton. He asked if she or her husband had heard anything of Mr O'Connor?

'No,' replied Mrs Manning, adding that Mr Keating and another man had seen him on London Bridge on the 9th. She described Mr O'Connor as 'fickle-minded', saying he often called at her home for a minute or two and suddenly 'jumped up' and went away. 'Poor Mr O'Connor,' she added, 'he was the best friend I had in London.' At this point Flynn fancied Mrs Manning's 'countenance changed', and that she turned pale. Later, Flynn went to O'Connor's lodgings where he knew O'Connor kept money in a cashbox in his bedroom. He forced the cashbox open, finding a few memorandums, but no money.

Poor Mr O'Connor indeed! This remark, together with the certainty that Patrick O'Connor would not simply disappear, was good cause to suspect foul play, and on 17 August, by which time the Mannings themselves had disappeared, the police were at the door of 3 Miniver Place. Constables Barnes and Burton, having obtained the key from the landlord, began searching for clues that would shed some light on O'Connor's disappearance. They looked through all six rooms and dug up the garden, but found nothing. They didn't give up though, and just as well, for their endeavours would lead them to the grim discovery of his body, and the ensuing pursuit of two murderers, the account of which would grip the nation.

In the kitchen, PC Barnes noticed a damp mark between two of the flagstones. The stones were square-shaped and heavy. The policemen prised them up, finding wet mortar underneath. They dug at the earth below, and about twelve inches down they saw some pieces of rag. 'There's the toe of a man!' exclaimed Barnes. They dug again, and unearthed a man's naked body. It was lying face down, with the legs drawn back and tied to the haunches with strong cord. The body was embedded in quicklime. They sent for Mr Lockwood, a surgeon.

Lockwood went to the house, where he saw the body, still in the hole. He removed a set of false teeth from the dead man's mouth. The constables then moved the body to the front kitchen, where Lockwood examined it and found a bullet inside the head, which had apparently passed through the right eye. There were extensive fractures to the back of the head, from which he extracted sixteen pieces of bone. The fractures might have been caused by being struck with a crowbar-like instrument.

Few people had false teeth in the mid-nineteenth century. They were relevant, therefore, for identification purposes, at least at first. The facts soon became clear: Patrick O'Connor had been murdered and buried in quicklime, so that his remains would quickly disappear. The Mannings had fled, but not together.

Maria de Roux, as she was, was a 'fine-grown handsome' Swiss woman, aged about 28. She had come to England where she worked as a lady's maid to Lady Blantyre, daughter of the Duchess of Sutherland, at her London home. As such, she would have tasted some of life's luxuries, whilst remaining poor herself. She met Patrick O'Connor through one of her trips abroad, he working for Customs in London's docks. He was about fifty. He told her he had invested in foreign railway stocks. But then perchance she met Frederick George Manning, a guard on the Great Western Railway, until his dismissal a year before when he was suspected of involvement in mail robberies for which two alleged accomplices were transported, but he, Manning, was never charged. He falsely told Maria he would inherit £600 on the death of his mother. Both men were visitors to Stafford House, and both, it seems, had wanted to marry Maria. She chose Manning. Her liaisons with both men continued, however, even when O'Connor learned the truth, and she was a regular visitor to his lodgings at Mile End. After taking a public house at Taunton, a failed venture, the Mannings ended up at 3 Miniver Place, Bermondsey.

On 18 August an inquest into the death of Patrick O'Connor was opened at the New Leathermarket Tavern, Bermondsey, before the coroner, Mr Carter. The jury saw for themselves the marks left through the body having been trussed up with rope and the discolouration of the face, neck and thorax caused by the quicklime, leaving only the projecting chin and mouth. Mr Odling, surgeon, confirmed that a bullet had passed through the right eye, but said the shot had not proved fatal, and that the cause of death was at the back of the head which had been 'fearfully beaten', probably by a hammer or crowbar.

Evidence showing the Mannings' murderous intent was provided by William Massey, a medical student, who lodged with them at 3 Miniver Place for fourteen weeks. He frequently saw Patrick O'Connor in the house, and said that Mrs Manning had told him O'Connor was 'a man worth £20,000', and that he intended to leave her the greater part of his property in his will. Frederick Manning had asked Massey if chloroform or laudanum would 'produce stupefaction or intoxication, so as to get a person to put his hand to paper', and had also asked him questions 'about the head', including which part would be most fatal to strike. A blow behind the ear was Massey's considered reply. He had asked him about the 'nature of an air gun', but Massey was unable to give an opinion. Manning even asked him if a murderer would go to heaven. 'No,' said Massey, who quit the Mannings' home on 28 July, at their request. 'They appeared anxious that I should go,' he said.

Six weeks before the crime, the next-door neighbours at No. 2 had heard 'unusual noises' – knocking and digging, and the sound of earth being thrown alongside the party wall. That the murder was premeditated there was no doubt, and Frederick and Maria Manning were both implicated. This would become even clearer when the police discovered that the lime was purchased about three weeks previously by Frederick Manning from Mr Wells, a plasterer and bricklayer. It was delivered to 3 Miniver Place, and deposited in the kitchen where the body was discovered. The police also discovered that Frederick Manning had bought a crowbar, and Mrs Manning had bought a shovel. The Mannings' descriptions were 'extensively circulated'; Frederick and Maria Manning were wanted for murder.

The Mannings had put their premeditated plan into operation on Wednesday 8 August, when Mrs Manning wrote a note to Patrick O'Connor, inviting him to dinner that afternoon:

Dear O'Connor,

We shall be happy to see you to dine with us today at half past five.

Yours affectionately,

Maria Manning.

Sending a note was the most practical form of communication then. Unlike today, it would have been expected to be delivered the same day it was posted, in this case to O'Connor's work address at London Docks. However, as it was not posted until 3 p.m. it was not delivered until the next morning, too late for O'Connor to see it on the Wednesday. Consequently, when he turned up on the Wednesday evening at the Mannings', accompanied by his friend, Pierce Walsh, he was unaware that he had been invited to dinner at 5.30 p.m. In any event, the two men stayed until midnight, when they left together. Walsh would later say that O'Connor was 'as friendly as a brother' with the Mannings.

If the Mannings' murderous plans had been thwarted by the late delivery of a note and the unexpected appearance of Walsh, it wouldn't deter them for long. The next day, Thursday, O'Connor was invited for dinner again, this time by a letter he did receive on time. That day he went to work as usual, leaving at 4 p.m. At about 4.45 p.m., when he was seen by his two work colleagues at London Bridge, he showed them the letter of invitation to dinner with the Mannings and said that was where he was going now. That very evening he was murdered, and his body was buried beneath the kitchen floor where it was found eight days later.

About 5.45 p.m. that Thursday – just after O'Connor was murdered – Maria Manning went to his lodgings in Greenwood Street, a normal occurrence, where she stayed in his private rooms until 7.15 p.m., before returning home, her appearance being noted as 'nervous and pale' by Ann Armes, O'Connor's landlady, and her sister, Emily. At Mrs Manning's trial, she would say the purpose of this visit was to look for O'Connor, who had not arrived for dinner; the prosecution would infer this visit to O'Connor's lodgings was to give the *effect* of looking for him, knowing perfectly well he was already dead. About 7.15 p.m. the same evening, Frederick Manning sat on the wall at the back of 3 Miniver Place, smoking and chatting to Sophia Payne, his next-door neighbour, which he did for some twenty minutes before jumping down suddenly, saying he had to keep an engagement.

About 5.45 p.m. on the Friday, Mrs Manning returned to O'Connor's private rooms, remaining there until 7.15 p.m. Her visit aroused no undue suspicion. On Saturday she hired 12-year-old Hannah Firman to clean her back and front kitchens, and a basket, which appeared to Hannah to have been filled with lime. She was unable to clean the basket, which Mrs Manning endeavoured to do herself, also unsuccessfully. Later that day, Frederick Manning went to a stockbroker's, where, purporting to be Patrick O'Connor, he sold twenty Eastern Counties shares for £110. He was given as payment a £100 note, which he changed at a bank for 50 sovereigns and five 10 shilling notes.

Four days after the murder Frederick Manning called on Mr Bainbridge, a broker, and offered to sell him all of their furniture. Bainbridge agreed to buy it for 13 shillings. Among the property Bainbridge removed from the Mannings' was the shovel. When Bainbridge collected the property, he found it included a dress, which Mrs Bainbridge washed. In her opinion there had been blood on it, and it had been 'imperfectly washed and dried'. Manning asked if he and his wife could lodge with the Bainbridges at 10 shillings per week; Bainbridge agreed, and Manning went to the house that same afternoon. He then sent a message to 3 Miniver Place, bidding his wife to follow. But Frederick Manning was in for a surprise when a message came back saying she was not at home. He 'made enquiries', only to discover she had left in a cab. What he made of his wife's unexpected disappearance we can only guess. Gone, she was, with O'Connor's money and his shares, and it would have been obvious to him that he was not part of her plans. He probably never had been.

In fact, about 4 p.m. that day, Mrs Manning, having helped herself to O'Connor's cash and shares, packed her bags into boxes, called a cab and went to London Bridge railway station. On the way she called at a stationer's, bought some cards and wrote upon them, 'Mrs Smith, passenger to Paris'. At the station she told the porter to nail the cards to her boxes, which she left at the station, and then told the driver to take her to Euston station. Frederick Manning fled too, to Southampton.

The search was on to find the Mannings. On 21 August *The Times* reported that the police believed they were on board the *Victoria*, an American packet ship, bound for New York. A steamer, with police on board, set off in pursuit. On 23 August, the *Victoria* was intercepted and boarded, her 300 emigrant passengers turned from their beds. They included a 'Mrs Manning', but it was not Maria, and the fugitives were not among the passengers. Then, suddenly, came news of an arrest; Maria Manning was in custody in Edinburgh.

Her arrest came about through the new 'electric telegraph'. Having traced the cab driver, Superintendent Haynes searched the two boxes, marked 'Smith', which Mrs Manning had deposited at London Bridge railway station, finding 'female wearing apparel', marked in her maiden name, along with some articles belonging to O'Connor, and several letters written by him to Mrs Manning. Haynes then went to Euston station, where he discovered a woman passenger in the name of 'Smith' had left on the 6.15 train that Tuesday to Edinburgh. He telegraphed the Edinburgh force, with the circumstances of the crime and a description of Mrs Manning, alias Smith, after which he went to Scotland Yard, where, scarcely an hour later he received a telegraph message in reply saying she was already in custody! She had been arrested in possession of seventy-three gold sovereigns, a £50 note, six £10 notes, five of which were confirmed through their serial numbers as being paid to her husband at the London stockbrokers the previous Saturday on the presentation of one of O'Connor's cheques, and the missing scrip (share certificates) of foreign railway companies belonging to O'Connor. *The Times* reported: 'A great deal of excitement prevailed in the neighbourhood of Scotland Yard …'You can be sure it did. And wasn't modern technology, the electric telegraph, wonderfully exciting too?

Maria Manning, on arrival in Edinburgh, hadn't wasted any time in her endeavours to raise cash on O'Connor's shares. Having taken lodgings as 'Mrs Smith', she went to a 'respectable stockbrokers' the following day, 21 August. She was told the shares she presented were foreign and 'not dealt with much in Edinburgh', but, the broker said, they would be able to process them through their London agents. She said she was 'much inclined' to invest cash in railway preference stock, and was advised that it was unsafe for her to travel with so much money; she should put it in a bank. She replied, pointing to her breast, 'I keep it here, where it is quite safe.'

She handed over a share certificate for a number of shares in the Huntingdon, St Ives & Wisbech Railway Company, on which £1 per share had been returned, and wanted to know if any further return could be made on them. The stockbrokers said they would correspond with their agent in London and let her know in a day or two. She left this certificate, together with a note of her Edinburgh address. The police could hardly have asked for more.

Two days later she returned to the stockbrokers and asked for the share certificate to be returned to her. She then asked for the return of the note bearing her address in Edinburgh. This was not to hand, and she left without it. Whether it could not be found, or the gentlemen she was trying to do business with smelled the proverbial rat, is open to question. In any event, the next day, when the company received a communication about murder and 'stolen shares in London', 'Mrs Smith' was soon connected with the crime in the capital. The police were told, Superintendent Moxey of the Edinburgh force attended and called at the address, so helpfully provided by Mrs Manning, where she was identified by one of the stockbrokers. When told she was believed to have murdered Patrick O'Connor on 9 August, she replied, 'Murder O'Connor? Certainly not! He was the kindest friend I ever had in the world. He acted the part of a father to me.' Told she was being arrested, she said, 'Well, if a murder was committed in the house on the Thursday it must have been during my absence, for I went out at four o'clock and I did not return till late in the evening.' Superintendent Moxey told her she was also charged with going into Mr O'Connor's lodgings and stealing his property on the Friday, and that it was impossible to get the property without his keys, which he always carried with him. She replied, 'I know nothing about the keys, but hearing he was missing I certainly went to his house and took the property, which was my own.' It was time to take a cab again – this time to an Edinburgh police station.

The following morning, at the Edinburgh Police Court, Mrs Manning did not betray the slightest symptom of agitation. The charges were read out to her, that she murdered Patrick O'Connor and stole his shares. In a low but distinct voice she replied, 'I have nothing to say.' After being taken to London and formally charged with murder, her reply was a request for a cup of coffee. She told the magistrates she was 'quite innocent' of the charge, and was remanded to Horsemonger Lane gaol. Among the letters found in her luggage was one written by Patrick O'Connor, expressing surprise that she was married, accusing her of 'faithlessness' and complaining bitterly at having 'lost an angel who might have been my guiding star through life'. Meanwhile, nearly three weeks after the murder, Frederick Manning was still at large. But on 28 August came news, again courtesy of the electric telegraph; Frederick Manning was in custody.

He was arrested at his lodgings at St Helier, Jersey, by 'detective police' from London, and would be brought to Southampton, and thence to London. The telegraph message stated that 'Manning had confessed his guilt' to the officers, adding that he was 'instigated to the deed by his wife', and stating that Mrs Manning fired the pistol shot at the unfortunate O'Connor. He said it was his intention to surrender himself the following day if he had not been captured.

It seems that Manning had arrived on Jersey on 16 August, and taken lodgings at the Navy Arms public house. He was recognised in St Helier by a young woman who knew him by sight, who at the time knew nothing of the murder but when she read the newspapers she reported her sighting to the authorities. Two detectives, Sergeants Langley (who knew Manning through the earlier police investigation into mail robberies) and Lockyer were dispatched to the island. Checking out the Navy Arms, they found Manning's box and some papers in the breast pocket of a coat. Manning had quit the Navy Arms and taken lodgings off St Aubin's Road. He had arranged to be taken to Guernsey, but slept in and missed the boat. Suspicions were aroused and the police came knocking.

'Is the wretch taken?' asked Manning, clearly indicating the blame lay with his wife. When told she had been, he said, 'I am glad of it, that will save my life.' He blamed her for the murder. It was she who dug the grave, she who invited O'Connor to dinner and to go downstairs to wash his hands, and she who shot him. He made no mention of the fact that the back of O'Connor's head had been smashed in. When charged before the magistrates in London, he replied, simply, 'I am innocent of the murder.' He was remanded to Horsemonger Lane gaol, where, not surprisingly, he asked to see his wife. His request was refused. Hearing of his detention, and that her husband was accusing her of shooting O'Connor at the bottom of the stairs, she declared, 'The villain! It was he that did it, not me.'

As the Mannings languished in gaol, the evidence against them mounted. The police discovered that on 26 July Frederick Manning had called at Evans' ironmongers shop, near London Bridge, asking to see a small crowbar. They had none in stock, he was told, but one could be made for him. On 28 July a newly-made crowbar was sent to 3 Miniver Place. Manning happened to call at the shop to see if it was ready, to be told a porter was on his way with it.

He hurried off and stopped the porter. Manning said, 'I suppose paper is scarce at your establishment. One doesn't want everybody to see such things.' He then went directly to a stationer's, and emerged with a sheet of brown paper and wrapped the crowbar in it. He wrote his name and address on the paper and allowed the porter to go on, alone, to deliver it. Mrs Manning took the delivery, complaining that it was sixpence more than she expected.

Awaiting their fate, the Mannings' demeanour stood out in marked contrast. She had recovered her poise, even asking after her husband: 'Poor boy, he ought not to have been taken.' Her satin dresses were returned to her, and she altered her bonnet 'so as to screen her from the vulgar gaze of the mob'. She was happy: 'I have plenty of room, plenty of air, plenty of food and am not without society.' She was grateful to Superintendent Moxey of the Edinburgh force for his gentlemanly conduct, saying 'I intend to go to Scotland as soon as I have got over this difficulty and I will call and see him.' In contrast, Frederick Manning became depressed. By mid September, Mrs Manning was a changed woman: 'Even under her veil the sickly hue of her countenance could be detected'. Her husband was worse than ever, his face 'pale and bloodless, filled with an air of mental suffering which he strove in vain to conceal'.

The trial of Frederick and Maria Manning opened at the Central Criminal Court on 26 October. Admission was by ticket only. Judge Baron Pollock presided, with the Attorney General, Sir J. Jervis, prosecuting. Frederick George Manning was represented by Mr Serjeant Wilkins, his wife by Mr Ballantine. No look of recognition was exchanged between the accused as they entered the dock, he wearing a black suit and black neckerchief and appearing restless, she in a dark dress fitting close to the throat, 'the cheerful buoyancy of spirits, amounting almost to levity, which she manifested at preliminary examinations, having deserted her'. Frederick Manning was charged with the murder of Patrick O'Connor, on 9 August, by firing a bullet from a pistol at him, and 'striking, cutting and wounding' him on the back of the head with a crowbar. Maria Manning was charged with aiding and abetting him. Both pleaded not guilty. Mrs Manning's defence argued that being an alien (a Swiss), she was entitled to have aliens on the jury, but this was overruled on the grounds that she was married to a British subject.

The prosecution's case was so strong it must have seemed difficult, if not impossible, for their barristers to defend them. In the Mannings' house, Patrick O'Connor had been shot and bludgeoned to death and buried under the kitchen floor, after which both accused had fled, she to Edinburgh, where she was caught trying to sell O'Connor's shares, he to Jersey, where his replies clearly indicated complicity in the crime. All that either could have hoped for was to persuade the jury that the other was the sole guilty party.

Serjeant Wilkins, for Frederick Manning, said, 'As far as the male prisoner is concerned, there is not a single fact from beginning to end to justify the hypothesis that he premeditated the destruction of O'Connor. History teaches us that the female is capable of reaching higher in point of virtue than the male, but that once she gives way to vice she sinks far lower. My hypothesis is that the female premeditated, planned and concocted the murder; she made her husband her dupe and instrument for that purpose.'

Regarding the purchase of the lime, counsel suggested she told her husband that it was necessary to destroy slugs in the garden. Frederick Manning had made no secret of its purchase. The crowbar – where did the male prisoner go for that? To the most respected ironmongers in London. It was absurd to suppose that it was purchased for the purpose of murder; there was a poker and a pistol in the house, he could have used either. There was nothing to show he acted in concert with his wife. The murder could have been done by one person. Likewise, the burying of the body. What motive could he have had? He was not the sort of man to be jealous; he allowed his wife night after night to visit O'Connor alone, and received him with great cordiality and friendship.

It was Mrs Manning who wrote the notes to O'Connor, inviting him to dinner, who was constantly with him at his lodgings, who had access to his secrets. Let the jury observe her hypocrisy, her falsehood, her consummate wickedness. How did she have possession of his cash and scrip? His box was locked, he always carried his keys in his pocket. How did she get those keys? She knew where O'Connor kept his property and was afterwards found in possession of it. Frederick Manning might have assisted in disposing of the body, but there was nothing to show he was aware of contemplated murder, or that he participated in the act.

Mr Ballantine said the allegations relating to 'this unhappy woman' had not been proved. The facts did not show that Mrs Manning was present at the time the murder was committed. He hoped the jury would come to the conclusion that she did not forget her sex, and do that which few women were recorded to have done – commit a cold-blooded and atrocious murder. Mr O'Connor had formed a connexion with Mrs Manning, the nature of which no one could doubt. He had reached middle age, the time when most men were weak enough to yield anything to a woman to whom they were connected. She would have had no need to commit murder to get possession of his property; she was a woman of kindly feelings and disposition. Mr O'Connor had been seen near London Bridge about five o'clock and would not have arrived at the Mannings' until after dinnertime, so she went to his lodgings to look for him. The Armes sisters, who lived at 3 Greenwood Street where O'Connor had lodged, said she arrived there at 5.45 p.m., and had left at 7.15 p.m. Mrs Manning could not have got home before eight o'clock, by which time the murder had been committed – by her husband.

A murder of this kind, said Mr Ballantine, was much more likely to have been committed by a man than by a woman, and this was a murder committed by one person. The prosecution alleged that she was party to the purchase of the crowbar, the lime and the shovel. The lime was for destroying slugs in the garden; the shovel was for use in the garden; why should she not purchase one? Mr Manning ordered the crowbar; she paid for it on delivery upon her husband's direction. He added that the marks on her dress were not blood, but 'ironmould'. As to her conduct after the murder, the criminality (sexual intercourse outside marriage) she had indulged in with O'Connor would operate powerfully upon her; she might believe jealousy by her husband was the groundwork on which the conception of the murder was raised. As for O'Connor's property – the shares and cash, found in her possession – she believed she was entitled to it.

Patrick O'Connor was murdered by both of them, said the prosecution; by one of them only, said defence counsel for each of the Mannings. Summing up, the judge said that if either of them committed violence against Patrick O'Connor with the knowledge and connivance of the other, and if they were both direct participators, then both were guilty. Patrick O'Connor was murdered sometime on 9 August and his body was found buried, the skull having been perforated by a bullet and the back of the skull fractured so that no fewer than sixteen pieces of broken bones were recovered. By whom was he murdered? Who was living in the house? The two prisoners, each blaming the other. The jury retired at 6 p.m. and returned at 6.45 p.m., finding both guilty of murder.

Justice Cresswell (who had replaced Baron Pollock) asked the prisoners why sentence of death should not be passed upon them. Mrs Manning, addressing the court with 'remarkable vehemence', said, 'There is no justice for a foreign subject in this country. I am unjustly condemned. My solicitors and counsel could have called witnesses to testify that shares were bought with my own money. Mr O'Connor was more to me than my husband. He was a friend and brother to me. He wanted to marry me. I am not treated like a Christian but like a wild beast of the forest. I am not guilty of the murder. If my husband, through jealousy, chose to murder him, I don't see why I should be punished.' Frederick Manning said nothing.

Passing sentence, the judge addressed them both. 'Under the pretence of friendship, or affection, you deluded the victim to a place where his grave was prepared and where the deed was committed. It appears a conversation passed between one of you and the witness Massey as to where the soul of a person who committed murder would go. You should ask that question again. I cannot hold out the slightest hope of commutation of the sentence I am about to pronounce. Your doom is irretrievably fixed.'

He then sentenced them both to death. According to custom, the bench in front of the dock was strewn with rue (a strong-smelling plant with greenish-yellow flowers, symbolic of repentance or compassion). Mrs Manning took some in her hand and threw it into the body of the court, and was then removed. Her husband simply bowed and left the court.

Post-Trial

Maria Manning had been taken from the court, but the sound of her voice was still clear enough as she railed against her legal adviser, the jury and England. 'Damnation seize you all,' she screamed, in rage and despair. Her husband, dejected and forlorn, remained quiet. Half an hour later they were taken in separate cabs back to Horsemonger Lane gaol, but in the confines of the cab, Maria still wasn't finished. 'I showed them resolution, did I not?' she declared, before turning her verbal assault upon her husband, whom she described as 'the unmanly wretch', kicking the seat opposite for good measure. When she saw the placards on public display, announcing a 'full report of the trial', her rage knew no bounds.

Frederick Manning maintained his wife alone was guilty, that she had shot O'Connor, and had threatened to shoot him also unless he helped her bury the body. He said the hole in the kitchen was dug the previous May. A shutter had been placed over it, but Maria couldn't pluck up the courage to do the deed. They told O'Connor they were making a drain. He must have walked over his own grave several times.

Manning wrote to his wife, urging her to confess. She wrote to him, saying he murdered O'Connor when she was out of the house at O'Connor's lodgings. He wrote to her again, imploring her to 'grant him an interview'. She replied by saying she would consent to see him, but only if he first admitted the crime, in writing. Manning told his brother, 'I never hurt a hair of O'Connor's head.' His brother's advice was simply, 'Make your peace with God.'

Later, Manning gave this account of events on the evening of the murder: In the parlour at Miniver Place, Maria said to O'Connor, 'Come downstairs and wash your hands before dinner.' O'Connor went downstairs into the back kitchen, closely followed by Maria, whilst he, Manning, remained in the front room. In a few minutes she came back upstairs, saying, 'I have done it – he is dead enough.' Manning said he was 'dreadfully frightened', and told her she was a 'dead woman', that she would hang for murder. She called him a coward, and pointed a pistol at him, and said, 'If you don't come to see him I will serve you the same.'

Manning said he went downstairs and was horrified to see O'Connor lying on his face, his head hanging into the grave that had been prepared for him. Then his wife struck O'Connor three or four times with the crowbar, screaming, 'You damned villain, you will never deceive me any more!' Manning then ran upstairs, followed by Maria, who took off her bloodied dress and washed her bloodstained hands. He told Mr Keane, the prison governor, that if he were executed 'the life of an innocent man would be taken'.

The public executions of Frederick and Maria Manning were scheduled for Tuesday 13 November 1849, at Horsemonger Lane gaol. Every window with a view was in demand, at prices between one and two guineas, whilst others paid for positions on rooftops. Scaffolding was erected in front of houses, and planks placed into position. Barricades were erected in front of the gaol, and 'four to five hundred constables' would be deployed to keep the peace.

Over 30,000 people gathered to witness the Mannings' demise. Men, women and children. The rich, viewing from the rooftops, some with opera glasses; ragtags and pickpockets, drunks and navvies, all faces turned upward to the gallows on the prison roof as the dreaded hour approached. Charles Dickens was present and later wrote to *The Times*:

> I believe a sight so inconceivably awful as the wickedness and levity of the immense crowd collected at the execution could be imagined by no man ... thieves, prostitutes, ruffians and vagabonds of every kind, with every variety of offensive behaviour. Fightings, faintings, brutal jokes, demonstrations of indecent delight when swooning women were dragged out of the crowd by police. A man had cause to feel ashamed ...

The Mannings came face to face in the prison chapel. 'I hope you are not going to depart this life with animosity,' said Frederick, 'will you kiss me?' She replied that she had no animosity, and they kissed. 'I hope we shall meet in heaven,' said Frederick. When Calcraft, the hangman, appeared, their time was up. Manning was pinioned; Mrs Manning nearly fainted, but recovered, thanks to a shot of brandy. She then took a black handkerchief from her pocket and asked to be blindfolded. Her request was granted. As the prison bell tolled, the two prisoners, man and wife, then proceeded to the scaffold. A 'ghastly pallor' spread over Frederick Manning's face, as he muttered, 'Lord, have mercy upon me'; his wife, still blindfold, walked with unfaltering step.

At 9 a.m. the procession emerged onto the prison roof. The crowd watched as Frederick Manning ascended the steps to the drop. His legs all but gave way, but he reached the scaffold where he seemed scarcely able to move. Calcraft placed a white hood over his head and adjusted the rope about his neck. Mrs Manning mounted the scaffold with a firm step, and stood 'as still as a marble statue' under the beam. The chaplain asked her if she wished to confess. She had nothing to say. After shaking hands, husband and wife were hanged together, their bodies remaining in situ for an hour before being cut down and buried within the gaol, their coffins partly filled with lime to ensure early decay, a process with which they were all too familiar.

Fours days before, Frederick Manning had made a 'full confession'. Its authenticity cannot be guaranteed, for he may have yet hoped for a reprieve in making it. Suffice to say he said his wife shot Patrick O'Connor in the kitchen, that he, Manning, on hearing the shot, went downstairs where, hearing O'Connor's moans, he battered his skull in with the crowbar. His wife then went to O'Connor's lodgings and took his shares. The crowbar was later recovered.

It had been deposited, wrapped in paper and addressed to 'Mrs Smith, passenger from Brighton to Lewes', at Lewes railway station. Opinion had it that Manning had left it in a carriage when he fled to Jersey, and it had been found and handed in to the authorities.

Author's Verdict

Maria Manning never confessed to playing any part in the murder of Patrick O'Connor. Nor was her conduct afterwards, when she took his property – his money and his scrip – and travelled to Edinburgh, direct proof that she was guilty of murder. But there was ample evidence to prove, beyond reasonable doubt, that she was guilty.

Her main defence was that she was not present when the murder was committed, that when O'Connor failed to arrive for dinner at 5 p.m., she went looking for him. She was seen to arrive at his lodgings at 5.45 p.m., and leave at 7.15 p.m. Prosecution counsel had 'instructed persons' to walk the distance; it took forty-two minutes. By omnibus it took thirty-five minutes; by cab twenty-five minutes. If O'Connor had arrived at 3 Miniver Place at about five o'clock, she would have had to shoot him immediately, as her husband alleged, wash herself of the blood, change her dress and go at once, by cab, to his lodgings to 'look for him', as she maintained. We know she was one for taking a cab, but, even so, the time is tight. Her alibi takes some discounting. Maybe that's why the indictment charged her with 'aiding and abetting' her husband.

But even if she didn't shoot O'Connor, and her husband alone did the deed, she was guilty. One doesn't have to be present to be guilty of murder, but act in concert. Some weeks before the act, she or her husband dug a hole in their kitchen floor, not for a drain, as they told their victim, but for his body when the time came. A shovel to dig the hole, a pistol to shoot him, a crowbar to smash his head in, lime to hasten the disappearance of his remains, telling their fee-paying lodger to quit the house. If either was innocent, as each claimed, what did he or she think the other was up to, other than murder? Her counsel suggested the crime was 'more likely to have been committed by a man than a woman', but the jury dismissed such nonsense.

Whatever happened, the Mannings' premeditated plan was to claim that, when O'Connor did not arrive for dinner, Mrs Manning would go 'looking for him', whilst Mr Manning would go into the garden to chat with a neighbour as though nothing had happened. O'Connor, ventured *The Times*, was 'a tool in the hands of his wife, whose uncontrolled temper and impetuous will worked upon his weak disposition, dragging him after her into the abyss of crime'. She had seen and enjoyed the fruits of life whilst remaining poor herself. Aspiring to riches of her own, Patrick O'Connor's considerable wealth would have been hers if she had got away with murder.

3

A Temporary Frenzy

Mary Ann Brough, Surrey, 1854

Completed in 1774, the grand mansion of Claremont House, near Esher, was later a holiday destination for Queen Victoria. On the staff was George Brough, a 'hard working, sober and honest man', who had worked for the Royal Palace at Claremont for years. Brough met his wife-to-be, Mary Ann, at Claremont, when she was interviewed for the position of 'wet nurse' to the queen, not an unusual situation at the time for respectable women with 'a good breast of milk'. Victoria was pregnant with her second child, and Mary Ann was duly installed at Buckingham Palace pending the arrival of the baby, the future Edward VII, who was born on 9 November 1841.

It seems a medical attendant at the palace decided that Mary Ann was not in a proper state 'to afford sufficient nurture' to the royal baby – meaning, in all probability, that she came from too low a class of society. She was dismissed, and returned to her husband at their small house at West End, near Esher. Despite rumours that they were unhappy, the couple's marriage lasted twenty years and by 1854 they had seven children – Mary Ann, aged 15, Georgina, 11, Caroline, 8, William, 6, Henry and Harriet (twins), 2, and George, 21 months.

If George Brough was content to soldier on in an unhappy marriage, his wife, it seems, was not. Mary Ann was making frequent trips to 'town' – London – where her husband suspected she was seeing another man for 'immoral purposes'. Consequently he sought out the services of a detective called Henry Field to keep observations on her on one of her visits to the capital. One day Brough sent the following note to Field: 'Please send tomorrow morning by the seven o'clock train, as the party is on the move, I expect, by the 9 a.m.'.

Field took the same train to London as Mary Ann, where, on arrival, she was seen to go directly into a public house where she met a man, before going to a 'questionable house' with him. This information was passed on to her husband, who told her he had found out and would no longer live with her. George Brough left home on Tuesday 6 June 1854, in a 'low and dejected state'. No doubt his strict Victorian values, added to the hurt and offence of his wife's infidelity and many years of unhappiness, prompted his decision to leave his family. But he did more than just leave; he and Field went to see a solicitor, who advised Brough to take legal action against Mary Ann for adultery.

On the evening of Wednesday 7 June, Brough asked a friend, John Birdseye, landlord of the Wheatsheaf public house, to accompany him to his house. As they approached, Mary Ann called from an upstairs window, asking her husband what he wanted. Just his nightshirt and nightcap, he said. She passed a bundle out to him and Brough and Birdseye departed. It would have been clear to Mary Ann that her husband was not coming back. Then she got wind of his intended legal proceedings against her, and a proposed meeting he had arranged with another solicitor for the Saturday with a view to getting custody of the children. Clearly, George Brough was not a man to tolerate adultery.

Mary Ann's illicit lover was a man called Woodhatch, who had a shop in Esher. Their affair had gone on for years; four years earlier, her eldest daughter, also Mary Ann, had copied a letter her mother had written to Woodhatch and taken it to a solicitor, evidently trying to institute legal proceedings against her. It may seem unusual for a youngster to take these steps, but infidelity was looked upon with a serious eye then, and young Mary Ann's sympathies lay with her father.

It seems reasonable to think George Brough must have suspected his cheating wife for a long time too. But when he left the family home and took the first steps to initiate legal proceedings he could not have foreseen the consequences, for within a week six of his children were dead by his wife's hand, slaughtered in their beds before she tried, unsuccessfully, to take her own life. Their eldest child, Mary Ann's namesake, alone would survive, being elsewhere at the time.

The inquest was opened at the Chequers public house, Esher, on 13 June, before the coroner, William Carter. After viewing the pitiful bodies of the children, the jury heard the evidence that would identify the obvious culprit. First to testify was Henry Woolger, a labourer. Woolger was on his way to work on Saturday morning, 10 June, at 5.45 a.m., when, passing Mary Ann's house he noticed a bloodstained pillow hanging out of a rear upstairs window. Alarmed at this sight, he waited, until he heard the noise of a gate. Looking round, he saw Thomas Peastley approaching. 'Look here, Thomas,' said Woolger, 'here is an awful sight.' The two men went to the front of the house and rang the bell, but no one came. Mrs Bergham, Woolger's landlady, came along, and rang the bell 'violently'. A woman, dressed in a half mourning shawl, came to the window and waved a towel, as if to beckon them. Woolger found a ladder, which he placed against the back window, and climbed up. As he did he heard someone coming up the stairs inside. He then saw Mary Ann, her body covered 'all over blood'. He saw a wound in her throat that seemed to be making a whistling noise. He descended the ladder and went for Dr Mott.

John Crockford, a neighbour, was in his garden when he saw those gathered at Mary Ann's house. He went to the back of the house, climbed the ladder and went into the room. The sight that awaited him was horrific. First, he saw a 'little child' with its throat cut. The child was dead. He went into the front bedroom, where Mary Ann was lying on a bed. Two children lay at the foot of the same bed, both with their throats cut, both dead. Crockford left the house then, and saw two men to whom he told what he had seen. He then went inside the house again, and found three more children, all with their throats cut. They were lying on another bed, all dead.

PC William Bedser went to the house, where, at the side of the bed upon which Mary Ann lay, he found a razor, open and stained with dried blood. He had known Mary Ann for years, and said he considered her 'as good a mother as ever lived, who kept her children well dressed and clean'. Superintendent Biddlecomb was the next policeman to arrive. On entering the back door he found a pair of women's boots and a pair of bloody stockings. Mary Ann received medical attention from Dr Mott, and the following day, Sunday, she asked to see Biddlecomb, who returned to the house where she was being detained. She said to him, 'I should like to tell you all about it.'

'I begged of her to be careful what she said,' said Biddlecomb, 'for it would be my duty to take down everything and produce it as evidence against her.' She then made a statement, which he took down in writing. The following day Biddlecomb saw her again, and told her he wished to read back to her what she had said, and if there was anything she wished to retract, to do so, adding that he would lay her statement before the coroner's jury that afternoon. He then read the statement to her, which she said was 'perfectly correct':

On Friday last I was bad all day. I wanted to see Mr Izod [her doctor] and waited all day. I wanted some medicine. In the evening I walked about, and afterwards put the children to bed, and wanted to go to sleep in a chair. About 9 o'clock Georgy [Georgina] kept calling me to come to bed. I came up to bed and they kept calling me to bring them some barley water, till near 12 o'clock. I had one candle lit, and I went and got another but I could not see. There was something like a cloud over my eyes. I thought I would go down and get a knife and cut my throat. I groped about in the master's room and found his keys and his razor. I went to Georgy and cut her first. I came to Carry [Caroline] and cut her. Then to Henry. He said, 'Don't mother.' I said, 'I must,' and cut him. Then I went to Bill. He was fast asleep. I turned him over. He never woke. I served him the same. The two children, Harriet and George, were awake. They made no resistance at all. Harriet struggled very much after I cut her, and gurgled for some time. I then lay down and did myself. I can't tell what occurred for some time after that. I seemed weak and found myself on the floor. That nasty black cloud was gone then. I was thirsty and got the water bottle and drank. I got up and saw the children, and it all came to me again. I wanted to call but could not speak. I did not know what to do. I went to the window and put something out to attract attention. I staggered back to my own bed, and lay till I heard someone ringing a bell. I went on my hands and knees to the window. It was Henry Woolger. I went down to unbolt the door. That is all I know.

Superintendent Biddlecomb said the statement was signed by the 'miserable woman', and added he did not believe she had made it to shield any other person. Later, Inspector James Martell said on that same morning Mary Ann made a similar statement to the first, adding, 'If there had been 40 I should have served them all the same, but what a pity it was I did not do myself first'. It was hardly surprising the inquest jury's verdict was 'that the deceased children were wilfully murdered by their mother'.

On 10 August, Mary Ann appeared at the Summer Assizes at Guildford, before Justice Erle, charged with murdering her six children. One indictment only would be heard, that of the charge of murdering Harriet, aged 2 years.

Opening his address for the prosecution, William Bodkin said Mary Ann Brough was charged with killing a child of her own body, and that there was no doubt that the only persons in the cottage that night were the prisoner and her six children. Her husband had felt 'justified' in leaving her, and there was not the slightest doubt that it was by the hand of the prisoner that the lives of the six children were sacrificed. He told the jury they would have to consider if, at the time, the prisoner was in such a state of mind as rendered her responsible for her actions. Every person was considered sane and responsible for his actions unless the contrary was made out. He would show that on the day of the 'fatal occurrence', and up to within a very short period of it taking place, the prisoner went about her affairs in an ordinary manner. He added that after Mary Ann had inflicted injury upon herself, she made a 'remarkable statement' to a woman (Sarah Waller) who was in attendance upon her. This was to the effect that her husband had left her without money and that he intended to take the children from her, and she intended he would not do so. In short, he said, Mary Ann was sane when she killed her children.

The first witnesses testified. These were Henry Woolger and John Crockford, who had been first to the scene. Then followed the police. Superintendent Biddlecomb said he took Mary Ann's statement 'originally in pencil', and it was copied afterwards, in ink, 'under my superintendence'. 'I have not got the original,' he said, 'but I swear I made a verbatim copy of it'. (A statement made by a suspect regarding six murders and the Superintendent hadn't kept the original!) PC Collett said that on 13 June Mary Ann told him she had wished her daughter, Mary Ann, had come, and she told the policeman to take a box from under the bed. He did so, and found it contained plate and jewellery. On top of the box was a piece of paper, which read as follows: 'All for my daughter Mary. Her father is only seeking to get money from them as I never injured him or done him any harm. Mary Ann Brough'.

On the same day, said PC Collett, the prisoner said to him, 'This would not have happened but for my daughter and Fred Foster. It is owing to a letter which they said they found and copied, and they took the copy to Kingston to Mr Jemmett.' She told him this had occurred three or four years ago. Mr Jemmett had said he could do nothing as they only had a copy of the letter. The letter was sent by the shopkeeper, Woodhatch – her lover – who left Esher immediately after the murders. The constable said Mary Ann had told him that if Dr Izod had come, 'it would not have happened'.

Sarah Waller nursed Mary Ann when she was suffering from the injury to her throat. She said she took her some brandy and tea on the morning of 10 June, when she asked her if any of the children had cried. Mary Ann had replied, 'No, they were all asleep, except the baby. He was awake and fetched three struggles.' She said her husband had left her without money and was going to take the children from her. Waller then had this to say to the court:

On the Saturday morning the prisoner said this to me, the doctor had only just sewn up her throat, but she was able to speak quite distinctively. She had an epileptic fit about a year and a half ago and lost the use of one side, and since then has not spoken so distinctively as before. She has constantly complained to me of her head since she had the fit, and she has told me she has felt a heaviness in her head – a 'tumbling' when she was stooping, as if she must fall, and a swimming. She had this fit after the birth of her last child. I was fetched to her one night, and I found she had suffered a great loss of blood from her nose. She appeared relieved in her head after the discharge of the blood. All this occurred before the birth of the child I have mentioned. The prisoner has suffered in the same manner since, but I have observed an alteration in her since she had the fit. I have frequently seen her laugh in a silly manner. She was always very kind to her children, almost too kind. She was a most indulgent mother.

Mary Ann's niece, Ann Yates, said that three of Mary Ann's children were 'very ill' with measles at the time of the murders. She said her aunt frequently complained of 'violent heaviness' in her head, over the eyes, and was relieved of this when bleeding from the nose.

For the defence, Mr Edwin James addressed the jury in 'a speech of great eloquence and power'. It was a most remarkable case, he said. 'A woman proved to have been a kind and devoted mother now stood at the bar charged with murdering six of her children. A woman who, in a moment of some unaccountable impulse, became a fiend, and destroyed the children to whom but a few short minutes before she had been attending with kindness and affection. Was it not clear that some mysterious agency, which no one could divine, must have been at work? Was it possible to believe she was mistress of her actions at the time?

The Almighty did sometimes take away from man his reason, and reduce him to the condition of an irresponsible being.'

He did not mean the prisoner at the present time was not perfectly sane, but he hoped to satisfy the jury that 'the deed was committed while she was under the influence of a temporary frenzy, which it was impossible for her to control'. He said that being relieved by the quantity of blood that escaped from the wound she had inflicted upon herself, the 'dark cloud' passed away, and for the first time she became aware of what she had done. She afterwards made no attempt to escape, but sought assistance and made a statement. There was nothing in the shape of an adequate motive. 'Her mind had broken down, and she was not conscious of the act she committed.' He called two witnesses in her defence.

Dr Izod had attended Mary Ann for years. In 1852, he said, she had suffered severe bleeding from the nose and had complained of 'great pain' in her head. He had had to administer 'certain medicines' and to 'blister her'. She had completely lost the use of her left side after the delivery of her last child, and her face became distorted. She had never entirely recovered. He had observed symptoms of a 'disordered brain' and had, in consequence, constantly 'advised her to avoid excitement of every description'. He was satisfied that any sudden excitement would be dangerous to her.

Dr Forbes Winslow said he had for years directed his attention principally to diseases of the brain. He had had a long interview with Mary Ann, and it was his opinion that the attack of paralysis suffered by her was the result of a diseased brain. Paralysis could exist without insanity, 'but it is always symptomatic of a disease in the brain.' Bleeding from the nose was a symptom of a congested brain, 'as it is considered an effort of the brain to relieve itself.' During his interview with Mary Ann he did not observe any symptom of insanity, but cases of *temporary* insanity resulting in desire to commit murder were common. It frequently occurred with mothers and children, he said. 'In such cases the patient suddenly suffers under a strong homicidal impulse which he cannot control.' He had no doubt Mary Ann's brain had been in a 'disordered state' ever since the attack of paralysis. 'In cases of transient insanity it is very common for a patient to say they had experienced the sensation of a dark cloud passing before their eyes, and during this paroxysm would not be able to distinguish between right and wrong.'

The judge was hardly sympathetic to Mary Ann. It was admitted, he said, that it was by her hand that these 'unfortunate children' met their deaths. The only question that remained was whether, at the time the deed was committed, the prisoner was in such a state of mind as rendered her responsible. 'A defence of this character ought to be looked at with caution, and the jury ought not to acquit the prisoner on the grounds of insanity unless there were circumstances surrounding it, totally irrespective of the enormity of the crime, leaving no reasonable doubt that at the time of its commission the accused was not in a condition of mind to distinguish between right and wrong.' The crime was committed under impulse, he said, but 'the object of the law was to control impulses.' If the jury thought there were grounds for supposing that at the time the prisoner committed the act she was not in a sane state, they would be justified in acquitting her.

'If, on the other hand,' said his lordship, 'you are of the opinion that, owing to the unfortunate relationship in which she stood with her husband, she was induced to meditate the commission of some act of violence, either towards herself or others, and this created an excited condition which, operating on her brain in its diseased condition, drove her to a state of temporary insanity, during which she committed the act, I am bound to tell you this would not excuse her from the consequences, and it would be your duty to find her guilty.' What the members of the jury understood of the 'expert' medical opinion they heard, if anything, as well as the explanatory words of counsel and the judge is debatable, but it took them two hours to return a 'not guilty' verdict on the ground of insanity. Mary Ann Brough was sentenced to be detained 'in safe custody' during Her Majesty's Pleasure.

Author's Verdict

From the moment of the grim discovery of the bodies of six little children, there was never any doubt that the culprit was their mother. One recoils at the horror perpetrated that night, as one by one she cut open their throats with a razor; six innocents who lost their lives in the dead of night in the place they should have felt safest: their home.

Mary Ann was a woman whose mind was in turmoil. She was nursing sick children, her husband had left her and had threatened to take the kids – and his income. Her lover had disappeared without trace; she was staring the workhouse in the face. Yet it seems accepted that up to the time she killed her children, and immediately after, she was quite sane. It was her state of mind *at the time* that mattered. 'There was something like a cloud over my eyes,' she said in her statement. 'Some mysterious agency must have been at work,' said her defence, and the 'cloud' passed away after she had lost blood from her own injury.

Mary Ann told Sarah Waller her husband had left her without money and was going to take the children, the implication being that she would kill her children in consequence. The judge seemed to make his views clear; he meant she deliberately murdered them out of spite and was not insane at all. Perhaps he was alluding to the fact that, before she killed her children, Mary Ann placed plate and jewellery into a box, along with a note, 'all for my daughter, Mary', an act suggesting premeditation and denouncing the 'cloud over my eyes' defence.

One wonders what the jury made of it all: the words of counsel and the judge, and the testimonies of the medical men, who talked about a disordered and congested brain, transient insanity and paroxysm. Sarah Waller's testimony about Mary Ann's sickness probably made more sense. Suffice to say they would have thought a woman who murdered her six children could not have been in her right mind and decided she was insane. Maybe she was.

4

Murder in the Glenkens

Mary Timney, Kirkudbrightshire, 1862

It was Monday 13 January 1862, just after midday, when young Agnes McLellan, who lived in a lonely part of the country known as the Glenkens, received a visit from Susan Timney. Susan had a message for her: her mother, who was poorly, would like Agnes to come to the Timneys' house and bake for the family. Agnes said she would, after she had eaten her dinner. The request was not unusual; only four days before she had looked after the Timneys' house whilst Mrs Timney went into Dalry.

To get to the Timneys', Agnes had to pass Ann Hannah's cottage, known as Carsphad Farmhouse. Agnes knew Ann well, and had been in the habit of popping in to see her ever since her mother died, a kindly and neighbourly gesture one might expect in such an isolated community. So it was that Agnes decided to call briefly on Ann, but when she arrived at the cottage and pushed open the door she was in for an unpleasant surprise. Ann was lying on the stone-flagged floor of the kitchen, with her arms crossed below her, her woollen cap lying a little distance away. 'Oh dear me, Ann, what's ado?' said Agnes, and when Ann did not reply she went at once to Knocknalling Lodge to seek assistance from Elizabeth Coates. Mrs Coates accompanied Agnes to the cottage, where she saw Ann's head resting on freshly-washed clothes, and pools of blood on the kitchen floor. She left to send her son for a doctor. Shortly afterwards, Mrs Coates' husband, Robert, and a labourer, John McAdam, arrived and lifted Ann on to her bed. As they did so she said, 'Oh dear, oh dear,' the last words she would utter.

Mrs Coates returned to the cottage, where she, her husband, Agnes and John McAdam, all waited for the doctor. They had plenty of time to look at what would be a murder scene. On the floor lay a butcher's knife, 'all bloody about blade and handle', and a piece of iron, used as a poker. There was blood and hair on the latter, the hair the colour of Ann's. The stone-flagged floor was broken in places, and blood had run into gaps and holes; it was also spattered onto the legs of the kitchen table. The washtub stood in its place by the window, with wringed-out clothes nearby. The dish Ann would have placed the clothes into lay upside down on the floor.

As they waited, they were joined by Mary Timney. 'Dear me,' said Mrs Timney, 'I think the likes o' this never happened here afore!' John McAdam asked her if she had seen anyone on the road. She said she had not. A strange thing it was, said McAdam, that something like this could happen so near her door, and her children about too. Mrs Timney said she had been poorly and not been at her door since her husband left that morning.

At 2.30 p.m. Dr Andrew Jackson arrived at the cottage. He dressed Ann's wounds, tearing away her dress to see if there were any other injuries, but finding none. Ann had been washing clothes when she had been struck on the head from behind, after which she had been struck again and suffered defensive wounds to her forearms in the process. The poker, the knife and a heavier instrument had been used. She died at 9.30 p.m. that evening.

Ann Hannah, aged 40, was single, and had lived at Carsphad, some three and a half miles north of New Galloway, keeping house, while her two brothers, William and Lockhart, went to work. The cottage was a simple building, having only two rooms: one, where the brothers slept, and the kitchen, where Ann cooked and the family ate, and where she slept. At another cottage, just fifty yards away, lived Mary Timney and her husband, Francis, a road-surface man, and their four children, whilst the next dwelling, Knocknalling Lodge, a quarter of a mile away, was occupied by the Coates family.

Some time after 8 a.m. on Monday the two Hannah brothers had left Carsphad and went to work at Greenloop, two or three miles away. Ann Hannah, then alone in the house, was seen alive and well at 9.30 a.m. by some children on their way to school. Later, when William Hannah arrived, having been told the news, Mrs Timney was seated by the fire, with her son John, aged eighteen months. The child was fractious, and William told Mrs Timney to go home. Some time later, Lockhart Hannah entered the house.

At six o'clock, Constable Robson arrived with Lockhart Hannah, who had gone to fetch him. They met at New Galloway, the constable having heard that 'something had happened at Carsphad'. There will be little doubt that what Lockhart had to tell him on the way will have thrown some light on events, although PC Robson would already have been *au fait* with at least some of the recent goings on between Ann Hannah and Mary Timney. Ann had told Lockhart of a quarrel she and Mrs Timney had had over Mrs Timney's collecting sticks on their land for firewood. William Hannah, too, had information for the policeman. He had lent Francis Timney 2 shillings and 6 pence that very morning, about seven o' clock. Timney had told him he was going away that day, to work, that there was no money in the house and that he wished to give some to his wife before he left. William confirmed Ann and Mrs Timney had had 'words' about the latter carrying away wood from the Hannahs' cottage. William himself had told Mrs Timney not to take away wood, and had advised his sister to avoid her, especially when she told him Mrs Timney had turned up one day in a field with a stone in her hand, saying, 'I will have your life.'

William Hannah had seen Mrs Timney at 8 a.m. on the day his sister was murdered. She – Mrs Timney – was going to the pig house at the end of her cottage. He thought someone had attacked Ann for 'plunder', as there was tea and sugar missing, and he could not find her purse. Instead, he found the bloodstained knife he had bought for killing pigs. The last time he saw it, it was on a shelf at the back of the house.

The Timneys' cottage consisted of 'one apartment', with beds 'boxed at the back' behind a partition. Having spoken with the Hannah brothers, Constable Robson went to the cottage about 6.20 p.m. He saw the Timneys' four children, and Mrs Timney herself, whom he found in bed, fully clothed. When she saw the constable she got up and said, 'What lies have you been telling on me today?' The constable asked her to give him her clothes, which she did. The flannel petticoat and shift she was wearing appeared to be bloodstained. He then made a search of the house, including the loft, which he got up to by climbing on top of a barrel. The floor was of loose boards laid upon joists, with turf laid on the boards. He found a tartan dress, a bed gown, and a child's night-dress, bloodstained on the right breast, all in the loft. The clothes were rolled up in the tartan dress, which was wet at the front. There were spots of blood on the other clothing, and the child's stained night-dress was also wet, and seemed to have been washed. In the room below he found a bonnet, recently washed.

On the left of the fireplace, PC Robson found a mallet, or 'beetle', as it was called, behind a barrel. It had also been washed, but there was what appeared to be human hair on it. He did not think it important, so replaced it. He also found 7 shillings and 7 pence in a glove on the dresser, and took possession of some tea and sugar, which was mixed together in a cloth. These he handed to the chief constable, John Johnstone. At ten o'clock that same night PC Robson arrested Mrs Timney, who was taken to New Galloway, and her children to her mother's at Dalry. Mrs Timney said it was 'a terrible business', but that she was innocent as she had been in bed all morning and not been out of the house at all that day. The following day she was taken to the gaol at Kirkudbright, where she denied ever having quarrelled with Ann Hannah. PC Robson later returned to the house and collected the mallet.

Two days after Ann Hannah was murdered, Doctors Jackson and Millman made a post-mortem examination of the body, finding extensive wounds to the head and face, ten in all. Ann's skull had been fractured as a result of being struck. There were several wounds to each forearm, probably caused by the piece of iron, and the fractures to the skull had been caused by a heavier weapon, such as the mallet, which had produced the fatal blows. The knife could have caused the cuts across the face. Francis Timney and his two eldest children readily identified the mallet, saying it had been in their house for years. Mrs Timney denied ever having seen it before.

That April, Mary Timney stood trial for her life at the Spring Circuit Court for Dumfriesshire and the Stewartry of Kirkudbright. Lord Deas presided.

The *Dumfries and Galloway Standard and Advertiser* described her as having 'a countenance that is by no means repulsive, exhibiting no trace of feeling, her face wearing an impassive aspect'. She scarcely seemed to realise the dreadful circumstances of her position until her advocate began to plead on her behalf, 'and then tears occasionally trickled down her visage'. The newspaper further reported, 'The prisoner's physiognomical outline decidedly indicates low intellect, and the likelihood that animal passion on being aroused might overbear her reason and hurry her on to deeds of violence'. Fortunately, her physical appearance was not a factor that could be given in evidence, which is just as well, given the twisted logic of those words.

The court was taken aback when Mary Timney, asked if she was 'guilty or not guilty' to murdering Ann Hannah, replied, 'Guilty, my lord – yes, I'm guilty.' Evidently she had not understood, so when asked again she replied, 'Not guilty.' The charge was then formally put to her, that she did 'wickedly and feloniously attack Ann Hannah, and did with a poker, or piece of iron and with a wooden beetle or mallet, or with one or other of them, strike her about the head, face and other parts of her person whereby her skull was fractured and she was thus murdered'. All those who attended the murder scene that day testified, as did Dr Shand, who had carried out a second post-mortem examination on 24 January, at the behest of the Procurator Fiscal, the body having to be exhumed for this purpose.

Dr Shand's was shown the iron bar, or poker. In his opinion, 'It might have produced some of the fractures on the head, but it was unlikely that it produced the larger. The mallet might have produced the larger fracture, and some of the smaller.' Whichever weapon did what, the good doctor was adamant about one thing: that the larger wounds could not have been produced by Ann Hannah falling on to the stone floor, not even in a struggle; nor could they have been caused by falling off a chair. He agreed the knife might have been used to inflict the wounds on her face. The judge thought the jury should consider the possibility of the wounds being self-inflicted.

'How could a person make a fracture behind one's head?' he asked.

'It might be possible,' replied the doctor.

'You have never tried it, I suppose?' asked his lordship. Not surprisingly, there was laughter in court.

Dr Shand was asked if a person could have stood on a table or chair, struck herself on the head and fallen to the floor? 'No,' he said, 'because the points of fracture were too many to have been by one fall and were on the side of the head, not the vertex.' The upshot of all the medical testimony was that Ann Hannah could not have inflicted upon herself the wounds that killed her. Her wounds were caused by being struck upon the head by the mallet, probably when she was washing her clothes. What happened after that we cannot know exactly; she may have turned to face her attacker, when the poker and knife might also have been used.

Mary Timney's clothes were bloodstained. If it could be shown the stains were Ann Hannah's blood, this would be damning indeed. Today, there would be no problem, but in the mid-nineteenth century, science was not so precise. The bloodstained clothing taken from Mary Timney, along with the mallet, was taken to Dr Maclagan, at Edinburgh. Although Dr Maclagan could not say conclusively that the blood on Mrs Timney's clothes and the mallet was that of Ann Hannah, he did say that it was human blood. Under the microscope he compared a specimen of Ann's hair with the hairs found on the mallet. These were 'quite the same in tint and average size ... It is in the highest degree probable, although it cannot be absolutely affirmed, that the hairs were from the same person.' On the green tartan dress, found in the loft of Mrs Timney's house, Maclagan found a brown stain on the breast, apparently that of blood, which had soaked through and stained the lining. There was another stain on the front of the petticoat, found with the dress. A bed-gown found in the same place was stained at the right breast, and on putting it with the tartan dress he found the stains corresponded, and could reasonably conclude that the two garments had been worn and sustained bloodstains at the same time.

Dr Maclagan subjected all the bloodstains to a microscopic test. Defence counsel, Mr Cowan, asked him what value such a test had. Dr Maclagan answered: 'If you get blood corpuscles you would find, if they were not round, that they were not those of a human being.'

'You mean that oval globules are such as in a fish or a bird?'

'Yes.'

'Blood corpuscles of the mammalia, that is, of animals which suckle their young, are round – such as those of a cow?'

'Yes.'

'Would you allow me in that part of your report where you mention "human blood" to substitute the word "mammalian"?'

'Certainly.'

'You mean it does not refer to human blood any more than to that of any other mammal?'

'Yes.'

Thus Dr Maclagan could not 'absolutely affirm' that the hairs found on the mallet were that of Ann Hannah; neither had he established the blood on Mary Timney's clothing was human, his only firm conclusion being that Ann Hannah had not been attacked by a fish or a bird. His evidence on the blood, therefore, was useless, except that the position of the blood on the clothing – on the chest – meant that it was not her attacker's menstrual blood. The doctor's evidence was hardly conclusive.

It was the rule that the prisoner, who could not testify, could make 'declarations'. Mary Ann Timney made three.

The first, made on 14 January (the day after the murder), was that, on the Wednesday before Christmas, when she went to gather sticks, Ann Hannah had stopped her and said she was not to gather them, calling her a thief and accusing her of stealing her turnips. Since that day she had neither seen nor spoken to Ann Hannah. She had not seen her on the day of the crime until she went with neighbours to the house where she saw her lying on the floor. She – Mrs Timney – had been unwell that day and had not left her house that morning or forenoon. She had never seen the knife or poker. She had worn the petticoat and shift on the day of the crime; the green tartan dress, petticoat, bonnet, bed-gown and other clothing were hers. She had not worn the bed-gown on the day of the crime. The tea and sugar had been bought by her eldest daughter at Smith's grocer's shop, Dalry, the previous Saturday. She said she was 'innocent of doing Ann Hannah any harm'.

In her second declaration, on 17 January, she said she had never seen the wooden mallet before.

Her third, made on 4 February, was quite sensational: in it, she said it was her own mother, Margaret Corson, who had murdered Ann Hannah:

My mother came to my house that Monday morning to wash some clothes for me. The other children were out gathering sticks … My mother took her frock off and put on my green tartan dress and my petticoat. She said she saw Ann Hannah going into or coming out of the yard, and said, 'Mary, I have a mind to give Ann Hannah her licks for setting your man against you when you were taken to Kirkudbright.' I replied she was not to mind Ann Hannah. She said if she thought Ann Hannah was alone she would go to her now. I said, 'Mother, don't go, for Ann Hannah is stronger than you and she'll fell you.' I could see her from my door go into Ann Hannah's. In about ten minutes my mother returned all over blood. I said, 'Preserve me, mother, has Ann Hannah killed you?' She said, 'No, Mary, but I think I have near killed her.' She took off my frock and petticoat and put on her own. She also took off her bed-gown, which I said was mine, but I now declare to be my mother's. She washed her hands and face in my tub, and said, 'Now, Mary, after what I have done to Ann Hannah I can neither stop to bake or wash, nor rest. I must be away home.' I saw her go down the road past Carsphad. I said, 'Mother, I hope ye haven't killed Ann Hannah.' She said she would never tell she had been to my house, that she had not been seen by anyone and had not passed the neighbours' houses as she came up the riverside, and would go back the same way. She then left. All of which is truth.

In reply to Mrs Timney's assertion that she had not left her house 'that morning or forenoon', William Hannah said he had seen her outside, going to her pigs. That she had sent her eldest daughter to buy tea and sugar on the Saturday, at Smith's grocer's at Dalry, was proved false by William Smith, the grocer, and by two others in the town, none of whom had served any Timney children that day.

The mallet was recognised by her husband and two of her children as having been in the house for years.

As to her third declaration – that her mother, Margaret Corson, murdered Ann Hannah – five witnesses testified to discredit it. They were Mrs Corson's husband and Jane Good, her daughter, both of whom were with Mrs Corson at her home in Dalry on the day of the murder; Erskine Fisher, the next-door neighbour, who saw Mrs Corson doing her washing that morning and hanging out her clothes at one o'clock; Jane Stevenson, who lived opposite, who saw her at her washtub; and Mary Douglas, who saw her at her door about 10.30 a.m. Mary Timney was proved to be a liar. And who, in any case, would have believed her mother would have worn her daughter's clothes to go and attack Ann Hannah?

The Advocate Depute said no single, accidental blow had killed Ann. 'Wound after wound, blow after blow was inflicted on that woman with considerable violence, so that her skull was fractured in four places, two of her ribs were broken and her arms discoloured with strokes.' Questions had been put as to whether she could have fractured her own skull, and that was impossible. 'It was not one fracture, but four distinct ones.' A single injury might have resulted in falling off a chair, but not another. The articles stained with blood were found in the prisoner's house, in the loft. There was clothing, not concealed, which had been wet, but notwithstanding being washed there was blood on it. Mary Timney took the mallet with her to the Hannahs' house. The taking of the money and the tea might not have been the object of the murder, but the idea of taking them might have occurred afterwards; she had none of these things immediately before, and they were found in her house later.

Mr Cowan, defending, said there had been much prejudice against Mrs Timney, and the evidence against her was circumstantial. With regard to her third declaration – Mrs Timney accusing her mother of the crime – he would not ask the jury to believe it, but it had been made after she had been more than a fortnight in prison. She did not know what she was doing, and no proof was shown that Mrs Timney had cherished malice against the deceased. There was a struggle, and the injuries the deceased had sustained might have been caused by her head coming into contact with a chair, a table, or the stone floor, or any hard object. It was possible, therefore, to return a verdict of culpable homicide.

The judge said, 'No human eye saw Mary Timney commit the crime, but nobody committed a murder intending to be seen'. It was not necessary to show motive, but there was no trace of any motive on the part of anyone else but she. Her husband had to borrow 2 shillings and 6 pence that morning, as they had no money in the house, yet she had 7 shillings and 7 pence soon after; they had no tea or sugar that morning, but did in the afternoon; there was fresh blood on the front of her clothing, none of it on the back. The jury would have 'no difficulty' in disbelieving her third declaration, that of accusing her mother. They were there to administer the law, and they would have no reflection upon themselves if they did their duty according to their conscience. They returned after thirty minutes when, in 'breathless silence', the foreman declared, 'We unanimously find the prisoner guilty of murder.'

His lordship told Timney, 'You were well acquainted with Ann Hannah. She and her brothers were your neighbours, and had been kind to you and your husband. On the very morning of her death one of her brothers lent your husband half a crown. She had accused you of taking wood, and you say she accused you of stealing her turnips. Whatever these causes were, they were miserably small to have produced such a result. You went to her house carrying with you that mallet, with which you must have inflicted repeated blows upon the head of that unfortunate woman till her skull was fractured, injuries enough to produce death. It now remains for me to pronounce the last sentence of the law ...'

As he spoke, Timney sobbed, 'My lord, it never was me, it never was me.'

'The time of all of us in this world is short, but it is necessarily short in your case. Your days are numbered ...'

'No, my lord. No, my lord.'

'I should betray my duty and hold out false hopes to you if I gave you the slightest hope that the sentence of the law might not be carried into effect ...'

'No, my lord. Give me forever a prison. Dinnae, dinnae do that.'

The judge donned the black cap, passed sentence of death and ordered Mary Timney be removed to the prison at Dumfries, there to be detained and fed on bread and water until 29 April, upon which day, between eight and ten o'clock in the forenoon, to be taken to a place of execution, and there, by the hands of the executioner, be hanged by the neck upon a gibbet till she be dead. He ordained her body to be buried within the precincts of the prison, saying, 'And may the Lord have mercy upon your soul.'

'Oh my weans. My lord, dinnae dae that. Oh my weans. Oh my weans,' sobbed Timney. Then, in a scene harrowing in the extreme, she was taken away, crying for her children: 'My weans, my weans.'

Post-Trial

After sentence, Mary Timney, in a written statement, said that she and her husband had lived happily together for ten years until they came to Carsphad. Then Ann Hannah acquired a 'great influence' over her husband, and she became jealous. On the morning of the 'fatal occurrence' Ann Hannah, seeing her, cried, 'Are you coming here to steal my sticks?' Blows were exchanged, after which she – Timney – returned to her house. But, still heated with the quarrel, she went back to Ann Hannah's house to give her a beating, but not intending to take her life. When she entered the kitchen, Ann Hannah kicked her in the knee and struck her with the mallet. When Ann dropped the mallet, Timney picked it up and struck her a heavy blow to the side of the head. Then, in a 'frenzy of passion', she followed up this blow with others. She 'positively affirmed' the mallet was not hers and was not taken by her to Ann Hannah's cottage.

A 'great change' came over the community, with a wish that Timney be spared. This was largely based on her lowly position in life, her ignorance, her want of education, her weak intellect, her children. It seemed there was hope, because 'the criminal pleaded for was female'. Her case was taken up by Mr Ewart, MP, who believed Ann Hannah might have lost her life in an affray, not murder. Two Dumfries women went to the Northumberland home of the Home Secretary, Sir George Grey, who said he would do all he could, 'compatible with his sense of duty and regard for law and justice'. Meanwhile, Dr W. Browne visited Timney in prison, and reported to the Crown Agent in Edinburgh that 'she was neither fatuous nor imbecile, but possessed the average intellect of her class, at the same time showing an entire want of moral training and education, while her life had been passed under conditions very unfavourable to moral development.'

Sir George Grey said that after the most careful consideration of facts, he could not justify recommending that the prerogative of the Crown should be interposed for the remission of the capital punishment. When Timney was told the news, she insisted that although she had quarrelled with Ann Hannah, she did not intend to take her life. On the day before the scheduled execution, in a heart-rending scene, she had to be dragged away from her children. If it was harrowing for her, what it must have been like for her family is beyond comprehension.

That night, a 'black-timbered gibbet' and scaffold were erected at the junction of St David Street – now Irish Street – and Buccleugh Street, Dumfries. A 7ft-high barrier was put up, and 200 special constables were sworn in to assist with any crowd problems. At 8.15 a.m. on 29 April 1862, 'a morning that dawned thick and heavy, with a dense mist shrouding the landscape', Mary Timney was taken from her cell to expiate her crime. A crowd of between 2,000 and 3,000 was gathered, mainly young lads and labourers. Calcraft was executioner, assisted by 'a seedy, barefaced fellow, who had taken to the business from a liking he had for it'. Timney had 'lost all composure and fortitude'. Begging not to be hanged, she was taken to the scaffold in a 'frantic and distracted state'. Her face distorted with terror, she gazed around her, then screamed aloud, in tones that brought a shudder to the gawping crowd, 'Oh no, no, no! My four weans, my four weans ...'

Suddenly, beyond the prison wall, someone handed the prison governor a letter. Was it a reprieve? Was the poor, wretched soul now staring death in the face to be spared after all? But no! The letter was a request from a news agency in London to be provided with details of the execution in time for the evening papers. As Timney was brought forward there were gasps of sympathy for the wretched woman. Then Calcraft placed the white hood over her head, so that now she could not see. At 8.23 a.m. he pulled the bolt, and Mary Timney dropped fifteen inches, a pathetically short, inhumane distance for one who was supposed to die without pain and distress. One of the gentlemen in the prison yard almost fainted, two of the militiamen opposite the courthouse 'fell from the ranks', whilst in the crowd 'a thrill of horror chilled every heart'. As the thick and heavy mist gave way to soft, spring sunshine, the crowd quietly dispersed, the special constables surrendered their batons and in Dumfries it was business as usual.

Author's Verdict

In a statement, post conviction, Mary Timney admitted killing Ann Hannah. But had she confessed to the crime? Hardly.

Far from showing remorse and telling the truth, her 'confession' was a clever ploy, contrived to have her crime reduced to culpable homicide – manslaughter, if you will. It was all about the mallet. She was saying she went to Ann Hannah's house to give her a beating, and that Ann attacked *her* with the mallet before she struck her with it 'in a frenzy of passion'. It was perchance that she came by the mallet at all, she was saying. If true, she may have had a case and been spared her life. But her husband and children said the mallet had been in the Timney household for years.

The bad blood between the two women was commonly known. The menfolk of the two families knew, the local policeman knew, and we can assume from her actions when she discovered Ann Hannah lying senseless, that Agnes McLellan knew. For where did she go to report her grisly find? To the next cottage, a mere fifty yards along the road? No, she sought the help of the Coates family, quarter of a mile away. She suspected Mary Timney, not a passing stranger, of attacking her friend.

Timney's actions were not those of one who was reacting to provocation or suffering attack. She left her front door and walked the fifty yards to the Hannahs' house, which she entered and struck her victim on the head as she was kneeling on the floor, washing her clothes. She also struck her with the iron bar. What, if anything, she did with the knife, we cannot know. In fact, we cannot know exactly what happened, except that poor Ann Hannah had her head smashed in. It was a cowardly, brutal attack, one for which the jury rightly returned a murder verdict.

The manner of Timney's execution was harrowing in the extreme. Pleading for her life and her 'four weans', she was carried, petrified with fear, up the steps to the platform, where Calcraft calmly went about his work. All this in front of thousands of people, there to witness the dispensation of justice – or whatever other reason each individual may have had to see such a spectacle. Of the fourteen women publicly hanged in Scotland in the nineteenth century, Mary Timney was the last.

5

A Murderous Liaison

Priscilla Biggadike, Lincolnshire, 1868

The 'miserable hut' the Biggadike family shared with two lodgers in the village of Stickney was, nonetheless, home. There was one first-floor bedroom with two beds, which stood side by side just eighteen inches apart, one for the entire Biggadike family – Richard and Priscilla and their three children, the eldest 12 years of age – and the other for their two lodgers, Thomas Procter, aged 31, and 21-year-old George Ironmonger. These were harsh living conditions indeed, even in mid-Victorian Britain.

The three adult males all worked. Richard Biggadike had a good income as a well sinker, whilst Procter and Ironmonger earned a living as rat catcher and boatman respectively. They had lived – and slept – with the Biggadikes for some months. Biggadike was always off to work early, leaving Procter and Ironmonger within touching distance of his wife. It was little wonder that he suspected one of them, Procter, of taking advantage, but surprising, perhaps, that he didn't show him the door, not even when he accused his wife of being 'too intimate' with him.

Thirty-nine-year-old Priscilla did not take kindly to her husband's accusations of infidelity on her part, and the pair frequently quarrelled 'loudly and passionately'. Jane Ironmonger, a neighbour, said she once heard Priscilla say that she wished her husband might be 'brought home dead', and on another occasion that he 'might come home stiff'. Still, things ticked along, but the situation was hardly satisfactory from Richard Biggadike's point of view, although why he allowed it to prevail, given his suspicions, is hard to imagine.

About 6 a.m. on Wednesday 30 September, Biggadike rose early as usual and went off to work. Procter and Ironmonger also went to work, albeit later, arriving home between four and five o' clock, then went off fishing, before returning at 5.30 p.m. Mrs Biggadike, the children, Procter and Ironmonger had their tea together, which included some shortcake that Mrs Biggadike had baked. Ironmonger then went fishing again, and Procter followed half an hour or so later. A piece of the shortcake was put aside for Richard Biggadike when he got home.

At 6 p.m., twelve hours after leaving the house that morning, Richard Biggadike arrived home. Not surprisingly, he ate a hearty meal of mutton, then the shortcake that had been kept for him, before sitting by the fire and lighting his pipe. Sadly for him, he would not enjoy the quiet evening he had earned and no doubt looked forward to, for just ten minutes later he was 'seized with violent sickness and purging'. He went outside where he began retching and was in great pain, then returned indoors only to go outside again, telling George Ironmonger, 'I can't live long like this. You must fetch the doctor.' Ironmonger went as he was bid and Dr Maxwell arrived about seven o' clock, by which time Biggadike was in bed, desperately ill. Mrs Biggadike told the doctor her husband had eaten 'nothing but what we had ourselves' – the mutton and the cake. Already forming his own opinion about Biggadike's sudden illness, Maxwell poured some of his patient's vomit into a bottle, and took it away for examination. He asked Mrs Biggadike to come to his house for some medicine.

Mrs Biggadike first went to the house of a neighbour, Mary Ann Clark, taking with her a piece of the shortcake. She told Mrs Clark that Dr Maxwell had said she had 'put something in the cake', and she was going to take it to him. The two women then went to the doctor's for the medicine, before returning to the Biggadike house; where they went upstairs, finding Richard bleeding from the mouth and nose, exclaiming, 'Lord, have mercy upon me.' About 11 p.m. Dr Maxwell returned, finding Biggadike vomiting blood and in a state of collapse. He left him to his fate. In truth there was little he could do.

About 6 o' clock the next morning Thomas Procter called at Mrs Clark's house, and said, 'Dick's worse. He's dying. Will you come in?' Mrs Clark did so, finding Mrs Biggadike and Ironmonger upstairs with the dying Richard. Mrs Biggadike said her husband had thrown a teacup at her, and had kicked her off the foot of the bed, then had got out of bed and knocked her down. We may assume by his actions that Richard Biggadike, like Dr Maxwell, had formed an opinion about the cause of his illness. He died even as his wife and the others were in his bedroom.

Dr Maxwell's suspicions about the cause of Biggadike's death prompted him to do two things: to inform the police, and carry out a post-mortem examination. Finding the internal organs in a 'very inflamed state', he removed the stomach, part of the intestines and other organs, which he gave, together with the vomit, in jars and bottles to Superintendent Wright, to be taken for examination by Professor Alfred Swayne Taylor, at Guy's Hospital, London. Maxwell's opinion, that Richard Biggadike had died through the effects of irritant poison, was corroborated by Dr Taylor, who told the jury at the resumed inquest on 26 October, 'I never saw a clearer case of death from poison. The case is so perfectly clear that portions of arsenic were found even in its perfect state.' It was impossible to state what the arsenic was taken in, he said, because it always mixes with whatever is in the stomach.

There were several people, all living nearby, who gave the police good reason to suspect Priscilla Biggadike of poisoning her husband. About three or four months before, Eliza Fenwick, Priscilla's sister-in-law, called at the Biggadikes' house with her husband on their way to go shopping. Mrs Fenwick drew Priscilla's attention to mice having eaten a hole in her flour bag. 'If you like,' said Priscilla, 'I'll give you a little white mercury to kill them.' She got up intending to fetch some, but Mrs Fenwick's husband, Edwin, stopped her, saying he would not have any of the 'old stuff' in the house as the children might be poisoned by it.

Susan Everington said she was passing the Biggadikes' on 24 September when she saw Mrs Biggadike standing at the door. 'I'm sorry you and your husband have got to live very uncomfortable together,' said Mrs Everington. 'I understand you disagreed when you went to Boston the other day and he put you out of doors. I hope it's not true, for he is a good looking man and a kind husband and father I hope.' She asked if her husband ever made a fuss with the children. Mrs Biggadike said that when he was 'in drink' he would say a child was not his, to which she would reply, 'Never mind whose it is, I know it's mine.'

Jane Ironmonger said on 28 September Mrs Biggadike called at her house and mentioned the poisoning case of John Garner of Mareham le Fen, Lincolnshire, and asked Mrs Ironmonger how he had 'got on', meaning what the sentence was. Mrs Ironmonger said she did not know. Mrs Biggadike said she thought Garner was transported, adding that she understood doctors and police could not find poison in the meal or sago. Mrs Ironmonger also said that Richard Biggadike could not read or write.

On 2 October, the day after Biggadike died, Eliza Fenwick went to the house. As she entered, Thomas Procter stepped outside and said, 'Here, I want you.'

'Do you mean me?' Mrs Fenwick said.

'No, I want Mrs Biggadike,' he replied. When Mrs Biggadike went to him, Mrs Fenwick heard him say to her, 'Now, mind what you say.'

'Do you think I'm a fool? Don't tell me no more than I know,' Mrs Biggadike replied.

Shortly afterwards, when Mrs Fenwick came downstairs, she said to Mrs Biggadike, 'They say you've poisoned him.'

'Yes, I know they do. It was that Dr Maxwell, but I'll give the devil for it,' she replied.

On 3 October, Superintendent Wright arrested Priscilla Biggadike on suspicion of murdering her husband. After being cautioned not to incriminate herself, she replied, 'It's hard work I should bear all the blame. I am innocent.' Near the railway station on the way to Spilsby police station, Superintendent Wright remarked, 'We have not been long coming from Stickney. The last train is not in yet.'

'I wasn't thinking about the train,' replied Mrs Biggadike, 'I was thinking what I should say that I haven't said. I found a piece of paper in his pocket, wrote upon, saying that he had done it himself, and the reason was stated he was so much in debt.'

'I understood your husband could neither read nor write,' said Superintendent Wright. 'What have you done with the paper?'

'I burnt it,' she replied.

On 15 October, by now incarcerated in the House of Correction at Spilsby, Mrs Biggadike applied to see the governor, John Farr Phillips. She was taken to his office, accompanied by the matron, where she told Phillips she wished to make a statement and 'tell all' about her husband's death. After cautioning her, Phillips took down the following statement at her behest:

> On Wednesday I was standing against the tea table and saw Thomas Procter put a white powder of some sort in a teacup, and then pour some milk into it. My husband at that time was in the dairy, washing himself. My husband came into the room directly after and sat down to the table and I poured his tea out. He drank it, and more besides that. About half an hour afterwards he was taken ill. He went out of doors and was sick, then came in and sat about ten minutes, and went out and was sick again, then went to bed. He asked me to send for the doctor, which I did. The doctor was about an hour before he came. I went to the doctor's about quarter of an hour after he left, and he gave me some medicine and ordered me how to give it him – two tablespoonfuls every half hour, and I was to put a mustard plaster on the stomach. He came no more till eleven o'clock at night. I came downstairs to go out of doors and asked Thomas Procter to go upstairs and sit with my husband. When I went upstairs into the room as I was going up I saw Procter putting some white powder into the medicine bottle with a spoon, and he then went downstairs and left me in the room with my husband. As soon as he had left the room I poured some medicine into the cup and gave it to my husband, and I tasted it myself. An hour afterwards I was sick, and so I was for two days after. What I have just stated about the medicine took place about two o'clock in the morning, after the doctor had gone.

Not surprisingly, on being given this information Superintendent Wright arrested Procter, who replied, 'I'm innocent. I know no more about it than I stated at the inquest.' Also unsurprising was that the jury, at the final inquest, decided both Priscilla Biggadike and Thomas Procter had a case to answer. The predjudist views of the Victorian press were exposed when Procter appeared on this occasion as a prisoner: 'The most uncouth-looking individual in the whole parish, his countenance is very repugnant; he has a high back and his legs appear to have a serious malformation'. As though his physical appearance could in any way be held in evidence against him. The pair were promptly taken before the magistrates and committed for trial, where Procter said, 'Well, gentlemen, I shall be innocent, take me where you like'. Priscilla Biggadike said nothing, except to apply in vain for bail.

That December, when the prisoners appeared at the Lincoln Winter Assizes, Justice Byles instructed the jury to dismiss the case against Procter. He was right to do so, since there was no evidence against him, save the uncorroborated statement of Mrs Biggadike that she had seen him put white powder into a teacup with milk, then spoon white powder into his medicine. His lordship probably did so with profound regret, but made a valid point in saying, 'As to Procter, there is considerable difficulty, for if the jury sent down a bill on insufficient evidence he would be acquitted with immunity for the future; but if they threw out the bill, he might be apprehended in future and put on trial.' It was the law until recent times that where someone has been charged with a crime, he cannot be tried again – 'charge' meaning imperilled before a jury. By dismissing Procter before he was 'charged', there might be a time, if new evidence came to light, that he could be tried later.

Priscilla Biggadike alone stood trial. Mr Bristowe, prosecuting, told the jury to dismiss from their minds any 'rumours or statements' they may have heard, and to carefully weigh the facts they would hear. The first witness, James Turner, testified that he had known Richard Biggadike to be in good health on the 30 September, and said he, Biggadike, could neither read nor write. Thereafter the witnesses testified, steadily building up the case against Mrs Biggadike, including Procter, who, not surprisingly, denied knowing anything about white powder.

Mr Lawrance, defending, accepted there was no doubt Richard Biggadike had died from poison, but the 'great and all-important question' was whether it was given to him by the prisoner. The prosecution had failed to show there was poison in the house, either at the time or months before, and even then 'white mercury' was mentioned though not seen. No adequate motive had been proved. Every single word Mrs Biggadike had said had been raked up against her to support the prosecution case to show she had bad feeling towards her husband, and it was not for the defence to suggest that any other person had administered the poison.

Then there were the statements she had made to persons in authority. Was there anything to fix the crime upon her without them? The jury could not believe them all, as they were not consistent; why should they fix on that which told most against her? The first, made to the coroner, gave account of the matter but implicated no one; in the second, made to Superintendent Wright, she said she had found a piece of paper in her husband's pocket containing a statement that he had taken the poison himself; in the third, she attempted to throw the blame on to Procter. The statements showed that, finding suspicion against her growing stronger every day, she tried to free herself from it by every means possible. She was a weak woman, labouring under suspicion, who told different stories, and this was accounted for by the terror she naturally felt. There was no proof that she did it, and the slightest doubt should turn the scale in her favour.

As ever, the judge had the last word. The crime was a secret one, he said; it was rare that any eye witnessed the poison being poured into a cup, except that of the person who did it. Such a case would be proved by circumstantial, not direct, evidence. Significantly, he added, 'As to the lodger, Procter, if she saw him put powder into the tea, and then into the medicine, it would not absolve her.' The jury unanimously agreed, returning a verdict of 'Guilty, but we recommend her to mercy.'

'On what grounds?' asked his lordship.

After consulting his fellow jurors the foreman said, 'Only because it is circumstantial evidence.'

'Your verdict is guilty,' said the judge, adding, 'And so say you all?' The men of the jury nodded assent.

Assuming the black cap, the judge said, 'Priscilla Biggadike, though the evidence is circumstantial, more satisfactory evidence I never heard. The sentence of the court is that you be taken from whence you came, and from thence to a place of execution, and that you there be hanged by the neck till you are dead, and may the Lord have mercy on your soul.'

Whilst the guilty verdict affected almost every person in the court, Biggadike seemed to have 'no terror', and it was only when the judge was passing sentence she seemed to realise her position, bowing her head upon her hands and remaining thus till the gaoler touched her. Whereupon she rose without comment, and walked firmly from the dock.

Post-Trial

Convicted and sentenced for murdering her husband, Priscilla Biggadike was to hang on 28 December at the county gaol within the walls of Lincoln Castle. During this time she did not see her children, or any friends. Her three sisters and one brother did visit her, exhorting her to confess to the crime. She never did, not to them or anyone.

Just before nine, the 'sad procession' emerged through a side door in the prison wall and made its way to where a new drop had been erected. As they walked, Biggadike moaned and leaned on her warders for support. The executioner was Thomas Askern, 'a tall, sombre-looking man dressed in good clothes'. They had about 200 yards to walk. At about halfway Biggadike asked, sobbing, 'How much longer is it?'

'Not far,' she was told.

'My troubles are nearly over,' she replied. Nearly, but not quite, for her death would be a protracted and painful one.

The chaplain, the Revd H.W. Richter, addressed her, saying, 'I want to ask whether you still persist in your declaration of innocence. Do you still say you had nothing to do with it, in thought, word or deed?'

'I do, Sir,' she replied.

The procession arrived at the foot of the drop, where, being five minutes early –
five interminable minutes for Priscilla Biggadike – she was provided with a chair
and made to wait. As she looked around with forlorn hope at the faces around
her, the chaplain addressed her again. 'You are soon to pass from this world into
another. What satisfaction it would be to your children, your friends and relations
to know that you had passed from death to life under the promise that your sins
were forgiven, and that you had been admitted into the blessed kingdom of God.
Had you made an open confession I should have done what I am authorised to
do: pronounced your sins, though many, forgiven.' To this final appeal to confess,
Biggadike had nothing to say.

Having ascended the steps, she was placed under the noose, and while it was
being adjusted and her legs were fastened together, she stood firm, moaning
and exclaiming, 'My troubles are nearly over. Surely my troubles are ended.' As
she dropped, she shrieked out loud, then nothing was heard but gurgling as the
wretched woman swung at the rope's end for three and a half minutes before
life was pronounced extinct. The black flag was hoisted as the clock struck nine.
A hundred people stood outside the gates, unable to witness events – a new
law meant executions were now carried out in private followed by an inquest
immediately afterwards.

This was a botched hanging, as the inquest would show. When the coroner
asked the prison governor, Mr Foster, 'Was the sentence carried out in accordance
with decency and humanity?', the answer came, 'It might have been done better.'

Mr Broadbent, the medical officer, said, 'The rope was adjusted in a different
way to what I have hitherto seen it. It was passed round the neck and the knot
came directly under the chin, which threw the head back and the convict
breathed for some minutes before she died. It is usual to apply the rope with
the knot at the side, but the executioner said that by hanging with the knot in
front all sensation is immediately destroyed.' Mr Broadbent said he preferred the
'old method'. How could Askerne, or anyone, know whether sensation had been
destroyed? Priscilla Biggadike was buried in the Lucy Tower within the grounds
of the castle, her grave marked by a small stone bearing her initials and the date
of her execution.

Author's Verdict

There was ample circumstantial evidence to incriminate Priscilla Biggadike with
the murder of her husband, not least her bringing up the subject of another
poisoning case in Lincolnshire – 'doctors and police could not find poison in the
sago', and the offer of 'white mercury' to her sister-in-law, Eliza Fenwick, to kill
mice, an offer only interrupted by Eliza's husband, who said he didn't want any of
the 'old stuff' in the house (and who could blame him?). She told Superintendent
Wright about a suicide note she alleged her (illiterate) husband had written, but
said she had burnt it when asked for it. She willingly offered the cake for analysis

because she knew perfectly well it did not contain arsenic. Other facts in these pages lend further weight to the circumstantial evidence.

But what of her assertion that she saw her lover, Thomas Procter, put white powder into her husband's cup, into which he poured milk and then she poured his tea, which her husband then drank? 'He drank it and about half an hour afterwards he was taken ill … he went out of doors and was sick.' And the white powder she said she saw Procter spooning into her husband's medicine, which she then gave him? It was as a result of this statement that Procter found himself in the dock, if only for a short time until the judge had no choice but to release him. If, as she alleged, Procter did these things, was she any the less guilty of the crime, given that she said she saw what he did?

In 1882, fourteen years after Priscilla Biggadike was hanged for murdering her husband, Thomas Procter, on his deathbed, admitted his part in the crime. He was guilty of murder all along – but wasn't Priscilla Biggadike also guilty? She poured her husband's tea knowing it contained white powder, and watched him become ill; she gave him his medicine, knowing the white powder was in it. She would have known perfectly well what that white powder was, and she admitted administering it. 'If she saw Procter put powder into the tea, and then into the medicine, it would not absolve her,' said the judge. Quite so.

6

'A Sort of Inhumanity'

Mary Ann Cotton, County Durham, 1872

Mary Ann Cotton
She's dead and she's rotten.
She lies in her bed
With her eyes wide oppen;
Sing, sing, oh what can I sing?
Mary Ann Cotton is tied up with string.
Where? Where? Up in the air
Sellin' black puddens a penny a pair.

(Children's rhyme)

Aged 40 and widowed, life wasn't easy for Mary Ann. With three kids to care for – two not even her own – she couldn't go out to work, and her live-in lover, Joseph Nattrass, a pitman, earned little at the local colliery. A better prospect would have been Mr Quick-Manning, the excise officer at the local brewery. He was free, but hardly interested in someone with so much baggage. Life in a small Durham village in Victorian England was hard for someone so ambitious.

But fate played a kind hand when Quick-Manning fell ill with smallpox and Mary Ann, a former nurse, was asked to look after him. Look after him she did, and she wasted no time in securing his affections. Soon they were lovers, and there was even talk of marriage. Quick-Manning was hesitant, but if the clutter in Mary Ann's life was a problem for him, it wasn't a problem for Mary Ann.

In the space of three weeks, from 10 March to 1 April, there were three deaths in the Cotton family home at Johnson Terrace, West Auckland. First, Frederick Cotton, aged 10, the son of Mary Ann's late husband (also called Frederick), apparently of fever; then Mary Ann's own son by Cotton, Robert Robson Cotton, aged fourteen months, evidently due to convulsions caused by teething; then Joseph Nattrass, apparently of fever. That left Mary Ann and 7-year-old Charles Edward Cotton, her remaining stepson and sole barrier, presumably, to

Quick-Manning asking her to be his wife. She would have been optimistic when, a fortnight later, she became pregnant by him. But then things took a turn for the worse for Mary Ann.

It all started on Saturday 6 July, when Thomas Riley, assistant overseer at West Auckland, came to call. By then Mary Ann and Charles Edward had moved to 13 Front Street, a small terraced house facing the village green. Riley wanted to know if she could look after a smallpox patient. Alas, she was unable to help, because, as she explained, she had to look after Charles Edward. In fact, she said, Riley could help her by making an order to have the boy put into the workhouse. He was not her child after all, and she had the opportunity of taking in a respectable lodger. Riley said he could make no such order unless she went to the workhouse with the boy. She would never go to such a place, she said.

By 'respectable lodger', Riley knew Mary Ann meant Quick-Manning. 'I have heard you might marry,' he ventured.

'It might be so,' replied Mary Ann, 'but the boy is in the way.' Then she added, 'Perhaps it won't matter, as I won't be troubled long. He'll go like all the rest of the Cotton family.'

'You don't mean to tell me this little healthy fellow is going to die?' said Riley.

'He'll not get up,' said Mary Ann, which Riley took to mean he would not reach adulthood.

The following Friday, Riley was passing again when he saw Mary Ann standing at her cottage door. 'My boy's dead,' she told him. She asked him if he would like to come in and see him. Riley declined, and went instead to the local police station where he saw Sergeant Hutchinson, after which he went to see Dr Kilburn. The doctor was 'startled' to hear of the boy's death, as he had seen him twice only the day before, and his assistant, Dr Chalmers, had seen him three times. Riley's suspicions persuaded Kilburn to postpone making out a death certificate, which was a bitter blow for Mary Ann, who needed it to claim the £4 10 shillings insurance money from the Prudential's agent when he called.

Sergeant Hutchinson reported the case to the coroner, who ordered an inquest. It was held in the pub next door to Mary Ann's house, the day after Charles Edward's death. But if they were looking for an accurate cause of death, they would be lucky to have it, as Doctors Kilburn and Chalmers only began their post-mortem examination an hour before the inquest opened – performed, bizarrely we would think today, on a table in Mary Ann's house. Dr Kilburn had no opportunity of making a chemical examination of the contents of the stomach or other organs. He believed that death 'might have been' caused by gastro-enteritis, and told the inquest jury so. A verdict of 'death by natural causes' was recorded. Charles Edward was buried, Mary Ann had her death certificate, and that, it seemed, was that.

But other forces were at work. Rumours that Mary Ann was a 'wholesale poisoner' appeared in the press and alarmed Quick-Manning, who promptly broke off relations with her. If that was bad news, she would have been mortified had she known what Dr Kilburn did. At the hasty post-mortem, he had no time to make a chemical examination, so he took the stomach and other viscera home, where he placed them into a cupboard. The following day he poured the contents of the stomach into a jar, which he kept. The rest was buried in the garden. Three days later he submitted the stomach contents to a Reinsch's Test. One can imagine the look on his face when he beheld the telltale deposit of arsenic. At midnight that very day he reported his findings to the police at Bishop Auckland, and the following day, Thursday 18 July, Mary Ann was arrested. She offered no comment and the police found no arsenic in her house.

On 26 July, the Home Secretary having granted the police permission to exhume Charles Edward's body, they dug up the coffin. They also dug up the remains from Dr Kilburn's garden. Dr Thomas Scattergood, an expert in forensic medicine and toxicology, made an examination and found arsenic in the stomach contents and bowels, as well as the liver, lungs, heart, kidneys and faeces, the latter having been preserved by Mary Ann Dodds, a suspicious neighbour, who had attended the Cotton household when Charles Edward died.

On 21 August Mary Ann appeared before the Bishop Auckland magistrates for committal proceedings. The charge was murder by administering arsenic to her stepson, or causing it to be administered, which she denied. A telling piece of evidence was that of a chemist, John Townend, who said a little boy, whose name he did not know, had come to his shop on 27 May for soft soap and arsenic. He would not serve him. Five minutes later, Mrs Dodds, came in, saying Mrs Cotton had sent her, and he sold her half an ounce to one ounce of arsenic. Mrs Dodds confirmed that Mary Ann had first sent Charles Edward to the chemist's for two penn'orth of arsenic and soft soap, and that she had gone for it when the chemist wouldn't serve the boy. She said about half of the mixture was rubbed on the bedstead, because Mrs Cotton said there were bugs in it. The remainder was put into a jug.

Mrs Dodds said that on 8 July Mary Ann had told her Charles Edward had taken ill. The following Wednesday he seemed 'quite ill', which seems to be an understatement as Mrs Dodds remarked, 'I don't think he'll be long here if he keeps at this.' On Friday the boy was dead. Dr Kilburn had last seen him on the evening before he died, when he said he looked 'pale and waxy', and was suffering from 'vomiting, purging and pains in the stomach'. The doctor had prescribed medicines, but to no avail. He made his belated examination of the stomach contents because of 'what he had heard'. Without rumours or suspicion, he probably wouldn't have bothered.

Dr Scattergood said that arsenic was present in the body, including more than half a grain of white arsenic in the stomach. 'Death was due to arsenic poisoning,' he said, unequivocally. Asked if she wanted to say anything, Mary

Ann whispered 'No' in a low voice. Alone, in the grand surrounding of the court, she would hardly have had the nerve to say anything. She was committed for trial for the murder of her stepson.

It was only a matter of time before the victims of the other deaths at West Auckland were exhumed. Joseph Nattrass was first. On 14 September they recovered his remains from the churchyard at St Helen, Auckland. Dr Scattergood found arsenic in the stomach, bowels, liver, lungs, heart kidneys and spleen. The arsenic in the bowels amounted to 17¾ grains, four being solid. He had no doubt that Nattrass had died as a result of arsenic poisoning.

On 15 October they were back at the churchyard, where they dug up the two children, Frederick Cotton junior and the baby, Robert Robson Cotton. Both had died of arsenic poisoning. The remaining body they sought was that of Frederick Cotton senior, who had died thirteen months before. Try as they might, the digging party could not locate the coffin among graves 'as thick and close as furrows in a field'. It hardly mattered. Mary Ann appeared before the magistrates again the following February, the delay caused by her pregnancy; she now carried the six-week-old baby girl she bore by Quick-Manning. She was charged with a further three murders: of Frederick Cotton junior, her own son Robert Robson Cotton, and Joseph Nattrass. She denied all charges.

Nattrass was 35. He had come to lodge with Mary Ann after the death of her husband in September 1871. The magistrates heard the testimony of several witnesses, including Nattrass's workmates, who said he had been healthy enough in the past. One, Thomas Hall, had wondered why Mary Ann had not had the baby Robert, who had died just three days before, buried, instead of keeping his body in the house. She said she might as well have them buried together, and even sent out for 'stockings and things' to lay Nattrass out when, as she obviously anticipated, he was dead too.

Phoebe Robson, a neighbour, was in Mary Ann's house often enough and had seen Nattrass, who was 'bad in the bowels' and sick. Mary Ann wouldn't let anyone near him and refused him food, explaining he couldn't keep anything down. Mrs Robson had seen Nattrass taking fits, when Mary Ann would hold him down. Sarah Smith said he had complained of his stomach and bowels, and had also witnessed the fits. 'He clashed his head against the wall and bedpost, and bent back his toes as if in cramp.' Mary Ann gave him tea from one of two teapots on the table – his and hers, no doubt. Jane Hedley had seen her giving him something to drink several times and was present when Nattrass expired. Dr Richardson, who attended Nattrass, said he considered his complaint to be inflammation of the mucous membrane of the bowels and high irritability of the neck of the bladder. These are symptoms of arsenic poisoning, but the good doctor had no cause to suspect Nattrass was being poisoned.

Mary Ann had also been seen giving her stepson, Frederick, drinks from a teapot. His stomach was 'much inflamed', with bright red streaks; there was more than a grain of arsenic in the stomach and bowels, nearly all dissolved, and nearly half a grain in the organs. On the Wednesday before he died he asked Elizabeth Atkinson if he could see her husband, Elijah. When asked why, he replied, 'Because I want him to pray with me.' On the Saturday Mrs Atkinson prepared some beef tea, which she took to the boy, but Mary Ann said he was not to have it, saying that it would do no good. In the afternoon of Sunday 10 March, Frederick asked for his cap, and he had it on when he died at five minutes to midnight. It was still on his head when his body was exhumed.

Robert Robson Cotton, Mary Ann's own son, was just fourteen months old. His stomach contained a quantity of mucous which, when diffused in water, produced a sediment of arsenic. Arsenic was also present in the bowels and liver. He died on 28 March, just three days before Nattrass. 'I saw the child retch very much,' said Jane Hedley. Sarah Smith put the boy's troubles down to teething, but when she went to the house one night and saw Mary Ann kneeling by the cradle, as Nattrass was dying in his bed, she thought the baby was dying too.

'Who shall I fetch?' asked Sarah.

'Nobody,' replied Mary Ann.

Throughout all these harrowing scenes, neither Dr Kilburn nor Dr Chalmers gave foul play a thought. But one might think the death of Joseph Nattrass, in almost identical circumstances and so soon after the children, might have stirred their suspicions.

Mary Ann Robson, as she was, was born at Low Moorsley, near Sunderland, in 1832, one of three children of Michael Robson, who worked in the Durham coalfield as a 'sinker', and Margaret, his wife. Tragically, Michael Robson was killed when he fell down a mineshaft, aged only 30. Mary Ann attended Sunday School and later took her own class there. At sixteen she became a nursemaid to the Potter family at South Hetton, after which she was a dressmaker. She was eighteen when she met William Mowbray, a labourer, whom she married in July 1852.

Almost certainly, Mary Ann was pregnant before they married, which would be why they married at the relatively distant Newcastle upon Tyne Register Office and not locally. Such was the perceived shame of Victorian times. The newlyweds even left the North-East altogether, moving to Cornwall, where they lived for a time in Penzance. Four years later they returned to County Durham with one child, although they probably also had three daughters who had all died as infants. In 1857, the Mowbrays had another child, Margaret Jane, the first to be born in the North East. She was dead before 1861.

In 1858 another child, Isabella, was born. Two years later the daughter who was born in Cornwall was dead, of gastric fever, the doctor said. A year after that another Margaret Jane was born. A boy, John Robert, was born in 1863. He died in 1864, not twelve months old. The following January, Mowbray died too, after an attack of diarrhoea. He was 47. Diarrhoea is a symptom of gastric fever; it is also a symptom of arsenic poisoning.

Mary Ann collected £35 insurance money on her husband's life – a lot of money then – and went to live at Seaham Harbour, on the Durham coast, where she met Joseph Nattrass, who was engaged to a local girl. Nattrass and Mary Ann had an affair, but he married his fiancée and they moved away. This was when the second Margaret Jane died, and Isabella went to live with her grandmother, which is probably why she survived, at least until she returned to the custody of Mary Ann when she was nine. For the first time in her life Mary Ann was on her own. She went to work in the Fever House at Sunderland Infirmary. Here, aged 32, she met and married George Ward, a patient. Ward was described as 'well proportioned and muscular'. They had no children and he died the following year.

In November 1866, James Robinson, a Sunderland shipwright, was widowed and was left to care for his five children. When he advertised for a housekeeper Mary Ann applied and got the job. Three weeks after she moved in to the household the baby was dead, gastric fever listed as the cause. Mary Ann became pregnant by Robinson, and was then called away to look after her mother. Nine days later her mother was dead. Mary Ann returned to the Robinson household, taking 9-year-old Isabella with her. Two more of Robinson's children, James, 6, and Elizabeth, 8, died, and 9-year-old Isabella died days later. All had the same symptoms: rolling about in bed, foaming at the mouth.

In August 1867, James Robinson and Mary Ann were married, and her child by him, another girl, was born the following November. She was christened Mary Isabella, but she died a few days later, an apparent victim of gastric fever, the fifth child to die when Mary Ann was living under the same roof as Robinson.

Robinson's own life must have been imperilled, but, as things turned out, he escaped death, along with two of his children and another Mary Ann had had by him. Wisely, he refused Mary Ann's suggestion to have the children insured, and he refused to insure his own life (at her suggestion), although she did try, unsuccessfully, to have his life insured without his knowledge. In 1869, his Building Society threatened court action when she increased the amounts being paid into the account by fraudulently altering entries in the passbook, and then she tried to borrow money, giving the names of Robinson's brother-in-law and uncle as guarantors. When his son said his stepmother had been sending him to the pawnbrokers, Robinson's patience snapped. He said they had to part, and she left, taking her surviving child by him.

There was speculation later as to why Mary Ann wanted money, other than to buy food and essentials. It seems she wanted others to do her housework, and wanted herself to be smart and attractive. To heighten her social standing, in fact, and to thus rise above her station in life. A commendable ambition, but one she sought to achieve by foul and wicked means. As for James Robinson, he never spoke to Mary Ann again, but at the end of that year, 1869, Mary Ann called at a friend's house in Sunderland and, saying she had to post a letter, she left her child and never returned. The fortunate child was returned to its father, James Robinson.

In 1870, Mary Ann was introduced to Frederick Cotton by his sister, Margaret, who probably knew her through working in service. The Cotton family lived at North Walbottle, a small mining village six miles west of Newcastle. Cotton had lived there with his wife, Adelaide, and their four children. But Adelaide died of consumption, and two of the children, both girls, died too. None of these deaths was attributable to Mary Ann. The survivors of the Cotton household were Frederick senior, and his sons, Frederick junior, aged 10, and Charles Edward, aged 5. All would later perish at the hands of Mary Ann.

Soon after Mary Ann visited the Cottons' home, Margaret, Cotton's sister, died of severe stomach pains. She was 38. Suspicion points at Mary Ann here. Did she want her out of the way? Mary Ann then became pregnant, by Cotton presumably, and Robert Robson Cotton was born in January 1871. Mary Ann then moved to Spennymoor, in County Durham, where she was employed as housekeeper to a German doctor. She was well regarded, and may have had designs on a man of his standing, but there were suggestions that she tried to poison him and she was dismissed. She went back to North Walbottle, and she and Cotton were bigamously married that September, at St Andrew's Church, Newcastle. Soon after the marriage, Mary Ann completed an insurance proposal form, insuring her two stepsons.

In 1871, Frederick Cotton and Mary Ann, his 'wife', left North Walbottle and went to live at Johnson Terrace, West Auckland. They brought with them the two boys of Cotton's first marriage, and their own baby, Robert Robson Cotton.

Why West Auckland? Probably because Mary Ann's previous lover, Joseph Nattrass, now widowed, was living there. That very year Frederick Cotton died unexpectedly. He was 39. The doctor put his death down to gastric fever. Three months later, Nattrass moved in with Mary Ann, but it wasn't long before she was casting covetous eyes in the direction of the excise officer, Quick-Manning. Then came those eventful three weeks when she decided it was time to have a clear-out. Cotton's eldest son, her own baby by Cotton and Nattrass: they all perished.

Mary Ann Cotton's trial opened at the Durham Assizes in March 1873. Sir Thomas Dickson Archibald presided. Charles Russell led the prosecution. Despite appearing for her life, no barrister was eager to defend her. Finally, Thomas Campbell Foster, a highly-regarded silk, agreed. Mary Ann appeared, as she had in all court appearances, wearing a black gown, a black-and-white checked shawl, hairnet and black bonnet. She looked 'depressed, careworn and anxious', but paid close attention to what was going on. There was 'much merriment' as the judge had difficulty understanding the Durham dialect, with even Mary Ann joining in the laughter on that score.

Of the four counts – the murders of Charles Edward Cotton, Frederick Cotton junior, Robert Robson Cotton and Joseph Nattrass – only one would be heard, that of the murder of Charles Edward, her stepson. Mary Ann pleaded 'Not guilty'.

Russell opened by saying that Charles Edward Cotton, seven years old, had been poisoned by Mary Ann, his stepmother. Mary Ann was a qualified nurse, and were it not for her stepson she could have found work; the child was a burden to her, and she was known to ill-treat him, using 'great violence'. His life (and others) had been insured with the Prudential Assurance Co., so that Mary Ann would receive payment upon his death. Doctors Chalmers and Kilburn had been called when the child was ill; they had not anticipated death, but he died on 12 July. Arsenic could not have been given accidentally; it had to be administered over two or three days to work. Mary Ann had acquired arsenic and soft soap from the chemist's. The motive, ventured Russell, was the insurance money, or the 'irksome tie' of the child not of her own flesh and blood. The apparent promise of marriage to Quick-Manning may have played a part in her scheme.

The evidence was circumstantial. 'If a mind were deliberately plotting to take away the life of an infant, such a mind would work out its plan secretly, in security, in darkness. From the very nature of the case, the jury would not expect direct evidence,' said Russell. No arsenic was ever found in Mary Ann's possession, but arsenic and soft soap could easily be separated by a simple chemical process, resulting in the production of pure arsenic.

'Great violence' used against Charles Edward by Mary Ann had been seen by more than one witness. Mary Priestly, a neighbour, saw her strike the boy with her hand, causing his head to strike the wall, and then kick him. There were other, similar assaults. Sometimes the boy would be locked out of the house from eight in the morning until late at night. At other times he would be locked in. William Davison saw Mary Ann thrashing Charles Edward with a 'double belt', yet she slept with him in the bed on the middle floor of the house.

When Russell was finished, the defence called no witness of their own. Instead, Campbell Foster focused on two issues: accidental consumption of arsenic; or, if it had been deliberately administered, there was no proof that it had been by Mary Ann. On 'accidental consumption', he said there was arsenic in 'fluffy and handsome' wallpapers of the type in Mary Ann's house. Dr Kilburn agreed that a hot fire could cause arsenic fumes to be 'thrown off', but only at a temperature of about 380 degrees. Arsenic can cause suffusion to the eyes, irritation of the nostrils and colic pain in the stomach, but Dr Kilburn didn't think it could cause death, certainly not from wallpaper.

'Do you know,' Campbell Foster persisted, 'that its effects have proved injurious to health, and even fatal, and that in Prussia it is prohibited?'

'I have heard of it,' replied Kilburn.

Dr Scattergood put paid to this line of defence, saying, 'The presence of arsenic in the stomach implies recent administration.' He had never heard of anyone suffering death through arsenic in wallpaper.

Campbell Foster complained that evidence in the three other cases where arsenic had been found, and for which Mary Ann was not being tried, was put before the jury. As to the prosecution suggesting she had poisoned her own child, 14-month-old Robert Robson Cotton, one almost revolted at such a picture. 'A mother nursing it, calling in the doctor, dancing it upon her knee, listening to its prattle, seeing its pretty smiles while she knew she had given it arsenic. A mother could do nothing of that kind. The jury should come to the conclusion the mother was not the cold-blooded fiend who would administer poison to her child.'

Justice Archibald drew the jury's attention to motive. The law did not take notice of motive, he said. What the law regarded was intention. The evidence was circumstantial; the jury had to arrive at certainty that excluded reasonable doubt. If there had been a single case they might have doubt about whether poisoning was accidental or not. But the prosecution was entitled, when other deaths occurred under similar circumstances, to refer to them. Dr Scattergood had said that for arsenic to be inhaled or absorbed, the symptoms would have been quite different. There had been repeated administrations, and no fewer than four persons were known to have died by arsenic poisoning. As to proof that administration was by Mary Ann, who else could it have been? If the jury were 'impelled irresistibly' by the evidence that it was the prisoner who administered the poison, they should find her guilty.

The jury took an hour to reach a unanimous verdict of 'Guilty'. When Mary Ann was asked to stand up to hear sentence, a 'deathly pallor overspread her face', and after whispering that she was 'not guilty', the judge told her, 'You have been found guilty of the murder, by means of poisoning, of your stepson, whom it was your duty to cherish and take care of. You seem to have given way to that most awful of all delusions, that you could carry out your wicked designs without detection. Whilst murder by poison is the most detestable of all crimes, it is one the nature of which always leaves behind it complete and incontestable traces of guilt.' He then passed sentence in the usual way, after which Mary Ann almost slipped into unconsciousness.

Post-Trial

Mary Ann Cotton's execution at Durham Gaol was set for 8 a.m. on Monday 24 March 1873. Five days before she was to die, her baby daughter was taken from her. She never confessed to the crime for which she would hang, nor any other. In a letter to William Lowry, who had lodged with her, she wrote, 'I never gave that boy Charles Edward any poison. It was in the arrowroot. I am going to die for a crime I am not guilty of.' She was suggesting a shopkeeper who sold her arrowroot carelessly mixed it with the arsenic. It is hardly likely. The Revd Mountford asked her if she wanted to confess. 'It is not one act, done upon one day. Months passed and those persons of your family died. How did those deaths occur in that way?' To this Mary Ann made no comment.

Despite her wicked crimes, Mary Ann was not without public sympathy. On 18 March one Martha Olive, of Dorchester, wrote to the Home Secretary: 'I have just heard with extreme horror that the poor woman Cotton is to be executed on Monday. Can it really be possible that there can be a law that would take the life of a mother who has a suckling child?' Others thought she should be spared because she had not confessed. The Home Secretary was unmoved, whilst the *Durham County Advertiser* opined, 'The best thing for society and for Mary Ann was that she should quit the earth.'

It was Mary Ann's bad luck that the man assigned to hang her was William Calcraft. Despite his forty-five years' experience at hanging people, he was inept nonetheless. As the death bell sounded on that grim March morning, Calcraft, with his assistant, Robert Evens, 'demanded the body'. Mary Ann's arms were grasped and held to her sides, and a broad leather belt was strapped around her arms and chest. Outside, in the exercise yard, two dozen reporters waited as the small procession – the Deputy Governor, men of religion, the bailiff and warders, and Mary Ann, sobbing and praying – made its solemn way to the gallows.

When Mary Ann caught sight of the gallows, she gasped and fell back into the arms of the warders. Calcraft and Evens led her directly on to the platform, situated at ground level, with the drop into a pit. Shaking uncontrollably, Mary Ann whispered, 'Lord, have mercy upon me. Lord, receive my soul.' Evens slipped the white cap over her head and pulled the noose about her neck, while Calcraft strapped her ankles. Without waiting for a signal, Evens pulled the lever, the platform doors opened and Mary Ann dropped down.

Thanks to Calcraft's short drop, her death was by slow strangulation. She twisted, she swayed, she turned as her hands, still clasped, moved up and down her chest. Calcraft steadied her by grasping her shoulder, but when he let go she turned again. She struggled for three minutes before merciful release.

'Here was the vengeance of the penal code, Christian England demanding an eye for an eye, ache for ache, gripe for gripe, pang for pang, torture for torture.' Thus reported the *Newcastle Daily Chronicle*, adding that 'she was not released until she had paid the uttermost farthing to the inexorable spirit of public vengeance.' When it was over, they raised the black flag for the benefit of the crowd outside, 200 or so. As she awaited the imminent arrival of the men who would hang her, Mary Ann whispered, 'Heaven is my home.' Whether Heaven was her home a few minutes later cannot be known. She was buried within the prison, and the men who hanged her left on the 3.05 train.

Author's Verdict

Whilst there was no direct proof that Mary Ann Cotton killed anyone, the circumstantial evidence was overwhelming. As prosecution counsel put it to the jury, when considering the murder of Charles Edward Cotton, 'Whose was the mind that conceived the idea of administering the poison, and whose was the hand that, directed by that mind, committed the act?' The same question might have been applied to the deaths of Frederick Cotton Junior, Robert Robson Cotton and Joseph Nattrass, and the deaths of others had their bodies exhumed from the earth.

Her usual motive was money. Many of her victims' lives were insured. Of her four husbands and her lover, only one, James Robinson, refused to insure his life, and he was the sole survivor. She also killed when someone was in her way – her mother, for example, who died when Mary Ann was getting set fair with James Robinson; or Frederick Cotton's sister, whom she may have considered a bar to Cotton taking up with her. As the *Durham County Advertiser* reported, 'There was no hatred [of her victims], just a sort of inhumanity which made her indifferent to everything except the attainment of her own paltry ends'.

Those whose deaths may be ascribed to her are: all eight children by her first husband William Mowbray, and Mowbray himself; her second husband, George Ward; her mother; three children of her third husband, James Robinson, and the first of her own children by him; Frederick Cotton's sister, Margaret, and Cotton himself; Cotton's two sons, including Charles Edward, the murder for which she was convicted; the baby boy she bore Cotton; and her lover, Joseph Nattrass. Of the twelve children she bore, only two survived: the child she had by James Robinson, whom she returned to him, and the daughter she bore by Quick-Manning, born in prison and adopted. It should be said that in days of high infant mortality rates, some of her earlier children may have died through other causes. We cannot know.

How did she get away with it for so long? Didn't someone, somewhere, suspect? They did, but Mary Ann was never in one place for long; she killed and moved on. From County Durham to Cornwall and back; to Seaham Harbour and Sunderland, then to North Walbottle in Northumberland; then to Spennymoor and West Auckland. She would have moved on again if the police hadn't come knocking. Even so, all those insurance payouts – what about the man from the Pru? One supposes their offices were small and scattered, with staff unaware of events elsewhere.

Mary Ann's victims, every one, all died in unspeakable agony. The harrowing accounts of those who witnessed their slow, lingering deaths make grim reading. Mary Ann Dodds, describing poor Joseph Nattrass's demise, said, 'He would clench his hands together, grind his teeth, turn the whites of his eyes and draw his legs up.' Others who saw the dying children spoke of 'rolling about in bed' and 'frothing at the mouth'. Blood relation or otherwise, it meant nothing to Mary Ann. Anyone who was 'in the way', or whose death would provide the insurance money she coveted, was doomed. She was a heartless, psychopathic killer. How heart-rending it is to think of 10-year-old Frederick Cotton asking Elijah

Atkinson to pray with him, when all the time the cause of his pain, his wicked stepmother, was poisoning him so that she could marry a man of greater social standing who could provide her with a better life. Nothing is heard of Quick-Manning after the arrest and trial. Such a pity; it would have been interesting to know his feelings when he realised what a close encounter he had had with death, for he too, surely, would have perished the moment Mary Ann fancied claiming the insurance money or decided to move on with her life.

7

'The Barnes Mystery'

Katherine Webster, Surrey, 1879

It was early in the morning of Wednesday 5 March when Henry Wheatley, who was walking by the River Thames, noticed the box. It lay by the water's edge, about thirty yards from Barnes Bridge. Curious, Wheatley went to the box, which was tied with cord. Cutting the cord, he gave the box a kick and it fell apart. He was shocked when he saw the contents appeared to be human remains, 'looking like meat'. He called the police, who called Dr James Adams, who confirmed Wheatley's grim discovery to be the body parts of a human being. The box and its grisly contents were taken to the mortuary.

On 12 March, Thomas Bond, a surgeon, examined the remains, identifying the upper part of the chest, with some upper ribs, the heart and part of the right lung, the right shoulder and part of the right upper arm, the left upper arm, the right thigh, cut off below the joint, the right leg, divided from the thigh at the knee and cut off from above the ankle, part of the pelvis with the uterus attached, and the left foot, cut off above the ankle.

Bond calculated that the soft parts had been hacked, and that the bones had been sawn, 'the division made without relation to anatomical structure.' The body parts had been boiled. The remains appeared to be that of someone who had been dead a week or a fortnight, but decomposition had not occurred due to the cold conditions. The head was missing, but he could say the remains were that of a woman, perhaps over 50. Who was she, and how had she come by her death? No one knew, but she would surely have died by foul means. The police began their enquiries, while the press labelled the story, 'The Barnes Mystery'. A mystery it would remain – for a while.

When Henry Porter, a painter, arrived home from work about 6 p.m. on Tuesday 4 March, he was in for a surprise. Waiting for him at his house at 10 Brickwood Cottages, Rose Gardens, Hammersmith, was a well-dressed woman whom he did not recognise until she spoke. Why, it was Kate, who had lived next door at No. 11, six years before. Since then she had married and was now Mrs Thomas, but sadly was widowed. 'I've been longing to see you,' she told Porter, 'I have lost my aunt, who is dead, and has left me a comfortable home at Richmond. I shall have to dispose of it, on account of being unfortunate in getting lodgings. Can you find me a respectable broker to buy it?'

Porter's son, Robert, aged 15, was also present. Both he and his father noticed that Mrs Thomas's black bag, which was under the table, had something wrapped in brown paper inside. After tea, Kate asked Porter if he would see her off on the train for Richmond. Robert picked up the bag and the threesome set off for the railway station, Kate explaining that her father had written to her imploring her to live with him as he was on his 'last legs'. Instead of heading directly to the station, however, she said, 'I've a friend to go and see at Barnes.' That was on the opposite side of the river. At first, Robert Porter carried her bag, then Porter senior carried it along Hammersmith Bridge Road. When they arrived at the Oxford and Cambridge pub, Kate suggested they should call in for a glass of ale.

After half an hour in the pub, Kate said, 'I shan't be long seeing my friend at Barnes,' and made to leave with her bag.

'Let the boy carry it,' said Porter.

'No thanks,' she replied, and went outside. Porter saw her walk towards the bridge, losing sight of her in the darkness. She returned about quarter of an hour later, without the bag. She then showed them three or four rings, saying they had belonged to her sister, who had died. She then gave Robert Porter two keys, and said, 'Mind these. They unlock the door.' He kept them in his hand and they went to the station, where she asked Porter if Robert could accompany her to Richmond. Porter agreed and saw them off from Hammersmith station.

On arrival at Richmond, Kate and Robert walked to 2 Vine Cottages, the house where she said she lived. Inside, she showed him two £5 notes, a Building Society book and a Post Office Savings book, saying they were her late aunt's. She then said she would like Robert to carry a box to Richmond Bridge, where she had to meet a gentleman. It was a small wooden box, tied up with cord. At about 11 p.m. they left the cottage and reached the bridge, where Robert carried it into a recess. 'Put it down and you be going towards the station,' said Kate. 'I'll catch you up.' As Robert walked back towards Richmond he heard a splash. He stopped at the sound of it, and looked round before walking on. Kate caught up with him near the Richmond end of the bridge. 'I've seen my friend,' she told him. 'Now we'll keep towards the station and get home.'

Young Robert was too late for the last train to Hammersmith, but that wouldn't have bothered Kate Webster, as she really was, for whom it had been a good day's work. The cut up and boiled remains of the real Mrs Thomas were now deposited into the river, out of sight and out of mind, at least until the next morning when

Henry Wheatley made his grim discovery. The head was missing, but that was in the river too, where Kate had thrown it after Henry and Robert Porter had unwittingly carried it for her.

The remains recovered from the Thames were that of Julia Martha Thomas, a widow, aged about 54. She had lived as a tenant at 2 Vine Cottages, Park Road, Richmond, since the previous September. She lived alone and went to chapel twice every Sunday. Her next-door neighbour, at No. 1, was Elizabeth Ives, Mrs Thomas's landlady. At first Mrs Thomas did not have a servant, but on 29 January Kate Webster moved into the cottage in that capacity. Webster, who was Irish, had an illegitimate son, whom she left with an old lady, Mrs Sarah Cresse.

Mrs Thomas attended the Presbyterian service at the lecture hall, Richmond, twice (as usual) on Sunday 2 March. She was seen by Julia Nichols on both occasions, the second of which Mrs Nichols noticed that Mrs Thomas arrived late. On the second occasion, Mrs Thomas left at 7.30 p.m. to return to her cottage. She was never seen alive again.

Just before noon on Monday 3 March, William Deane, a coal merchant, called on Mrs Thomas. Opening the door only wide enough to see who the caller was, Webster told Deane that Mrs Thomas was not in. Emma Roberts, Mrs Thomas's friend, called at the cottage about 6 p.m. She noticed a 'strong light' in the hall, but her knock was not answered. Mary Roberts, Miss Ives's apprentice, had seen Mrs Thomas on 27 February, when Mrs Thomas left her a message about the roof. On Tuesday 4 March, Mary called at Mrs Thomas's house. Webster answered her knock by opening the window over the door.

'Who's there?' she enquired.

'I've come from Miss Ives to tell you the man will come to see after the roof,' replied Mary.

There was no need, said Webster, as the 'wet' had only been snow penetrating. Webster had her sleeves rolled up, as though she was cleaning. About eight o'clock the same evening, Mary heard sounds like people moving about in the cottage (which adjoined No. 1), someone poking the fire and someone 'thumping' the piano, though not actually playing.

At six o'clock on 5 March, when Henry Porter came home from work, Webster – Mrs Thomas, as she said – was waiting for him. She reminded him of her need to dispose of 'her home' and sell the furniture. She showed him some artificial teeth set in gold, saying they had belonged to her aunt. Could he dispose of them? she asked. The pair went to a jeweller's, a man named Rudd, who gave Porter 6 shillings for the gold. He gave the money to Webster who gave him a shilling in return. On 7 March, Porter spoke to John Church, a publican, about the furniture.

On 8 March, Henry Porter went to 2 Vine Cottages where he saw the furniture. The next day he introduced John Church to Webster as 'Mrs Thomas', as he believed her to be. Church lived at the Rising Sun beerhouse, Rose Gardens,

Hammersmith, just a few doors away from Porter, with his wife and 7-year-old child. The day after, Church went to the cottage, telling Webster he had come to examine the furniture. Webster told him her aunt had died and left the furniture to her, but she was going to live with her father in Scotland, who, she explained, was in bad health. She showed him a photograph, which she said was of her father. No arrangements were made about the furniture on that occasion, but something else was in the process of development: a budding relationship between the pair. If only John Church had known the mortal danger he was letting himself in for. Meanwhile, on 10 March, George Court, a gardener, who was spreading manure on an allotment at Twickenham, found a human foot. It would later be matched to the ankle of the deceased woman, Julia Martha Thomas. How it ended up in Twickenham will forever remain a mystery.

By 12 March arrangements for the collection of the furniture were underway, as were Webster's plans to vacate the area. That day she went to Mrs Cresse's house to collect her son whom, she said, she was sending to her cousin in Glasgow that evening by the eleven o'clock train. Later, when Webster stood trial for the murder of Mrs Thomas, Mrs Cresse broke down in the witness box, 'excessively overcome', upset at having lost the little boy she had cared for.

The next day, Porter went to the cottage to find Church and Webster already there. Church valued the furniture at £50, but Webster did not think this was enough and £68 was agreed. Later, Porter, Church and Webster went to Hammersmith, Webster carrying plate and candlesticks, which she left at Church's house before accompanying Porter to his. She said her son would 'want something', meaning to eat. It seems the little boy was now staying with the Porters.

On Saturday Church went to the cottage again, this time accompanied by a Mr Henderson, who wanted to see the furniture. Webster made her way there alone, and Porter followed later, he and Henderson returning to Hammersmith by cab. This left Webster and Church alone in the house. So many people, so much to-ing and fro-ing, and still no sign of the real Mrs Thomas. On Sunday, Webster, Church, his wife and child and Porter, went boating. One imagines they all needed time off from their endeavours.

On Monday, Church and Webster went to see Mr Woods, a jeweller. Webster, as Mrs Thomas, bought a pair of earrings for £1, which Church paid for. They then went to the cottage together and remained there until 10 p.m. when Church left, having 'fetched' a bottle of brandy. Their relationship was in full bloom. The following morning Church went to see a man called Maryon about assistance in moving the furniture. Later, Church, Maryon and Webster left together and went to the bank, where Church drew cash for £50. He had ample funds, with over £200 to his credit. He, Maryon and Webster then went to the cottage, where they prepared the furniture for removal. Henry Porter came, then furniture vans arrived between 6 and 7 p.m. As well as Webster, Church and Porter, there were van drivers and others to help move the furniture. Was Miss Ives watching? She was.

Three or four items of furniture had been placed into a van when Church heard someone was enquiring about Mrs Thomas.

'Who is it?' asked Webster.

'It's the lady next door,' replied Church. She went next door, and Miss Ives asked her where the furniture was being taken.

'Mrs Thomas has sold the things and a man can show you the receipt,' said Webster.

'Where is Mrs Thomas?' asked Miss Ives.

'Don't know,' was the best reply Webster could muster.

'Cannot you give me Mrs Thomas's address?' asked Miss Ives.

'No,' replied Webster, whereupon Miss Ives shut the door. Webster returned to the cottage, 'greatly agitated and excited', and said to Porter, 'Harry, come upstairs with me and take some dresses off the pegs. I must send them to Hammersmith.' Porter fetched the dresses and gave them to her. She threw them into the van, along with a bonnet box.

Church had something to say to her too. 'You have deceived me,' he declared, 'I will have nothing to do with the goods. Put them back again!'

The man with the vans wasn't best pleased either. 'It's all very well for you,' he said, but who is to pay me?' Alas, no one, least of all Webster. All the furniture that had been loaded was returned to the cottage, after which the men left in the empty vans and went to the nearest pub. Webster walked off, went to Church's house where she borrowed a sovereign from Mrs Church, then to the Porters' to collect her son – and disappeared.

The following morning Porter and Church called on Miss Ives, who was not able to help their enquiry concerning Mrs Thomas, as they believed Webster to be called. Things might have drifted on, the mystery remains found in the river unidentified, but for Church's wife, who found a letter in the pocket of one of the dresses Webster had thrown into the van. The letter had been sent by the wife of Charles Menhennick of Finsbury Park, a friend of Mrs Thomas. Church thought it right to make enquiries of the sender. When they did they came to the conclusion that Kate Webster was not Mrs Thomas at all, but must have assumed her character 'for some purpose or other'.

As a result of the visit, Charles Menhennick communicated with W.H. Hughes, a solicitor. Hughes's brother was Mrs Thomas's executor; he had known her for thirty years. On 22 March, Hughes went to Menhennick's address, where he saw John Church, who showed him a purse (also found by his wife in one of the dresses). The purse contained some rings. Porter was sent for and the three of them – Church, Porter and Hughes – went to Richmond police station, then to 2 Vine Cottages. Inside, Church made a remark about a large photograph, saying he had been told by 'Mrs Thomas' that it was of her father. Hughes, the solicitor, recognised the man in the photograph to be *his* father!

The police began an examination of the cottage. They found charred bones under the copper, and more in the grate. Some parts of Mrs Thomas's body had been boiled in the copper, and there had been an effort to reduce it by calcifying the bone by fire. The body, or some of it, had then been packed into the box, one portion boiled, the other not boiled, perhaps because of a change of plan as to the means of disposal. There could be no doubt that the remains were that of Mrs Thomas, and to add to the certainty was the identification of the box by Mrs Edith Menhennick, who had stayed with her once and recognised a box she had seen in the house as the same one found in the river.

Meanwhile, since Webster's disappearance, nothing had been seen nor heard of her. But it wasn't difficult for the police to track her down to her native Enniscorthy, in County Wexford, Ireland. She had been in trouble often enough, in prison even. Suffice to say communications took place to have her detained pending the arrival of officers from England, and on 29 March Inspectors Dowdell and Jones, of Scotland Yard, went to Enniscorthy. Told she would be taken to London and charged with the murder of Mrs Thomas and stealing her property, she made no reply. But if the case against her looked straightforward, she was far from throwing in the towel. On the steam packet between Dublin and Holyhead she made a series of statements, which Dowdell wrote down as one when they arrived at Richmond. Abridged, it reads:

Richmond police station, 30 March 1879
I have known John Church for nearly 7 years. I got acquainted with him when I was living two or three doors from him. He used to take me to London and various public houses. I met him again some months ago. He came to my mistress's house one night the worse for drink. I told him he would have to go, as I expected my mistress home from church. She came home and I let her in. Church had told me to say he was my brother.

A few days later, he called again. He said, 'Could we not put the old woman out of the way?'

I said, 'What do you mean?'

He said, 'Poison her.'

I said, 'I'll have nothing to do with that.'

He said, 'We could have her things and go off to America together, as I am getting tired of my old woman.'

He came again on Monday night, 3 March, and had tea with Mrs Thomas. I waited on them. After tea I asked Mrs Thomas if I could go and see my little boy. She said, 'Yes, you need not hurry back.'

When I returned late that evening I noticed the light was turned down. I knocked three times, and Church opened the door. I saw Mrs Thomas lying on the mats in the passage, struggling and groaning.

I said, 'What have you done?'

He said, 'Never you mind. I have done it for her, and if you say a word about it I'll put this knife into you up to the handle.' It was a carving knife.

I said, 'No, John, don't. I won't tell.' He offered me what I thought was a glass of water, but I said, 'No, I am better now,' thinking it was poison. Shortly after, we left the house together, leaving Mrs Thomas there, and took a cab. I told him I could not stay in the house by myself. He saw me into Mrs Porter's and I remained there for the night.

Early next morning I went to Church's house. Church said I should not go back to the house by myself. We agreed to meet at the Richmond Hotel. I took the boy [Robert Porter] with me and as I passed the hotel I saw Church inside. I asked the boy to go on a short distance and wait. I went into the hotel and saw Church. He gave me the keys to the house and said I was to go there and take the boy. I would find a box in the back room, which he had packed and tied with cord. The boy was to assist me to bring it away. We carried it to the bridge. The boy went away and Church appeared.

I said, 'What are you going to do with the box?'

He said, 'That is my business.' Then he said, 'Follow the boy.' I did so and heard a splash in the water.

I joined the boy Porter at the foot of the bridge. We went to the station but the last train had gone. I said, 'You shall come home and sleep with me.' In the kitchen I found the carpeting rolled up and the table with a leaf let down. The boards were wet as though they had been washed, and there was a fire and a large saucepan on it full of water. About two days after I saw blood on the carving knife. A meat saw usually hung by the fire. I found it on a box in the scullery ...

Webster said Church had told her not pay any bills, saying, 'Pay Mrs Ives, the landlady, to keep her quiet.' He said, 'I'll go to Porter and say I think there's something wrong about this. Don't move the things,' and told her to 'clear out'. He gave her a card with his business address and said she was to write to him, and he would 'stop at home and brazen it out'. He would send her money to return to England, and they would go to America. She reached her uncle's house, in Ireland, the following night. Webster said she had nothing to do with murdering Mrs Thomas, but that Church 'had done it'.

Not surprisingly, the police wanted to speak to John Church. When Webster's statement was read to him he laughed, and said, 'The lying woman, how can she say that about me?' He may have found the allegation preposterous or even funny, but he was now a murder suspect. What's more, when he was searched he was in possession of a gold watch and chain, and £39 in gold and other items, and when Detective Henry Jones went to his address at the Rising Sun beer house, he found the receipt marked 'March 18, 1879. Received of John Church the sum of £68 for furniture, part effects of Mayfield Cottage [another name for 2 Vine

Cottages], Park Road, Richmond'. Church declared, as he believed, that the property belonged to Mrs Thomas. He always spoke of Webster as 'Mrs Thomas'. That is who he thought she was.

Charged with the murder of Mrs Thomas and stealing her property, Church replied, 'I was not in Richmond at the time. I can prove that.' Inspector Pearman went to his house and recovered some of the property belonging to Mrs Thomas: the rings, the plate, her purse, dresses and curtains, and a bonnet in a bonnet box.

In her statement, Webster alleged that on the evening of Monday 3 March, Church and Mrs Thomas had taken tea at the cottage and she, Webster, had waited on them; and later the same evening she had seen Mrs Thomas lying in the passage, struggling and groaning, and Church saying he had 'done it for her'. Could Church refute this allegation, one that could send him to the gallows? He could, and he did. Church was treasurer of the Oak Slate Club, Hammersmith. The club met on Monday evenings. On Monday evening, 3 March, George Harris, the club steward, and John Taylor, saw Church at the club and were easily able to provide an alibi for him.

Clearly, Webster could not substantiate the allegation made in her statement concerning Church on 3 March. And she had another problem: Henry Porter and his son, Robert, could testify that she had come to their house, falsely calling herself Mrs Thomas, and between them they had carried the bag and box containing human remains recovered from the Thames. There was only one thing for it: to change her story. And so, whilst on remand, she made another statement, in which she changed the date of the murder to 2 March, the Sunday, and also incriminated Porter:

> At five o'clock on Tuesday 4 March, when Porter came home, he said, 'Church is to meet me at Hartley's [public house] in Richmond.' Porter, me, and the boy went down Hammersmith. We had something to drink about seven o'clock.
>
> I said, 'We must be gone if we are going to Richmond tonight.' We went to the station, and Porter said we might walk to Shaftsbury Road.
>
> When we got there the boy said, 'Ain't you going home now, father?'
> Porter said, 'Yes.'
> Porter asked me to go to a pub with him, but I said, 'No, I'll miss the train if I do.'
> The boy was waiting and Porter hurried him on and said, 'Kate will catch you in a minute.'
> I went to Richmond with the boy. I saw Church at Hartley's. I told the boy to go on in front and I went in and told Church that Porter was coming on the next train. He gave me two keys, one for the side door and one for the back of the house, and said, 'You'll find a small box in the back room between the sofa and bookcase. It ain't very heavy. I think the boy and you can manage it. Bring it to Richmond Bridge. I'll be there before you. I'll wait here till Porter comes.'

I left Church in the pub and joined the boy up the street and went to the house with him. After a short time we left, carrying between us the box mentioned by Church.

In the middle of the bridge I said to the boy, 'You go on to the station and I'll catch you.' He did, and Church came up. I left Church, and following the boy I got a short distance away when I heard a splash in the water. We then went to the station. The last train had gone. [She went on to say she and Robert Porter went to 2 Vine Cottages.]

In the kitchen I found a large fire, a large iron saucepan full of water, the table had one leaf let down and was moved to one side of the kitchen, the carpet pushed back. The floor was wet, as if it had been washed and scrubbed. I missed the meat saw [found afterwards in the washhouse], and the carving knife on the scullery floor, with streaks of blood on it.

I saw Church and Porter next evening. Porter said, 'Do you know how to act, Kate?'

I said, 'I know when you tell me.'

He said, 'If anyone comes and asks for Mrs Thomas, say she is gone to the country for a few days.'

I said, 'She pays the bills every week.'

Church said, 'We'll be moved before the bills come in. Let us get what we can. It's no good being too honest in this world.'

So, on 2 March, the day of the murder, Porter was at the house too! It was Church, she said, who drew her attention to the box, and Church who threw it into the river. She was also saying she was at Porter's house *all day* on Monday, 3 March, yet she was seen at the cottage by William Deane the coal agent, who spoke to her. Webster, for all her endeavours to wriggle free of a murder charge and implicate two others, could simply not substantiate any of the facts she said were true. She must have realised the game was up when John Church was released from custody.

Katherine Webster stood trial at the Central Criminal Court on 2 July. She pleaded 'Not guilty' to the murder of Julia Martha Thomas. Justice Denham presided. The Solicitor-General, Sir Hardinge Gifford, went through the evidence. The facts were: at 7.30 p.m. on 2 March, Mrs Thomas was still alive. She had not been seen alive since, and on the following Tuesday the dead body of a woman was taken from that house and the person who disposed of it was Katherine Webster, who went on to attempt to dispose of the dead woman's property. She had been seen with a black bag, which had never been found, and of which she had never given any account. She had been helped with the box and its grisly contents, found in the Thames the following day just yards from the bridge from which it had been deposited. She had made statements containing lies in an attempt to incriminate others. But for Church's visit to Charles Menhennick, whose wife's letter was found by Mrs Church in one of Mrs Thomas's dresses, the so-called 'Barnes Mystery' may never have been solved.

But the prosecution had a problem: without an identifiable body, how could anyone prove Mrs Thomas had been murdered? Addressing the jury, defence counsel, Warner Sleigh, said the case was clogged with 'doubt and difficulty'.

'Are you sure the bones found are the bones of Mrs Thomas? And if they are, can you be sure she died by violence?' There must be proof, he said. The head was missing, along with some body parts. Was there any evidence Mrs Thomas did not die of natural causes – heart disease, apoplexy, a burst blood vessel? There was no evidence as to the identity of the bones, no evidence to prove she came to her death by violent means. The jury was being asked to take a leap in the dark.

The prosecution had a final say. Mrs Thomas was seen alive on the evening of Sunday 2 March. On 5 March a box of human remains was found in the river, at Barnes. The box came from Mrs Thomas's house, and it was the box carried to Richmond Bridge. The remains were those of a woman who had been cut up and boiled. There was the 'dumb testimony' of the state of the kitchen: the range, the copper, burnt human bones in the fireplace. The evidence suggested Mrs Thomas was murdered on the Sunday night and early on Monday the process of destroying the body began. In Webster's final statement she substituted 2 March for 3 March. Why? Because Church could prove he was elsewhere on the latter date. He implored the jury to give a 'true verdict', and sat down.

Justice Denham said that Webster said she saw Mrs Thomas dead in the house. Two or three days later, boiled human remains, mixed in with a portion of a woman's body which had not been boiled, were found on the banks of the Thames in a box identified by witnesses, and the prisoner mentioned carrying a box. Was there any doubt the remains were those of Mrs Thomas? Mrs Thomas had seen the witness Rudd to order new artificial teeth. The plate afterwards found at the jeweller's had been taken there by Porter and Webster, and had raised 10 shillings on the gold. The plate fitted the cast Rudd had of Mrs Thomas's mouth.

As to 'natural causes', Webster had alluded to 'violent death', saying Church told her he had 'done it'. Yet she had said, 'I know nothing about the death. I had no hand in murdering her.' On 18 March the vans came to remove the furniture. When Miss Ives suspected there was something wrong, Webster 'disappeared suddenly' and went to Ireland.

'If,' his lordship concluded, 'you come to the conclusion that this murder cannot have been committed except either by her alone, or by someone in concert with her, you will have to find her guilty.' The jury found Katherine Webster guilty as charged. Asked if she had anything to say, she made the following statement from the dock:

I am not guilty, my lord. When I was taken into custody I was in a hurry and I made a statement against Church and Porter. I am sorry for doing so, and I want to clear them out of it. The man who is guilty is not in the case at all. There was a child put in my hands in 1874. I had to thieve for that child and go to prison for it. The father of that child is the ruin of me, and he is the instigation of this. I do not see why I should suffer for a scoundrel who has left me after what he has done.

Justice Denham told her, 'You tell us now, for the first time, you were instigated into the crime by someone who is not in custody, and you have made some reparation by exonerating from all charges the two persons who might have been sent to the scaffold on the statements you made against them. You say you ought not to suffer because another instigated you to the crime. That is a consideration which will not warrant me one moment from hesitating to pass upon you the sentence of the law.' He sentenced her to death, after which, having the last word, she said, 'I am not guilty, sir.'

Only it wasn't her last word, for she then said she was pregnant. Pregnant women would not be hanged, so it was important to find out if this was true. Mr Bond, the surgeon who had testified, was then called upon to examine Webster, and did so in the jury room, his verdict being that she was not 'quick with child'. Katherine Webster had twisted and turned, used every ploy imaginable to escape justice, even after the jury had passed a guilty verdict. She said, falsely, that Henry Porter had asked her if she could act. She certainly could, but for Kate Webster the gallows would be the final stage.

Post-Trial

In a confession made to Father McEnry, in Wandsworth Prison, Kate Webster said, 'I alone committed the murder of Mrs Thomas. I was excited by having taken some drink, and when my mistress came home I was aggravated by her manner. I pushed her downstairs and then strangled her.' Father McEnry asked her about her statements, about the names of 'certain men' – John Church, and Henry Porter, and though she did not name him in court, the man Strong, the father of her child. She admitted all the statements were 'not true', that she alone committed the crime.

At 9 a.m. on 29 July 1879, Katherine Webster was taken from her cell and hanged by William Marwood. Father McEnry read the Roman Catholic service. As he uttered the words, 'Jesus, good Shepherd, come,' Webster responded loudly, 'Lord, have mercy upon me.' They were her last words, for at that moment Marwood drew the bolt. The procedure was accompanied by the sound of the prison bell, and ended with the raising of the black flag. After being viewed by the inquest jury, the coffin was filled with quicklime.

Author's Verdict

In her confession, Webster said she was 'slightly excited' through drink, and was 'aggravated' by her mistress's 'manner', and that she 'pushed her downstairs and strangled her'. Even so, she may have been protecting Strong. We will never know. Although Church and Porter knew everything was not exactly above board but sought a quick shilling – whilst Church was also enjoying his bit on the side – they were clearly innocent when it came to murder. Despite trying to incriminate them to save her own neck, at least she cleared their names at the end of the trial and in her confession.

There was a hint of unfairness about her trial, in that the prosecution had two bites at the cherry: an opening and a closing address. That said, there can be no doubt that Webster, alone or otherwise, murdered Julia Martha Thomas and afterwards cut up and boiled her body parts before throwing them into the Thames, even commandeering the help of another in the disposal process. This was a dreadful crime. One can surely have no sympathy for her.

8

'A Bad End'

Catherine Churchill, Somerset, 1879

It was a fine March morning, perfect for George Whatley, who began work at 7.30 a.m., ploughing the field behind Samuel Churchill's cottage. It was picturesque scene, the ploughman and his team abusy on the gentle English landscape, with no interruptions, and no distractions other than a well-earned cup of tea.

At 8.30 a.m. Eliza Whatley left her cottage with her husband's breakfast. To access the field he worked in she had to walk along a muddy lane in front of the cottage, then turn left to the field, which lay just beyond the garden. As she made her way by the hedge at the back of the cottage she distinctly heard a man's voice cry 'Murder!' several times, followed by groaning, after which another voice was heard to say, 'You brute!'

Mrs Whatley went on a little further to a gap in the hedge, through which, from a slightly elevated position, she had a clear view of the back of the cottage. It is important here to understand the topography. On this bright, spring morning, the sun was positioned in the south-east, behind Mrs Whatley and shining directly through the window she could now see through. Even so, her view of anything or anyone inside the cottage would have been restricted, except that on the far wall of the cottage there was another window. What she could see, therefore, was anyone positioned between the two windows, illuminated by the sun's rays.

What she saw was the figure of a woman, identifiable by her head and shoulders and the dark dress she was wearing, although her facial features were unseen. The woman was in a 'stooping position', with her back to her, and seemed to be dragging something towards the fireplace. Mrs Whatley watched for two or three minutes, before going into the field and giving her waiting husband his breakfast. He asked her what it was that had drawn her attention to the cottage. She told him about the cries of 'Murder!' but neither of them felt any need to do anything, because everyone knew the Churchills quarrelled, and this would be no more than another of their arguments. Walking home again Mrs Whatley made her way around to the front of the cottage where, as she passed, she heard the door being locked by the sound of someone turning the key from the inside.

Around 9 a.m., 14-year-old James Millar, who worked for Mr Vincent of Woodhouse Farm, saw 50-year-old Mrs Churchill walking towards the Ship Inn at Chard, about a mile and a half away. Shortly afterwards some schoolchildren on their way to school noticed a smell of burning, or a 'stink', as one would describe it, coming from the direction of the cottage. Young James Millar then saw Mrs Churchill returning to the cottage, shortly after 9.30 a.m.

At 10 a.m. George Whatley, still working in the field, heard Mrs Churchill calling out to him from the hedge at the back of the cottage. 'Do'ee come in, Samuel has fallen into the fire,' she cried, whereupon Whatley abandoned his horses and ran to the cottage. As he reached it he saw Mrs Churchill take a cupful of water from the well, then she entered the cottage by the back door, closely followed by Whatley. She went directly to the fireplace and threw the water over Samuel Churchill, her husband, who was lying on the floor, flat on his back with his head on the left side of the fire-dog, his legs bent under him, his hands 'spread abroad'. Seeing his prostrate and obviously dead body, George Whatley declared, 'This is a bad job.'

'I don't know anything about it,' said Mrs Churchill. 'I have been to the Ship Inn. I left him in the corner smoking his pipe and I suppose he must have had a fit and fallen into the fire.'

Whatley noticed a small fire 'scattered about' in the grate, although Churchill's body was clear of the fireplace. Mrs Churchill urged him to fetch Charles Forsey, who lived nearby. When Whatley went to do so he found the front door locked. Mrs Churchill unlocked it so that he could proceed.

Whatley and Forsey, together with Enoch Cox, returned to the cottage. When the three men looked at the dead form of Samuel Churchill, they saw he was wearing corduroy breeches – the ones they knew he usually wore for 'best' – along with a flannel shirt and black stockings. Charles Forsey unhinged a door and they laid Churchill's body upon it. As they did so they noticed he was 'very much' burnt about the back of his head, and his right shoulder was burnt to the bone. His back was also burnt, as were his breeches. Whatever had happened, Charles Forsey was not happy about it, for he left the cottage to find a policeman.

Samuel Churchill had lived at Knowle St Giles almost all his life. His first wife had died about twenty-five years before. Their daughter, Sarah, married George England, a labourer.

Almost immediately after his first wife's death, Catherine (Kitty) Waldron, as she was, came to live with Samuel in the cottage, which he owned. At that time he was almost 60 years old, she a mere 28. She was described as 'young and good looking', a young woman 'who did not bear a very high character'. She and Churchill had a son, whom they named Samuel, after his father, although he took his mother's surname. Samuel lived with his parents until August 1877, when he moved out, although he still called for his breakfast before going to work. Living together 'in sin', as the Churchills did, was frowned upon in Victorian times, and moreso when that couple had a child. Nevertheless, Samuel and Kitty continued thus for about fifteen years, until the clergyman of the parish persuaded them to unite in holy matrimony. Their lives, before and after marriage, had been laced with constant strife, their quarrelling well known to their neighbours.

A third person lived in the cottage. She was Mrs Churchill's mother, who was in her nineties, bedridden and nearly blind. She lived upstairs. She had no knowledge whatsoever of events that morning, and played no part in any of the investigation or subsequent court proceedings.

Samuel Churchill had made a will. Its existence played an important part in the trial of Mrs Churchill for her husband's murder, being seen as providing a motive for the crime. The will was made out favourably to her and young Samuel, for Churchill had left just £5 to his daughter, and the cottage to Kitty to remain in throughout her widowhood, with young Samuel to benefit on her death.

Eliza Whatley, who had watched through the gap in the hedge, went to the cottage at 11 a.m., accompanied by Jane Forsey, having heard that old Samuel was dead. What was the matter with the old man this morning at half past eight when she heard him crying 'Murder!'? Mrs Whatley asked Mrs Churchill.

She replied, 'I went upstairs to my mother and heard him down here grumbling.'

'Perhaps Kitty was gone to the Ship Inn then,' ventured Mrs Forsey, to which Mrs Whatley retorted, 'She was not gone to the Ship Inn then, for I looked through the window and saw her from the gap, and when I came round to the front I heard someone lock the front door.'

Mrs Churchill said, 'I wasn't gone then. I went when the train went up.' This was the train from Ilminster to Chard which ran along the now-disused line.

Just after midday, George England – Mrs Churchill's son-in-law, although they were of similar age – arrived at the cottage, by which time Mrs Churchill was the only person present, save for her dead husband, his body still lying on the floor. England also noticed the old man was wearing his 'Sunday breeches'. When the police arrived, in the form of Acting Sergeant Joseph Williams, Mrs Churchill told him, 'My husband got up this morning about eight o'clock. We had breakfast and my husband then had a pipe and sat down on a stool at the left-hand side of the fireplace. I put on a good fire and left the house. When I left he was all right. I went to the Ship Inn, Chard, after some bread and bacon. When I returned to the house I found my husband lying on the fire burnt to death. I pulled him off the fire and put him by the side of it and went to the back of the house and called George Whatley. I threw some water over my husband's clothes to put the fire out.'

Acting Sergeant Williams told Mrs Churchill, 'Leave everything alone as I must get a doctor.'

She said, 'I have not hurted [*sic*] the old man.'

Williams then sent someone for Superintendent Gerity, before looking for Churchill's pipe, which he found by the fire grate. It appeared to have spots of blood on it. He then saw what appeared to be fresh spots of blood on the floor. He remained in the house until Superintendent Gerity and Dr Charles Munden arrived at four o'clock. Before that, however, Mrs Churchill was seen at the back door, washing things and hanging them out to dry. Hardly the actions of a woman who had just been widowed in tragic circumstances that very day – unless, of course, she was washing clothing or cloths to get rid of bloodstains.

Superintendent Gerity looked at the body of Samuel Churchill, and then, looking about the room, he saw a spot of blood on the floor, near a chair, and more spots of blood on the floor, near the fireplace. Then, searching the room, he found a billhook (an axe-like tool used for cutting hedges) under a chair. There appeared to be fresh bloodstains on both sides of the blade of the billhook, which was very sharp. Gerity found bloody finger marks on a screen close to the table by the fireplace. Later these were scraped away by someone in an obvious attempt to destroy them.

Acting Sergeant Williams noticed spots of blood on the front of Mrs Churchill's skirt. When he drew her attention to them she said, 'They may have come off my husband's hand when I took him off the fire.'

Superintendent Gerity then said, 'Now, Mrs Churchill, listen to what I am going to say. I am going to charge you, and anything you may say I shall give in evidence against you. I now charge you with having murdered your husband.' Mrs Churchill replied, 'I never injured him.' She was then taken outside where she climbed aboard the superintendent's trap. On the way to the police station at Ilminster her son, Samuel, was seen to approach across a field. He was in tears. She said to him, 'Don't cry, Samuel. Go and take care of the house.' Then, as he moved away, she called out, 'See to the will, and mind they don't cheat you out of the money.'

When Dr Munden arrived at the cottage he examined the body of Samuel Churchill. He noticed a deep cut to the forefinger and a slight wound to the index finger of the left hand. The cut on the forefinger extended to the bone, with two small arteries severed. Blood was still flowing from the wound, and he formed the opinion that it had been made on the morning of the same day. He thought the wounds to the hands could have been inflicted by the billhook. Turning to Mrs Churchill, he said, 'Well, Kitty, how came this blood on the hook?'

'I don't know,' she replied. 'He was chopping sticks yesterday and he might have cut his finger then.' But Munden considered the blood on the billhook to be fresh, not quite dry in fact. Munden found the back part of Churchill's head 'very much burnt', and on opening the skull a large portion of the back of the head fell on to the floor. It was 'perfectly impossible' to ascertain if the head had been cut with any instrument. The right arm was nearly burnt from the body, and the cut on the finger must have been produced by considerable force.

At the cottage the following day, Acting Sergeant Williams gave Superintendent Gerity Churchill's bloodstained corduroy trousers, and Sarah England, Churchill's daughter, gave him a dress stained with blood on the right sleeve and the front of the skirt. That same day, PC Hill found a dress on a barrel in the cellar. It was spotted with blood and the sleeves were damp, as though they had been washed. He also found a damp cloth at the back of the house. He gave these items to Superintendent Gerity, who took the clothing, cloth and the billhook to William Stoddart, county analyst at Bristol, for analysis.

The results of Stoddart's examination were protracted; suffice to say he found blood on everything. There were smears of blood on the sleeves of the dress, suggesting that something heavy must have rested on the arms of the wearer. Some of the clothing was burnt. There were stains and smears of blood on the billhook, the smears indicating that some blood had been wiped off. Also on the billhook was a white human hair, which under the microscope was seen to have been cut with a sharp instrument. There was also the hair of a hare, and a downy feather, which indicated the billhook had been used on animals and birds.

The question, of course, was whether the blood was human. Human blood could be distinguished from horse's blood, but not from, say, a pig's. It was known old Churchill had kept pigs, and killed them from time to time. Much importance was put on the bloodstains at Catherine Churchill's trial, and no wonder. The police concluded that she had murdered her husband, and so did the inquest jury, taking just fifteen minutes to arrive at their unanimous decision.

When Catherine Churchill appeared before the magistrates, she was asked to show Mrs Whatley the dress she was wearing that day, but Mrs Whatley was unable to say whether it was the same one that Mrs England found upstairs. Mrs Whatley then spoke of an occasion when Samuel Churchill had come to her house three or four months before. There had been a knocking at her door, and when she opened it Churchill was there, lying on the ground. Charles Forsey came and helped the old man up and Mrs Churchill was sent for. When she came she said, 'It serves the old rogue right. I wish the old devil was dead.' She then went home, leaving her aged husband in the care of others.

Mrs England, Samuel Churchill's daughter, said on 30 August, in the year before his death, her father had called on her. He said, 'Sally, I am come to tell you how the villains have served me this morning' – meaning his wife and son. They had torn his shirt, which he showed her, and he was now going to Chard to get his will and burn it. They had attacked him through the night, he said.

Mrs Churchill, in the dock, interrupted Mrs England, saying, 'That's not right. I went to bed and he came up and beat me. When my son came home he said, "Why don't you let mother stay in bed?" Sam took him by the collar and shook him.'

Continuing her testimony, Mrs England claimed that Mrs Churchill had said, 'You know, the old rogue ought to have been dead years ago,' and 'It's no more harm to shoot him than a cat or a dog.' He told her he would burn his will in her presence.

Mrs Churchill, interrupting proceedings again, said, 'I never knew what his will was. I did not know what was in it.'

Mrs England then told the court she had found the bloodstained dress between two old beds, the day after her father's death.

'That's a lie, Sally' said Mrs Churchill, 'that dress was left hanging on the banister.'

It was between the two beds, insisted Mrs England, and the coroner told Mrs Churchill to be quiet.

'I can't be quiet and hear that nasty, stinking liar,' screamed Mrs Churchill.

James Farmer, solicitor's clerk, said that on 7 November 1877 he had made a will for Samuel Churchill, who had left £5 and a Bible to George and Sarah England, and his cottage to Samuel, his son, and his wife to live in during her widowhood. Two months before his death, however, Mr Churchill had told Farmer in the street, 'I shall want to see you again soon to alter my will.' He had not seen him since. Two months after Mr Churchill made his will, Farmer saw his wife in the street. She asked him if he would tell her the content of the will. He said he could not.

Dr Munden told the court he was unable to say if the billhook caused death – the back of his head had burnt away so that no injury could be detected. He thought it possible it could have caused the cut to his hand. He did not think the injury was caused the day before death. Of the marks on it he said, 'I will not swear that there is blood on the billhook; I will not swear that it is not iron rust'. He had known Samuel Churchill for years, and said he had suffered from fainting fits for which he had prescribed medicine. If he had attempted to get up from his chair he might have fallen back on to the fire, but he would have had to turn around first. Presumably the doctor was alluding to the nature of the injuries, and the position the body was in. William Stoddart, the analyst, was asked about the vital question of bloodstains. His testimony would come under greater scrutiny at Catherine Churchill's trial.

The trial opened at Taunton Assizes that May before Baron Huddlestone, of whom the *Chard and Ilminster News* reported:

> None who looked on him could fail to be impressed with a conviction of his fitness for the solemn duties devolving upon him. It was not along the intellectual power seen in his grave, earnest face, nor the dignity which marked his whole bearing that arrested attention; it was the evidence that those qualities were combined with moral perceptions which enabled him to discern aright the bearing of the most trivial circumstances, while recognising the solemnity of his duty as judge, ever to be regarded of tenderness and mercy.

Guided by this regal figure were the prosecution and defence counsel, Messrs Hooper and St Aubyn respectively, and the jury, whilst Catherine Churchill was the 'most unmoved individual in the assembly', sitting in the dock wearing the clothes she had worn when she was arrested, including a waterproof cloak and a white sun bonnet. 'Hard and rigid and solid, she sat there, the only signs of life or emotion being the restless movement of her fingers and the constant tapping of her feet'. She pleaded 'Not guilty' to the wilful murder of her husband.

There were two main issues in proving the case: first, that Samuel Churchill was murdered at all, and second, if so, that he was murdered by his wife. Describing the scene, and events that spring morning, Mr Hooper told the jury that the only person who 'saw or heard anything' that day was Eliza Whatley, when she took her husband his breakfast. The figure she had seen through the window was a 'stooping woman', he said, although she had not seen her face. Mr Churchill's daughter, Sarah England, said Mr Hooper had found the brown dress between two beds, and this was the dress Mrs Whatley had seen the woman wearing when she had seen her through the window. This was a complete untruth, for at the magistrates' court Mrs Whatley stated clearly that she could not identify the dress.

The prosecution also called 23-year-old Samuel Waldron, the Churchills' son.

Samuel Waldron said he left the family home in August 1877, after having 'words' with his father. He was sure his father had not killed a pig for some weeks, thus eliminating the possibility that the recent bloodstains were those of a pig. He admitted scraping marks off the screen after his mother was committed for trial. On the day before his death he had seen his father trimming spur-gads (willow branches) with a billhook. He saw his father in fits sometimes, and said that about two years before, when his father was eating his dinner, he 'dropped away', and he caught his arm to prevent him from falling onto the fire.

Jane Forsey was once a dressmaker. About a year before she had made a dress for Mrs Churchill. It was the one found between the two beds. Mrs Churchill was wearing it when Mrs Forsey went to the cottage on the morning of her husband's death. Sarah England reiterated the evidence she gave at the magistrates' court, including her father's stated intention to go to Chard and burn his will. On many occasions since he had complained of his wife's conduct, and the last time she saw him alive he said, 'I know I shall come to a bad end.'

Dr Munden said the blood that had flowed from the wound on Samuel Churchill's hand was fresh; it was still oozing out even after death. He was questioned about the possibility that Churchill had fallen onto the fire from the stool, or from a standing position. He related the injuries to whatever position he might have been in before he fell, but none of this line of questioning was conclusive. He said the blood on the billhook was also fresh, which contradicted what he had said at the magistrates' hearing, when, under oath, he had said, 'I will not swear that there is blood on the billhook; I will not swear that it is not iron rust.' When asked by Mr Aubyn about the billhook, he replied, 'I did not examine the billhook carefully. I will not swear the marks were fresh.' He agreed Mr Churchill had had a weak heart, and had suffered from fainting fits.

William Stoddart, the analyst, confirmed he had examined the corduroy trousers, the dress and other items. All had blood on them, described in great detail by Mr Stoddart. Blood obviously played a major part in the thrust of the prosecution's case. Mr Aubyn had much to say to Stoddart about it.

'You can't say it was human blood?' Mr Aubyn enquired.

'No.'

'It might be a pig's blood?'

'I don't think it was.'

'There are no means of distinguishing human blood from the blood of some animals?'

'I am sorry to say there are not.'

'It is not a question of sorrow. It is a question of fact I am asking you. Have you said you can't distinguish human blood from the blood of a horse but might of a pig?'

'That is what I say.'

A juryman asked, 'The blood must have come from a fresh wound?'

'Yes.'

Summing up, Mr Hooper ventured that on the morning of his death, Samuel Churchill had put on his best breeches with the intention of going to see his solicitor to change his will in favour of his daughter. His wife became angry and struck him with the billhook as he sat smoking his pipe. He put his hand up and sustained the deep cut to it, and had then caught hold of the screen with his bloody fingers, shouting 'Murder!' Having killed him, she dragged him to the fire. She saw Mrs Whatley pass by the back window, so locked the front door. Having cleared up the blood, as she thought, she called in George Whatley and said the old man must have fallen on the fire when she was at the Ship Inn.

Mr Aubyn asked, 'Why would she kill her husband?' Here was an old man, long past 'ordinary age', with one leg in the grave. Was it hard to say that she would desire his death when in the course of human events he must die in a short time? Because they nagged and quarrelled, was that a reason why she should murder him? You could walk the streets of any town and hear threats of violence without concluding that because people wished someone dead they intended to murder them. He questioned the testimony of Mrs Whatley. Could she really have seen anything at all through 'that window'? Was it not possible that the cries of 'Murder!' were simply loud words, such as 'Oh dear,' passing between husband and wife? It was extraordinary that she did not go and see what was the matter. He suggested the old man cut his fingers the day before, chopping wood; the 'fresh blood' found on the day of his death was from reopened wounds.

His lordship told the jury they had before them 'a chain of circumstantial evidence', but said that sometimes circumstantial evidence was 'far more satisfactory' than direct testimony, and the circumstances could scarcely lie. He concluded that both mother and son had been afraid that Samuel Churchill would alter his will. The jury asked whether, if there had been a struggle between Samuel Churchill and his wife, where a blow had been struck by Mrs Churchill in order to defend herself which had resulted in her husband's death, could it be considered manslaughter? His reply was that there was no evidence of any blows passing; their verdict must be one of murder or acquittal. The jury then returned a verdict of 'guilty of murder'.

Telling Mrs Churchill he did not desire to aggravate the position in which she stood by making any 'observations', his lordship put on the black cap and sentenced her to death. She was 'utterly dazed' by the sentence and turned a 'ghastly pale'. Asked if she had anything to say or any reason to give why the execution should not be carried out, she replied, 'I am not guilty.' The question referred to any possible 'condition' she might have – meaning pregnancy – in which case sentence would be deferred. She had not understood, so a female warder explained it to her. To this she replied, 'I am not guilty of it, sir, not in the least. What they swore is false, especially that there Whatley's wife. I can kiss the Bible to it with a clear conscience. I am innocent of it, innocent as a babe unborn, there now.' She was then removed from the dock.

Post-Trial

Despite the murder conviction against Catherine Churchill, there were many who thought a conviction of manslaughter was more appropriate, not least because that had been the wishes of the jury who were directed to decide otherwise by the judge. Mrs Churchill's solicitor wrote to Peter Taylor, MP, highlighting this point of view. He was supported by the Mayor of Chard and some townspeople, who felt that she should not suffer death. A Memorial was sent to the Home Secretary, which (abridged) read:

> The undersigned pray that her most Gracious Majesty the Queen may be advised to exercise her royal prerogative of mercy towards Catherine Churchill … The memorialists believe there are extenuating circumstances which may be recognised by mercy as a powerful plea for commutation of sentence of death. Among these circumstances the character of the deceased man cannot be overlooked. It was exceedingly bad. Having first dragged the prisoner to the lowest depths of womanly degradation, he treated her very often with great cruelty. They lived on the most miserable terms, and violent disputes and quarrels were very frequent. The unhappy woman may have been provoked and aggravated by the deceased, but she has won the character of a hard-working woman. The deceased had been the means of dragging her to her present position, and she might have killed him without premeditation or immediate intention. The memorialists feel that punishment short of death will fully meet the requirements of this sad case, and give the wretched prisoner time for repentance and amendment.

Awaiting her fate, Catherine Churchill was visited by the Revd Phillips, who asked if she was afraid to die. 'Why not,' she answered, 'I am innocent. My life has been sworn away.'

Samuel Waldron, her son by her murdered husband, and her daughter, Mrs Priddy, also visited. The two women sobbed bitterly, Mrs Churchill asserting that she should be in her 'own home', as she had been wrongly imprisoned. Samuel told her of the efforts being made to obtain a reprieve to which, brightening up, she answered, 'Well, they didn't ought to hang me, for I ben't guilty.'

Just before 8 a.m. on Monday 26 May, Catherine Churchill was led from her cell to the place of execution in Taunton Gaol. The hangman was William Marwood. He reported afterwards that she died without a struggle, saying 'She did not move a finger'. A crowd of 500 waited outside the prison, the black flag indicating that she had expiated her crime. Marwood was asked whether he found women 'more affected' than men when they were being led to execution. He never observed any difference, he replied, adding that 'women appeared to possess the same amount of nerve and courage as men'. He said that Catherine Churchill did not confess to the crime on the scaffold. She was buried within the precincts of the gaol.

Marwood, who had decided to leave Taunton immediately afterwards, found himself in a somewhat unpleasant situation as he awaited his train. Standing on the platform, he was recognised, and 'so mobbed' that he had to beat a retreat into the compartment of the first train that happened along – not the express he was waiting for. This train was shunted into a siding to allow the express to pass, then rolled back into the station again where an inquisitive crowd gathered round it. Whilst people sought to catch a glimpse of him, no one wanted to be his travelling companion. It seems being a hangman had its own hazards.

Author's Verdict

There was little direct evidence to prove that Catherine Churchill murdered her husband. No one saw her do it, and the fire destroyed any injury to his head caused by being struck by the billhook, if indeed he was. He had a possible defensive injury to his hand, and there were bloodstains on the floor, screen and clothing. Human blood? It could not be proved that it was. There was the testimony of Eliza Whatley, who said she heard 'Murder!' and saw a woman through the window, dragging something. Much importance was put upon what she could see from the gap in hedge, and the physical appearance of the room. So why didn't they – judge, counsel, jury – go and look at it for themselves? Churchill said Whatley's evidence was false, but what reason would she have to lie?

The cottage was a crime scene, but you wouldn't have thought so. On the day of the crime Mrs Churchill was seen washing something outside the cottage. On the day after the crime we have the victim's daughter (who might have been a suspect) handing the superintendent a bloodstained dress, which, she said, she had found upstairs. PC Hill found clothing elsewhere, also the following day. The prisoner's son admitted scrubbing marks – bloodstains, presumably – from the screen.

There were important inconsistencies in some witnesses' testimonies. At the magistrates' court, Mrs Whatley could not say the dress worn by the woman she saw was the brown one found by Mrs England; at the trial she identified it as the same dress. At the magistrates' court, Dr Munden could not swear the marks on the billhook were blood; at the trial he said otherwise. It was as if their earlier evidence had been given honestly, but later was structured to fit the charge. Stoddart, the analyst, did his best to persuade the jury the blood was human when he knew perfectly well he could prove no such thing.

This case highlights again the unfairness of the law at the time, which prevented an accused testifying in his or her defence. One imagines Catherine Churchill would have had something to say had she been allowed to say it. Instead, the jury had to rely on what the police and witnesses said she said. She may have been provoked that morning – not that that is a reason to kill. The verdict here is that Catherine Churchill murdered her husband, who was sitting on his chair, smoking his pipe when she struck him with the billhook, and the motive suggested by the prosecution – preventing him from going into Chard to change his will – was accurate. She compounded the crime by dragging him to the fireplace to destroy the evidence of the wound, saying he fell into the fire. But the Home Secretary should have commuted her sentence to life imprisonment. The wording of the Memorial provides all the reasons one needs to come to this conclusion.

9

A Murderous Solution

Florence Elizabeth Maybrick, Lancashire, 1889

Thursday 29 March 1889, Grand National day. James Maybrick, 50, a cotton merchant, is not best pleased when his young wife, 27-year-old Florie, leaves their carriage to walk up the course with Alfred Brierley. When the Maybricks arrive home it is obvious to their servants that they have quarrelled. Florie sends for a cab but James declares, 'If you leave this house, you will never enter it again.' Florie reluctantly stays and Alice Yapp, the children's nurse, makes up a separate bed for her to sleep in that night.

The next day Florie goes to see a family friend, Matilda Briggs, and tells her of the quarrel she had with her husband. Mrs Briggs notices that Florie is sporting a black eye. Mrs Briggs' advice is to see Dr Arthur Hopper, which she does that very day, telling him she intends to see a lawyer about a separation. The following day, when Dr Hopper sees the Maybricks at their home, Battlecrease House, Aigburth, an affluent part of Liverpool, Mr Maybrick complains of his wife 'going off with a gentleman' at the racecourse, even though he distinctly told her not to. Mrs Maybrick says she feels 'repugnance' towards her husband. However, thanks to the good doctor's involvement, the couple appear to be reconciled.

What James Maybrick and Dr Hopper didn't know was that earlier that month, Mrs Maybrick was in communication with an hotelier in London, intimating that her brother-in-law and his wife, Mr and Mrs T. Maybrick, were coming to town. Sure enough, a Mrs Maybrick arrived at the hotel on 21 March, being joined that evening by an unknown man who, it was believed, took her to the theatre. The following morning, at breakfast, Florie– for it was she – was seen in the company of another man, whom staff took to be her husband, since they both remained in the hotel as 'man and wife' until 24 March.

On 13 April, James Maybrick went to London himself to consult Dr Charles Fuller about his health, and complained of pains in the head, numbness, and being 'apprehensive of being paralysed'. Dr Fuller said he was suffering from indigestion, and wrote two prescriptions for an aperient and a tonic.

When her husband was in London, Mrs Maybrick went to a chemist's shop locally and bought a dozen flypapers, telling the chemist that flies were 'troublesome in the kitchen'. Although she had an account, she opted to pay by cash. A few days later, Bessie Brierley, a housemaid, noticed the flypapers in the Maybricks' bedroom and told Alice Yapp about them. Yapp went into the bedroom and saw a towel on a plate, which she lifted and saw a basin containing the flypapers. She would have been puzzled, for there were no problems with flies in the house.

Meanwhile, returning from his consultation with Dr Fuller, James Maybrick took his prescriptions to the chemist's. The prescriptions were made up into two bottles, and handed to him on 24 April.

Thus we have James Maybrick, a hypochondriac, who'd been told by a London physician that his only illness was indigestion, now taking his prescribed medicine; and Florie, his wife, who was having a clandestine relationship with one man, perhaps two, who found her husband repugnant.

In 1873, James Maybrick and one of his brothers, Edwin, formed Maybrick & Co., cotton merchants. A year later James established an office at Norfolk, Virginia, after which he commuted between England and America in the course of the business. In 1880, after arriving in Norfolk, he contracted malaria, which led him to taking 'Fowler's Solution', a mixture of white arsenic, carbonate of potash and lavender water of such strength that 100 parts represents one part of white arsenic. Fowler's Solution was considered a suitable treatment for diseases such as malaria and syphilis, even though arsenic is addictive. Nor was arsenic used for purely medicinal reasons, since it was considered to be an aphrodisiac. We may assume the possibility, likelihood even, that James Maybrick used it to boost his sex life.

In March 1880, Maybrick left New York for England, a routine journey, but on this occasion he met Florence Chandler, an American woman who was travelling to England with her mother. James was twenty-three years older than Florie, but age didn't matter, for by the time they reached Liverpool they were very much an item. They were married on 27 July the following year. Thereafter the couple commuted regularly to America, taking with them James, their infant son, but when times got rough because of a slump in the cotton industry, James Senior, with increasing money worries, became depressed. He may have turned to arsenic and other substances for relief.

In 1886 the Maybricks had a second child, a daughter, and in early 1888 they moved to Battlecrease House. By then it was rumoured that he had several mistresses, whilst Florie was having an affair with Alfred Brierley, her 'husband' at the London hotel. If James was taking arsenic, for whatever purpose, he seemed

Sarah Dazley's house in Wrestlingworth.

The Chequers Inn, Wrestlingworth, venue of the inquests into the death of William Dazley. (Paul Heslop)

THE
EXECUTION
OF

SARAH 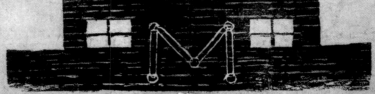 DAZLEY,

Who was Executed on the New Drop in front of the County Gaol at Bedford, on Saturday the 5th of August, 1843, for the Wilful Murder of her husband, William Dazley, at Wrestlingworth.

The Prisoner's maiden name was Reynolds, and was the daughter of Mr. P. Reynolds of Potton, hair-dresser. The first husband of this unhappy woman was named Simeon Mead, by whom she had a daughter, which when 9 months old died very suddenly. About five months after the death of Mead she was married to William Dazley, her unfortunate victim, who was buried in Wrestlingworth Church-yard, with the following remarkable verse on the tomb stone.

> " The strong may think their house a rock,
> Yet, soon as Jesus calls,
> Some sickness brings a fatal shock,
> And down the building fails."

Since the condemnation of the unhappy woman she has been confined in the condemned cell, and attended by a female both night and day, with whom she has frequently conversed in a light and cheerful manner, appearing to think the sentence would not be carried into execution, and that it was merely for the purpose of extorting a confession. On being visited on Wednesday by her friends in the presence of the Chaplain, they wished her to make a full confession of her crime, when she is reported to have said, " I won't make a confession I did not do it, he (meaning Dazley) poisoned the child, and afterwards poisoned himself.

At the hour of 4 o'clock this morning the workmen commenced preparing the drop for the execution and the people from the neighbouring villages began to arrive, amongst whom were a great many from Potton and Wrestlingworth, the scene of her crimes, and to whom she was well known. About 10 o'clock she attended the Chapel and the usual service was performed. On the arrival of under-sheriff (with an escort of javelin men,) the body of the unfortunate woman was demanded and they then proceeded to the press-room where the operation of pinioning her was performed. The procession consisting of the Under-Sheriff, Chaplain, Gaoler, Turnkeys, and Javelin-Men began to move the Chaplain reading the burial service, commencing with " I am the resurrection and the life." On arriving at the place of execution she joined the Chaplain in prayer and shook hands with the attendants thanking them for their kindness and attention, no extraordinary emotion or trepidation being perceptible in her manner, a slight sigh appeared to escape from her when the cap was drawn over her face and the rope adjusted, the executioner then retired leaving her standing alone on the drop, when the signal being given the bolt was drawn and the unfortunate woman was launched into eternity. She was observed to struggle for a few seconds when life became extinct. The body after hanging the usual time was removed for burial within the precincts of the Gaol, according to the sentence of the learned Judge. May the Lord

COPY OF

Farewell my friends and children dear,
Eternally farewell,
The pain I feel on your account
No tongue on earth can tell.

A guilty wretch I am proclaimed,
By vilest passions led,
To murder child and husband too,
My soul is filled with dread.

The fatal ars'nic n
My husband took
And lull'd into the
It made his spirit

In Town of Potton
Of parents good
Who taught me
And the Lord to

J. S. & W. MERRY, Printers,

A broadsheet showing the gallows at Sarah Dazley's execution. (Courtesy of Bedfordshire and Luton Archives)

Execution of Mrs REI? or TIMNEY, at Dumfries,

For the Murder of Ann Hannah, on the 13th of January last. 1862

The execution of Mary Timney. The illustration incorrectly shows the crowd next to the gallows.

Maria Manning.

The old gaol, Dumfries.

TRIAL AND EXECUTION
PRISCILLA ° BIGGADIKE,

For the wilful Murder of her Husband on the 1st of October, 1868, who was tried before the Right Hon. Sir John Barnard BYLES, Knight, on Friday, Dec. 11th.

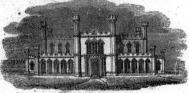

COUNTY HALL, THE CASTLE, LINCOLN.

She was Executed in private at the South End of the County Hall, Lincoln Castle, MONDAY morning, DECEMBER 28th, 1868.

[witnesses giving evidence.]
THE TRIAL.

THE STICKNEY MURDER.

PRISCILLA BIGGADIKE, widow, 29, was charged with the wilful murder of Richard Biggadike, her husband, at Stickney, on the 1st of October, 1868.

Mr. Bristowe and Mr. Horace Smith appeared on behalf of the prosecution; Mr. Lawrence defended the prisoner.

Mr. Bristowe, at considerable length, detailed to the jury all the principal facts of the case, and the circumstances under which the murder was committed revealed a depth of moral depravity and social degradation we could fain hope has no parallel elsewhere in the county of Lincoln. The following witnesses were examined :—

James Turner said he knew the deceased and he always appeared to enjoy excellent health.

George Ironmonger said : I lodged in the house with deceased. Mrs. Biggadike, Proctor, and I had tea together before deceased came home on Wednesday evening, Sept. 30th. We had two "short cakes," which were made by Mrs. B., who did all the cooking. I went out after tea, and when I returned deceased was just finishing his tea, and seemed quite well. He got up a few minutes after and went to the privy, and I heard him retching, and very sick. After he had returned he went again, and then he said, "I am very bad ; I can't live long this how ; send for the doctor." I fetched the doctor immediately. Deceased died at six next morning. I was upstairs once during the night.

Peter Maxwell, surgeon, deposed : I was called to the deceased at seven o'clock on Wednesday evening, Sept. 30. I found him in great pain in bed, sick, and violently purged. He had all the symptoms of poisoning by some irritant poison. I sent him suitable medicines, and saw him again at eleven o'clock, when he was collapsed and rapidly getting worse. I heard he died early next morning. On the 2nd October I made a post-mortem examination of the body. The head and chest were perfectly free from disease. I removed the viscera and contents of the stomach, placed them in jars &c., duly sealed, and handed over to to Supt. Wright. I believe deceased died from the effects of poison.

Supt. Wright, of Spilsby, deposed : On the 2nd October I received one jar and three bottles, sealed and secured by Dr. Maxwell. On the 6th I delivered them to Dr. Taylor, at Guy's Hospital. I apprehended the prisoner and then charged her with wilfully murdering her own husband. I cautioned her very strongly not to criminate herself. She [said] 'a hard work I should bear all the blame alone.'

Dr. Alfred Swaine Taylor stated that he was a Fellow of the College of Physicians, and Professor of Medical Jurisprudence at Guy's Hospital. On Tuesday the 6th of Oct. he received certain jars from Supt. Wright, containing the contents of the stomach of Rd Biggadike. Dr. Taylor's evidence was very lengthy, full of the usual scientific details, and showed that he had not the slightest doubt that the deceased had died through the administration of arsenic, which was the only conclusion he could draw from the results of his analysis.

Mary Ann Clarke said : I am a widow residing at Stickney, and close to Biggadike's. On the 30th I heard a noise in their house as of many people talking, and went to see what was the matter. Procter sat against the door, and he said, "Dick's very bad since he got his tea." A short time after the prisoner came to my house with a piece of cake in her hand, and she said, " the doctor says I've put something into the cake which I ought not to have done, but I hav'nt. I heard deceased in his agony say, "the Lord have mercy upon me." He died while I was there.

Jane Ironmonger said : I saw deceased in bed very sick and bad. I asked the prisoner if she had sent for his brother, and she said, " No, it does not matter, for they have not been on very good terms lately." I fetched his brother. We found the prisoner and two lodgers in the lower room. I was there when he died. On one occasion I heard the prisoner say she hoped her husband might be brought home dead, and another time she said she wished he might be brought home stiff. She then asked me how the murderers Garniers (of Marehani-le-Fen) got on about their poisoning case. She said they searched the meal and sago.

Thomas Proctor said : On the 30th of September last I lodged at Biggadike's. On that day I went fishing with George Ironmonger, a fellow lodger. We came home together to tea, and afterwards went fishing again. Ironmonger went first, leaving Mrs. Biggadike, and the child in the house. I never put any white powder in a tea cup, neither on that occasion or any other. I had no white powder or poison in my possession. I am a rat-catcher, and keep ferrets, but never keep any poison. When we came home from fishing, Mrs. Biggadike was in the house and her husband. He was taken very ill, and continued so all night. I remained with him until he died. The prisoner prepared our food.

The jury, after a consultation of only a few minutes, returned a verdict of GUILTY, accompanied by a recommendation to mercy, but upon the Judge asking upon what grounds, the foreman of the jury seemed perplexed, and again consulted with his fellows for a short time, and then said that the only ground for such recommendation was that the evidence was entirely circumstantial.

His Lordship then put on the black cap, and amidst the most solemn silence passed the sentence of death upon the unhappy woman. In addressing her his Lordship said : Priscilla Biggadike, although the evidence against you is only circumstantial, yet more satisfactory and conclusive evidence I never heard in my life. You must now prepare for your impending fate, by attending to the religious instruction you will receive, to which, if you had given heed before, you would never have stood in your present unhappy position. The sentence of the court is that you be taken to the place from whence you came, and thence to the place of execution, there to be hanged by the neck till you [are dead] and may the Lord have mercy upon your soul ! [She was] to be buried within the precincts of the pri[son]. [She] then walked firmly away from the [dock ...] lasted seven hours.

[...]ION[...]
[...]v, Dec. 28th, 1868.

cution of Picket and Carey, ni[...] were inserted in the wall in [...]

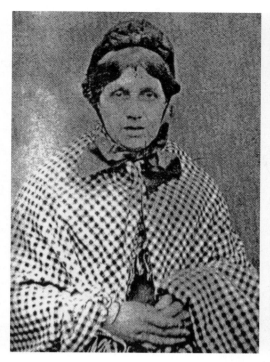

Above left: *A photograph of Mary Ann Cotton, taken while in custody.*

Above right: *Mary Ann Cotton's house, West Auckland. (Paul Heslop)*

Right: *Sergeant Tom Hutchinson, the arresting officer in the Cotton case.*

Kate Webster.

Justice Hewart, who turned down Charlotte Bryant's appeal against conviction.

Above: *The cottage at Knowle St Giles, where Catherine Churchill murdered her husband. (Paul Heslop)*

Right: *Florence Maybrick.*

Mary Wheeler.

Pathological killer: Amelia Dyer.
(Courtesy of Thames Valley Police
Museum)

The officers in the Amelia Dyer investigation. From left to right: Sergeant James, Superintendent Tewsley and Detective Constable Anderson. On the table is the carpet bag that contained the bodies of Harry Simmons and Doris Marmon, along with the white tape, string and bricks, all recovered from the River Thames. (Courtesy of Thames Valley Police Museum)

*An artist's impression of the
hanging of Mary Ann Ansell.
(Reproduced by kind permission
of Hertfordshire Archives and
Local Studies. Document reference
HALS Off Acc. 688)*

*An artist's impression of Caroline
Ansell, murder victim.*

Leavesden Hospital, Hertfordshire (since demolished).

Emily Swann and John Gallagher in the dock at Leeds Assizes.

Left: *Edith Thompson.*

Below: *From left to right:
Frederick Bywaters, Edith
and Percy Thompson,
in the garden at the
Thompsons' Ilford home.
(Solo Syndication Ltd)*

Above: *Inscription on Edith Thompson's grave, Brookwood cemetery: 'Sleep on Beloved'. (Paul Heslop)*

Right: *A woman demonstrates against the hanging of Thompson and Bywaters.*

Susan Newell.

Charlotte Bryant.

A murdered husband: Frederick Bryant.

Ruth Ellis and David Blakely. (Solo Syndication Ltd)

The other man: Desmond Cussen. (Solo Syndication Ltd)

used to whatever effects they were having on his system. But on Saturday 27 April 1889, when he attended the Wirral race meeting, his health went downhill rapidly. He complained of 'numbness', and was sick before he went out. It rained at the races, and he got a soaking. The next day he was 'very ill' and Dr Humphreys was called. Mrs Maybrick told the doctor that her husband was 'taking white powder' which she thought was strychnine. Maybrick complained to Humphreys about his heart, saying his tongue was 'furred', his legs were stiff and he had felt in a 'peculiar state' at the races. Humphreys prescribed prussic acid and advised him to drink nothing but soda water.

Humphreys returned that evening to find his patient still suffering from stiffness in the legs. He gave him another prescription, ascribing his stiffness to *nux vomica* (strychnine), which was in one of Dr Fuller's prescriptions. The following day Maybrick complained of a 'furred tongue' again, but Humphreys diagnosed indigestion. Meanwhile on Monday Mrs Maybrick bought another two dozen flypapers, paying for them, but not for some lotion, which was charged to her account.

Edwin Maybrick had witnessed his brother's condition, lying on the sofa at home, complaining of numbness in the legs. He saw him at his office on 1 May, when he seemed unwell, and again after lunch when he seemed worse. That day Edwin took a parcel to James's office given to him by Florie, who told him, 'This is your brother's dinner.' The parcel contained a small brown mug. James warmed its contents in a saucepan, poured them into a basin and ate the food.

On 3 May Dr Humphreys was called again, and this time told Maybrick directly, 'I really cannot see anything the matter with you.' Yet at midnight, called again, he found Maybrick in bed with 'great pain' in his thighs. He told Mrs Maybrick to apply moistened handkerchiefs to his mouth. The following day Maybrick could not keep anything down. The constant feature about his condition was his 'furred tongue'. Humphreys prescribed prussic acid and told him to take Valentine's Meat Juice, but this did not agree with him, and he was therefore told to stop taking it. He was finally prescribed Fowler's Solution.

The next time Edwin Maybrick saw his brother was on Sunday 5 May, when he was ill in bed. On Monday, Nurse Yapp heard him moaning in the bedroom. She went in and found him flushed and hot, moving from one side of the pillow to the other and complaining of numbness in his hands. She suggested sending for another doctor, but Mrs Maybrick declined. On Tuesday Yapp saw Mrs Maybrick on the landing, apparently pouring medicine from one bottle into another. The same day Edwin Maybrick called in Dr William Carter, a complete stranger to the Maybrick family. He found Maybrick in bed, very weak. Carter examined him thoroughly, finding his throat, which was inflamed, the only thing wrong with him. As he was being examined, Maybrick kept kicking the bedclothes away, evidently in distress. Carter diagnosed dyspepsia – indigestion – caused by 'improper food or drink', and prescribed a diet and a mouthwash.

On Wednesday Mrs Briggs, the family friend, called, and after speaking to Nurse Yapp went into the Maybricks' bedroom, followed by Mrs Maybrick. Maybrick tried to speak to Mrs Briggs, but his wife asked her to leave the room, which she did. Mrs Briggs suggested that she should send for a nurse, but Mrs Maybrick said she could nurse her husband herself. Dr Humphreys called that day and at Mrs Briggs's behest he sent for another nurse. Nurse Gore arrived the next day. Mrs Briggs also sent for Michael Maybrick, in London, asking him to come at once to Liverpool.

About three o'clock on Wednesday, Mrs Maybrick handed Nurse Yapp a letter, asking her to send it by the 3.45 post. Once on her own, Yapp opened the letter and read it, and instead of posting it she handed it to Edwin Maybrick. The letter was to Alfred Brierley, Florie's lover. Yapp later said she accidentally dropped it in the mud and opened it to put it into a clean envelope – an unlikely account, but one that indicates suspicion of her employer's wife. The letter was in reply to one that Mrs Maybrick had received from Brierley just two days earlier, when he wrote:

> My Dear Florie,
> I suppose now you have gone I am safe in writing to you. I should like to meet you, but dare not move. We had better not meet until the autumn. I think I shall take a trip to the Mediterranean, unless you wish me to stay in England.
> A.B.

The letter is much abridged. Mrs Maybrick's letter in reply, opened by Nurse Yapp, (also abridged) read:

> Dearest,
> Your letter under cover came to hand just after I had written to you. I have been nursing M all day and night. He is sick unto death. Both my brothers-in-law are here and we are terribly anxious. I cannot answer your letter fully today, my darling, but relieve your mind of all fear of discovery. M has been delirious since Sunday and I know he is perfectly ignorant of everything. Don't leave England until I have seen you again. Excuse this scrawl, my own darling, but I dare not leave the room for a moment.
> Yours in haste,
> Florie.

These letters hardly show any criminal intentions on the part of either Mrs Maybrick or Brierley towards James Maybrick, but clearly prove their covert liaison. The words she wrote, 'sick unto death', would have serious ramifications later.

About 7 p.m. the same day (Wednesday) Nurse Gore was looking for a glass, and found Mrs Maybrick in the lavatory putting medicine into another glass.

As soon as she had gone Gore threw the medicine away. Again, staff were suspicious. The following day Dr Carter went to the house to find Maybrick suffering from tenesmus (straining ineffectively to relieve the bowels). Nurse Gore gave Maybrick some Valentine's Meat Juice, which she had been given by Edwin Maybrick. James Maybrick complained that other meat juice, given to him by his wife, had made him sick, but he was not sick on this occasion.

On Friday morning, at half past midnight, Nurse Gore saw Mrs Maybrick pass through the bedroom and take away a bottle of meat juice from which Gore herself had fed Maybrick. Mrs Maybrick went to the dressing room for about two minutes, after which she brought the meat juice back and asked Gore to go for some ice to put in water to bathe her husband's head. Mrs Maybrick put the bottle of meat juice on the table. When Maybrick woke up his wife went into the bedroom and moved the bottle from the table to the washstand. Gore did not give Maybrick any of the meat juice, but when relieved by Nurse Callery she pointed out the bottle, which Callery subsequently gave to Michael Maybrick. Clearly, staff had grave suspicions about Mrs Maybrick. That afternoon, Dr Carter came again, and Michael Maybrick gave him the bottle of meat juice he had been given by Callery. Later, Carter examined its contents.

Subjecting the meat juice to a Reinsch's Test, he discovered a 'marked metallic deposit' on the pieces of copper foil. It was arsenic. The following day (Saturday) Carter returned to the house and told Dr Humphreys. By now James Maybrick was delirious and weak, and at 8.40 p.m. he passed away. That night Carter took the bottle of meat juice to Edward Davis, an analytical chemist, who applied a Marsh's Test; this likewise revealed crystals of arsenic.

When James Maybick died, Michael Maybrick directed staff to 'look and see what they could find'. They found a chocolate box, in which was a parcel labelled 'Arsenic – Poison', and written after it 'for cats', and a handkerchief which was found to be laced with arsenic. The following day, two hatboxes were found in a dressing room. They contained men's hats and at the top of one of the boxes some meat essence; this did not contain arsenic, but it was a strange place, nonetheless, to find a bottle of meat essence. Significantly, they also found three other bottles, all containing arsenic in the process of being converted into liquid form. The police came, and Inspector Baxendale took possession of bottles, glasses of liquid and other articles, including a bottle he found in the lavatory bearing the label of Messrs Clay and Abraham, chemists, and containing a dark mixture. He also took possession of the flypapers, which, along with everything else, he submitted for forensic examination. That day Martha Hughes, Mrs Briggs's sister, found the letter written to Mrs Maybrick by Alfred Brierley in a drawer of the dressing table in the Maybricks' bedroom.

On 13 May, a post-mortem examination was carried out on James Maybrick. Traces of arsenic were discovered in the bowels and intestines, and the stomach was acutely inflamed, as if by an irritant poison. There were traces of arsenic in the kidneys and liver, and the cause of death was put down to arsenical poisoning. Dr Stevenson and Edward Davis, who had 'large experience in these matters', said that if there were repeated doses of arsenic, as this case seemed to show, and if for a day or two before death no arsenic was given, that would be precisely how they would expect to find the body. Florence Maybrick was arrested on suspicion of murdering her husband.

At the inquest, Edward Davis, the analytical chemist, spoke of the Valentine's Meat Juices he received from Dr Carter. He had found a 'strong deposit' of white arsenic on the copper.

'There is no doubt in your mind that there was arsenic in the Valentine's Meat Juices given to you by Dr Carter?' asked the coroner.

'I am absolutely certain,' replied Davis.

He said that arsenic, when added, must have been by solution. He had examined the jug Edwin had been given by Mrs Maybrick, containing James's dinner. 'There must have been a considerable quantity of arsenic in it.' He had also examined bottles containing arsenic in the process of being converted into liquid. One contained dark liquid, with enough arsenic to kill two or three people. A second contained a saturated solution of arsenic, with solid arsenic at the bottom, and a third several drops of arsenic in a solution sufficient to prove fatal.

The coroner said, 'You are not talking about the chronic use of arsenic?'

Davis replied, 'No, a single dose. To put it on the safe side, we will say there is one grain in the bottle.'

'Would that quantity produce unpleasant solutions without causing death?'

'It would depend on a person's idiosyncrasies. I cannot take much of a dose myself' (laughter).

Davis went on to say that a fourth bottle contained fifteen to twenty grains of arsenic. The tumbler found in the second hatbox contained some milk, in which was a handkerchief. He squeezed the handkerchief and tested the liquid for arsenic, and found a very large quantity. He took the remainder of the fluid, which weighed 430 grains and contained practically 3 per cent arsenic, equal to 20 or 30 grains in the whole tumbler. He explained the box marked 'Arsenic – for cats' contained arsenic mixed with powdered charcoal. His examination of a bag containing Maybrick's lunch contained two pieces of farinaceous substance (cereals). He tested the contents by Reinsch's Test, finding arsenic. It seems Maybrick had cooked his lunch in an enamelled pan. To be certain that the arsenic did not come out of the enamel Davis bought an identical pan, and after boiling distilled water in it he found the contents free of arsenic. He found two grains of arsenic in the flypapers.

The coroner asked, significantly: 'Is it absolutely necessary to find a fatal dose in the body in order to conclude that death was due to arsenical poisoning?'

Davis replied, 'No.'

The inquest jury had no problem in finding that Florence Elizabeth Maybrick wilfully murdered her husband. Her trial took place on 31 July at Liverpool Assizes. Justice James Stephen presided. One might wonder what defence

Florence Maybrick could put forward, given the amount of arsenic found and motive to kill, her affair with Alfred Brierley. But she was not the only person in the Maybrick household with the opportunity to poison James Maybrick, and her defence counsel would challenge that he had been poisoned at all.

Mr Addison, for the prosecution, described arsenic as mineral poison, taken sometimes as a solid powder, sometimes in solution:

A single deadly dose to kill a man by one administration would be two grains, which would "take away a life" in about twelve hours. Symptoms are nausea, purging, vomiting without relief, burning pains in the throat and stomach, cramp in the thighs and stomach, a "furred" tongue, intense thirst and tenesmus. The same symptoms are produced by small doses, half or three-quarters of a grain. In a day or so the patient seems to get better, but continued dosage is fatal. Arsenic does not collect in the system, but passes away. It is the arsenic that passes away that kills, not that which remains in the system. Symptoms may not be recognised as being peculiar to arsenic, especially if taken in liquid form in small doses, and except in the liver you will not find extensive traces of arsenic.

Sir Charles Russell, for Mrs Maybrick, called several witnesses. Their testimonies, long and protracted, threw doubt on the prosecution's case. First, Dr Rawdon Macnamara was asked if, in his opinion, James Maybrick had died through arsenic poisoning. Dr Macnamara replied, 'Certainly not. He died of gastro-enteritis.' He said that where a person affected or troubled with a weak stomach – dyspepsia – was exposed to wet, the result is that blood from the surface of the body is driven to the internal organs, producing congestion, resulting in gastro-enteritis. Dr Frank Paul, Professor of Medical Jurisprudence at University College, Liverpool, had examined the glazed pan and said he found arsenic in the glazing. He had examined four such pans, all producing arsenic. He considered the minute quantities of arsenic found in Maybrick's body was consistent with someone who had been taking arsenic medicinally. 'I think it's a case of gastro-enteritis.'

Hugh Jones, a chemist, was asked if there was a use for arsenic as a cosmetic. 'Ladies buy flypapers when no flies are about. There is an impression in the trade they are used for that purpose.' James Bioletti, a hairdresser of thirty years' experience, said arsenic was used a 'good deal' in the hair and as a face wash. 'There is an impression among ladies that it is good for the complexion.' It was used for removing hair from the arms. He would mix it with lime and keep it in a bottle with nothing to show there was arsenic in it.

Mrs Maybrick then made a verbal statement (abridged):

My lord, I wish to make a few remarks in connection with the dreadfully crushing charge that has been made against me, the deliberate poisoning of my husband, the father of my dear children. I wish to speak principally of the flypapers and the bottle of meat essence. The flypapers were bought with the intention of using them as a cosmetic. I have been in the habit of using a face wash prescribed to me by Dr Grace, of Brooklyn. It consisted principally of arsenic, elderflower water and other ingredients. At that time I was suffering from slight eruption of the face and thought I would try a substitute. Many of my friends use a solution derived from flypapers, applied to the face when well soaked together. To avoid evaporation of the scent it is necessary to exclude the air and I put the papers under one towel folded up and another towel on top.

Referring to the bottle of meat essence on the night of Thursday 9 May:

After Nurse Gore had been in with my husband, I sat on the bed by his side. He complained of being very sick, weak and depressed, and asked me to get him the powder he referred to earlier in the evening, which I had declined to give him. I was overwrought, anxious, unhappy, and his distress unnerved me. He told me the powder would not harm him and I could put it in his food. I had no one to consult and no one to advise me. I took the white powder into the inner room and pushing the door I upset the bottle, and to make up the quantity of fluid spilled I added a considerable quantity of water. On returning to the room I found my husband asleep, and I placed the bottle on the table by the window where he would not see it. It remained there till Mr Michael Maybrick took possession of it.

Referring to the period after her husband's death:

It was only when Mrs Briggs alluded to the presence of arsenic in the meat juice that I was made aware of the nature of the powder my husband had been taking. For the love of our children and the sake of their future a reconciliation had taken place between us and on the day before his death I made a free and full confession of the fearful wrong I had done him.

Sir Charles said there were two questions for the jury to consider: was it proved that this was a death caused by arsenical poisoning, and did Mrs Maybrick cause that death? James Maybrick, he said, was a man who suffered from chronic derangement of the stomach. He was a hypochondriac, chronically dosing himself. In 1886 he told Dr Hopper he was taking unknown powders that had not agreed with him. He told Dr Humphreys the same in March 1889. On Grand National day Mrs Maybrick had forgotten her self-respect and duty to her husband. A stormy scene took place and she dressed to leave home, but was persuaded to stay by a servant. His wife had met and become 'intimately acquainted' with Alfred Brierley. Moral faults in a man were too often regarded as venial; in the case of a woman it was an unforgivable sin. She was regarded as a leper (by her family). Nothing save the purchase of flypapers occurred up to the date of the Wirral races. On that day her husband had taken a double dose of medicine containing *nux vomica*. That day he had got wet, and the next day was taken ill. What did his wife do? Send for the doctor!

Then there was the question of whether her husband had been poisoned by arsenic at all. The doctors agreed that death by arsenical poisoning never occurred to them until it was suggested. The symptoms were not distinguishable from gastro-enteritis. The quantity of arsenic found might be attributable to that taken before the fatal illness: one tenth of a grain, a minute quantity, was found. In the case of a man in the habit of taking arsenic, one might expect to find as much. Mr Maybrick, he suggested, got wet at the races, he felt cold, and was not particular in his diet, the combination of which brought on gastro-enteritis.

Supposing death was caused by arsenical poisoning. Was Florence Maybrick the person who administered it? Traces of arsenic were found in the glazing pan (according to Dr Paul), and other items. As to the alleged tampering with the meat essence, they had heard Mrs Maybrick's statement. If the jury was satisfied that James Maybrick was in the habit of taking arsenic, it would be sufficient to account for the amount of arsenic found in his body.

Mr Addison said the evidence showed that the arsenic taken by Maybrick in America was used simply as a 'pick-me-up', that he was first taken ill two days after the purchase of the first of the flypapers. There were no obvious diagnostic symptoms in taking arsenic; such symptoms were common to all irritant poisons, but arsenic was found in the liver. It was barely a fatal dose, but if the case depended upon the 'niceties and refinements' of medical evidence it might be difficult for the jury to come to a conclusion. The meat juice containing arsenic would have been given to Mr Maybrick but for the vigilance of Nurse Gore. The handkerchief applied to the mouth of her husband to assuage his thirst was steeped in arsenic, and found in a tumbler in the lavatory. Her adultery was proof that she was capable of 'duplicity, deceit and falsehood'. The jury should set aside any sympathy they may have with her, and if they considered the case proved they must say so.

Justice Stephen pointed out that Mrs Maybrick had said flies were 'troublesome in the kitchen', but this was untrue. In the medications by the chemist there was no arsenic, yet arsenic was found in them. Dr Humphreys had prescribed Fowler's Solution, the only arsenic prescribed during this fatal illness, and the deceased had taken only one amount to an equivalent of one 250th of a grain of arsenic. On 8 May he was 'going on favourably'. The defence view, said the judge, was that the illness, however caused, attacked Maybrick's weak stomach and extended to the bowels and caused death by natural causes. But arsenic was found in the liver, and other places, although in small quantity. Who put it there? Mr Maybrick may have put it there himself. If criminally, it was not suggested it was by anyone but the prisoner.

On the question of motive, his lordship said there was no doubt Mrs Maybrick had carried out an adulterous relationship with Brierley; she had admitted it.

But Brierley was not the only one; some man was with her, in London, before Brierley came. There was a letter signed, 'Your dear friend, John', which had been recovered. He was probably the man who took her out on her arrival in London. Also, it was evident that she wished Brierley to believe her husband was likely to die. 'To put it bluntly, was her letter not a strong and cogent reason to believe that she wished to be free, and to be rid of her husband in order to live with the man for whom she had made the greatest sacrifice a woman could make?' Dr Davis had said he believed the arsenic he found in the meat juice had been put in solution. And who, his lordship asked, would want all the arsenic that had been found in solution in the house? The jury retired for forty minutes, returning to declare that they found Mrs Maybrick guilty.

His lordship put on the black cap and said she had been convicted after a 'most prolonged and patient investigation'. The law gave him no discretion but to sentence her to death. A large mob had assembled outside and showed much indignation at the verdict. Counsel and witnesses were hooted, and the judge had to be guarded by police as he was driven off. On the other hand, rousing cheers were raised as the van containing Mrs Maybrick departed, guarded by mounted police.

Post-Trial

If the trial was over, the issue wasn't. The legal profession, the press, ordinary people in Liverpool and elsewhere felt there was sufficient doubt to justify the Royal Prerogative of Mercy. Several memorials to the Home Secretary were prepared. One (abridged), by Members of the Bar, read: 'We humbly pray that you will recommend Her Majesty to commute the death sentence, on the grounds that conflict of medical testimony leaves much doubt, and that the evidence of medical experts was so conflicting a guilty verdict is unfair'. Another, by the Liverpool public (through solicitors, also abridged), read: 'There was no direct evidence of administration of arsenic by Mrs Maybrick ... the case against Mrs Maybrick on the general facts was unduly prejudiced by the evidence of motive, and there is room for grave doubt whether the circumstantial evidence relied on by the prosecution was weighty enough to justify conviction ... there was a strong body of medical testimony on behalf of the defence that death was ascribable to natural causes, and having regard to the conflicting nature of the medical evidence and the widespread doubt as to the propriety of the verdict it would be in the highest degree unsafe to permit an irrevocable sentence to be carried out. We humbly pray that you will advise Her Majesty to respite the sentence of death with a view to commutation or reprieve.'

In America, the *Colorado Spring Gazette* highlighted Dr Macnamara's testimony, that James Maybrick's death was due to gastro-enteritis, mentioning his taking poisonous medicines habitually and commenting on Mrs Maybrick admitting she had put white powder into her husband's meat juice. 'As her husband said the powder was harmless, she consented'. The *Fort Wayne Weekly Sentinel* reported that 3,000 American women had signed a petition for the release of Mrs Maybrick, and intended to send it to the Princess of Wales as the Home Secretary was 'prejudiced'.

Support for Mrs Maybrick grew. Five thousand people met outside St George's Hall, Liverpool, agreeing to petition the Home Secretary. Her mother, Baroness von Roque, wrote to a barrister, asking why she had not been called to testify, saying she could corroborate her daughter's assertion that James Maybrick used arsenic as a cosmetic, and that her daughter used flypapers containing arsenic against 'corruptions of the skin'. She added that 'John', the man who had first met Mrs Maybrick at the London hotel, and whom the judge had implied was a 'lover', was a family friend who had known her daughter for years. Letters poured in to newspapers, nearly all demanding the sentence be commuted.

Then, finally, came news: the Home Secretary, 'after taking the best legal and medical advice', had commuted the punishment to penal servitude for life, 'inasmuch that although the evidence leads clearly to the conclusion that the prisoner administered arsenic with intent to murder, it does not wholly exclude reasonable doubt whether death was caused by its administration'. Florence Maybrick served fifteen years of her sentence, and was released in 1904. She returned to America where, amazingly, she published her memoirs, *My Fifteen Lost Years*. She died in 1941, aged 79.

Author's Verdict

The two main factors in this case were the flypapers and the meat essence given to James Maybrick by his wife. Mrs Maybrick recognised this in her statement to the court, saying the flypapers were to provide the arsenic required to apply to a solution when she was suffering from 'eruption of the face', and the meat essence she laced with the 'white powder' at her husband's behest.

There is much to support Mrs Maybrick's assertion that she was innocent, or at least that the case wasn't proved. Putting white powder into her husband's food might have been done without intending to kill him. He'd been using the stuff for years, after all. Then we have the first man she met in London, evidently called John, whom the judge wrongly suggested was another lover. This was a serious issue, for a woman to have a relationship outside marriage in Victorian times was an 'unforgivable sin', as counsel had said. The judge added unfair weight to the prosecution case here.

Yet there is much to support the jury's decision to convict. As his lordship remarked, 'Who would want all the arsenic that had been found *in solution* in the house?' Mrs Maybrick's affair with Alfred Brierley and her 'repugnance' of her husband were possible ingredients for a motive to kill. In her letter to Brierley she urged him not to go abroad, saying her husband was 'sick unto death', meaning it was only a matter of time till she was free. The phrase, 'sick unto death', brought sharp response from her American supporters, who said it was a common expression used by Americans, meaning, simply, feeling ill. Similar, perhaps, to what we say today, that we're 'sick to death' about something.

It seems the testimony of Edward Davis, the analytical chemist, that no arsenic came out of the enamel pan after boiling distilled water in it, was cancelled out by the evidence of Dr Paul, who found the opposite. But never mind the experts' testimonies: the jury heard evidence of arsenic being found in solution in separate bottles secreted in hatboxes, of Mrs Maybrick paying cash for flypapers when she ran accounts, of an arsenic-laced handkerchief being found in a tumbler, her carefully contrived statement, aimed at eliminating the points she knew were her undoing – the flypapers and the white powder. Yes, her husband had taken powder for years. But suddenly he dies in circumstances typical of arsenical poisoning. The judge's summing-up, in part, was unfair, but before he made it, hadn't the jury heard enough? Here was a woman who had poisoned her husband. A guilty woman. The verdict, not the sentence, was their sole concern.

The sentence, not the verdict, was the concern of those who petitioned in support of Mrs Maybrick. It reflected the feelings shared by people in Liverpool and beyond, including America; it is unlikely the issue would have arisen if Mrs Maybrick had been convicted but not sentenced to death. There was too much doubt to accept that hanging her was right. But whilst the public's knowledge of the case was gleaned through newspapers, the jury's verdict was based on witnesses' testimonies.

10

Loss of Rational Control

Mary Eleanor Wheeler, Kentish Town, London, 1890

It was ten o'clock on Friday night when Frank Hogg, a furniture remover, got home from work. Hungry and tired, he was ready for his dinner and the welcome company of his wife and 18-month old daughter. Sadly, the house was empty, although Phoebe had left a note on the table: 'Look in the saucepan. I shall not be long'. His dinner was indeed in the saucepan, but locating the whereabouts of his wife and child took priority, and Hogg hurried round to the house of Mary Pearcey in nearby Priory Street, Kentish Town, to see if they were there.

Mrs Pearcey had recently made acquaintance with Phoebe Hogg, but when Hogg arrived at 2 Priory Street he found no one there, although a light was burning in the parlour. He left a note and went home.

At 6 a.m. the following morning, Hogg went to work, but came home for his breakfast at eight o'clock. Home was the first-floor apartment of 141 Prince of Wales Road, Kentish Town. There was still no sign of his wife and daughter, but he was not unduly worried. Phoebe, he concluded, would have gone to Chorleywood, near Rickmansworth, Hertfordshire, where her father was very ill, and the arrangement was that she would go at once if she received information that he might pass away. Naturally she would have taken their daughter, also called Phoebe, but affectionately known as Tiggie, with her. Hogg took the train to Chorleywood, but Phoebe and Tiggie were not there. There was nothing for him to do but return home.

When he got home he asked his sister Clara to call at Mrs Pearcey's to enquire about Phoebe and Tiggie. Clara lived with her mother on the ground floor of 141 Prince of Wales Road, below the Hoggs. She had seen Phoebe on the Friday afternoon, about 3 p.m., pushing the pram in the direction of Priory Street, where Mrs Pearcey lived. That Saturday morning, at her brother's request, Clara called at Mrs Pearcey's, who admitted her to the bedroom.

'Did you see Phoebe yesterday?' asked Clara.

'No,' replied Mrs Pearcey.

Clara asked her again, adding that her sister-in-law had not been home that night.

'Well,' replied Mrs Pearcey, 'as you press me I will tell you. She did come about five o'clock and asked me if I would mind baby a little while. I refused, and she asked me if I would lend her some money. I said I could not. I did not tell you before because Phoebe wished me not to let anyone know anyone had been here.'

Clara went home, but half an hour later, Mrs Pearcey came to her house, and told her she had scratched her hands killing mice. They were 'running all over the place', she said, adding that her dressing table was covered in mouse blood.

'Don't be frightened,' said Clara, 'but my landlady has just told me about a dreadful murder at Hampstead. I hope it isn't Phoebe, but from the description, I think it is.'

Mrs Pearcey fetched a newspaper, and told Clara to read it. Clara did so, and said she thought the victim must be Pheobe, by the description.

'Oh no,' said Mrs Pearcey, adding, 'Frank will bring her home from Rickmansworth. It is not her.'

Clara said she'd go to the mortuary to see for herself. The two women went to Hampstead police station and thence to the mortuary where they saw the body of the murdered woman. 'That's not Phoebe,' declared Mrs Pearcey. But Clara recognised her sister's clothing, and when blood was washed from her face she confirmed that it was indeed her sister-in-law. When she touched her hand, Mrs Pearcey, in hysterics, screamed, 'Don't touch it. Let us go out.'

'Don't drag me, you go out. It is Phoebe,' said Clara. Both women were taken to the police station, where Clara was shown and identified a pram as Phoebe's.

At 6.50 p.m. that Friday, Phoebe Hogg's body had been found in 'a dark part' of Crossfield Road, Hampstead, by Somerled Macdonald, who went for the police. PC Gardener went to the scene where he saw Phoebe lying on the footpath, with her cardigan across her face. Her throat had been cut. At 10.30 p.m. the attention of PC John Roser was drawn to a pram standing close to the wall outside 35 Hamilton Terrace, about a mile from where Phoebe's body was found. A rug lay over the top of the pram, and when he removed it he saw the pram appeared to be stained with blood. He took the pram to the police station. Inspector Holland also examined it, finding hairs adhering to the sides and 'a great deal' of blood, 'not nearly dry'.

Just before 7.30 a.m. on Sunday, baby Tiggie's body was found by a hawker, Oliver Smith, lying face down among nettles in the Cock and Hoop field, off the Finchley Road. The body was taken to the mortuary.

Mary Pearcey, as she called herself, was a 24-year-old woman who had lived in the area for some years. Mary Eleanor Wheeler, as she really was, lived with John

Pearcey, whose name she had taken, for about three years before they parted in 1888. At 9.30 a.m. on 23 October, Pearcey was passing when he saw Wheeler standing at the door of her house in Priory Street. Noticing her blinds were down, he enquired why. 'My young brother is dead,' she explained. Pearcey bade her good morning and went on his way, but the significance of their encounter was that he recognised the cardigan she was wearing was one she had worn when they lived together.

Frank Hogg had known Wheeler, or Pearcey as she still called herself, for about five years. He thought she was a married woman. When Wheeler left Pearcey and moved to Priory Street, Hogg visited her there, but would deny his visits were anything other than for friendship. In November 1888 Hogg married Phoebe, his now late wife, who did not know Wheeler. Tiggie was born six months later. That Christmas, Hogg took Phoebe to Wheeler's house and they spent Christmas Day and Boxing Day there, after which Wheeler on occasion visited Phoebe at the Hoggs' house. They became quite friendly.

What Phoebe didn't know was that, after their marriage, her husband was visiting Wheeler in secret. The visits were of an 'intimate nature', their affair lasting from January until October 1890. He would call once a week at least, perhaps more. He had the key to her front door, and would let himself into the back parlour, which also served as a bedroom. This arrangement suited Wheeler who, without Hogg's knowledge, was also entertaining Charles Chrichton, a man of 'independent means', who lived at Northfleet, Kent. He, also, knew her as Mrs Pearcey.

Towards the end of January 1890, Phoebe was taken ill. She was nursed by Wheeler, who called round one night and suggested she look after her and take care of the baby. Thereafter Wheeler stayed on occasion, sometimes for a few nights, until some time in February when Phoebe's sister, Martha Styles, and niece, Elizabeth, took her to Mill Hill. This followed a disagreement between the Hoggs, but they made up and he brought her home. Wheeler did not visit again, although she did ask after Phoebe when Hogg paid his secret visits to her house.

When Phoebe Hogg's body was found at Crossfield Road on the Friday evening, Dr Poulett Wells attended the scene, and formed the opinion she had been dead a few hours. Her throat had been cut, so severely her head was merely hanging by a piece of skin, and there were compound fractures to the back of the head, caused by a heavy instrument. There were other injuries, but those to the head alone would have caused death. Having no doubt that Phoebe was murdered, the police were bound to have had their suspicions aroused by the conduct of Mary Wheeler at the mortuary.

Detective Inspector Banister and Detective Sergeant Nursey went with Wheeler to her house, 2 Priory Street, where they found the kitchen 'blood-spattered'. They found a bloodstained poker and bloodstained clothing. Two carving knives in a drawer were bloodstained too. Two panes of glass in the kitchen window had been broken from the inside and curtains found in the washhouse were also bloodstained. A card case, address card and cigarette case, all belonging to Frank Hogg, were found in a bonnet box, proving the association (they also found the latchkey in his house). Bizarrely, as the police searched her apartment, Mary Wheeler sat in an armchair, whistling, and assuming 'the greatest indifference'. DI Banister returned to the location where Phoebe's body was found four days later, and found a button, which matched those on Wheeler's jacket.

It was hardly surprising the police suspected Wheeler of murdering Phoebe Hogg, and no surprise either when they arrested her. On 25 October, at the police station, when Sarah Sawhill was searching Wheeler, the latter, who, by then, had been charged with two murders, said, 'I wrote a note to Mrs Hogg and gave it to a boy to take to her. I was to invite Mrs Hogg to my place on Friday afternoon to tea, as I should be home that afternoon.'

'Did Mrs Hogg come?' she was asked.

Wheeler replied, 'Yes, between four and a quarter past, and as we were having tea, Mrs Hogg made a remark I did not like. One word brought up another …' Wheeler stopped there, and said, 'Perhaps I had better not say any more.'

The last person known to have seen Phoebe Hogg alive was Clara Hogg, on the occasion she saw her pushing the pram, presumably containing Tiggie, in the direction of Priory Street, at 3 p.m. on the Friday afternoon. Between four o'clock and half past, Charlotte Priddington, who lived next door to Wheeler and who had borrowed a dress stand from her, went into her garden and placed the dress stand over the fence into Wheeler's garden. Just before doing so she heard the sound of breaking glass, and called out 'Mrs Pearcey' five or six times. There was no reply. She then heard a child cry, as if in pain, before going indoors. She came out again five minutes later to find the dress stand had gone.

Sarah Butler lived in the same house as Wheeler, on the second floor. She knew Wheeler (as Mrs Pearcey), and also Hogg by sight. Another man who called regularly on Mondays Wheeler said was her father – Mr Crichton, presumably.

On the Friday morning, Mrs Butler saw Wheeler sitting in her kitchen by the fire, reading a novelette. Butler saw a mouse scurry across the floor and said, 'Why don't you buy a trap?' Wheeler went out and bought one.

At 6 p.m., when it was dark and there was no light in the passage, Mrs Butler stumbled against the pram. Wheeler was in the passage too, by her sitting room door. 'Mind,' she cautioned.

Mrs Butler said, 'Alright. I can feel what it is.' Squeezing past the pram, she noticed Wheeler had her hat on. Ten minutes later, when Mrs Butler came downstairs, the pram had gone. The time is significant: between ten and a quarter past six.

The following morning Mrs Butler came downstairs at about six o'clock and noticed that two panes of glass had been broken from the inside of Wheeler's window. The washroom floor was swamped with water, with a large apron thrown on to two zinc baths, as if to dry. At 10.30 a.m. she came down again and looking into one of the baths she saw two lace curtains, which Wheeler had only put up a few days before. There was blood on them. In the copper was a pail half filled with water with two stained cloths in it.

Some time after six o'clock, Elizabeth Rogers, of nearby Priory Place, saw Wheeler pushing a 'bassinette perambulator', which was heavily loaded. She knew Wheeler; there was no mistake. She was pushing the pram along the middle of the road. The load was higher at the hood end of the pram than at the handle, and was covered over with something black. She was having a 'hard job' in pushing it, with her head dropped over the handle. She saw her turn left, towards Camden station.

About 6.30 p.m. Annie Gardner was crossing Crogsland Road to Prince of Wales Road when she saw a woman pushing a pram. She identified the woman as Wheeler. She noticed the pram was 'heavily loaded', which drew her attention to it. The load was covered with a black shawl, and Wheeler was having difficulty pushing the pram.

Martha Styles, Phoebe Hogg's sister, last saw Pheobe alive about ten minutes past six on the Thursday evening at Finchley Road station. She and Phoebe had visited their niece, Elizabeth, at the house where she worked in service. Phoebe had Tiggie and the pram with her. She told Martha she had received a note from Mrs Pearcey – Mary Wheeler – which she showed to her. It read, 'Dearest, come round this afternoon and bring our little darling. Do not fail'. The note was unsigned, but clearly believed by Phoebe to have been sent by Wheeler. Three weeks before, Phoebe had received another note asking her to go and see the writer by a public house, and when she got there she saw 'Mrs Pearcey' who invited her to go with her for 'an excursion to the seaside to look over an empty house'. Phoebe thought the place mentioned in the note was Southend. Wheeler had said to leave the baby with her nurse, but Phoebe didn't know who that was. In any event, she declined her offer. The letter was put on the fire, and Phoebe remarked, 'If I had gone to Southend no one would have thought of looking for me down there in an empty house.' She was clearly suspicious of Wheeler.

Referring to what Wheeler said when she was being searched, the boy she gave the note to was William Henry Holmes, of 138 Prince of Wales Road. At about 11 a.m. on the Friday morning, young Holmes was by his gate when Wheeler spoke to him. Would he take a note for her? She gave him a penny and the note, and told him to take it to 141 Prince of Wales Road, and to ring the top bell. He was to be sure to give it to Mrs Hogg. He went to the house and rang the top bell. A woman came to the door and he gave her the note. Later he saw Wheeler at the corner of Crogsland Road. She asked him if he had given the note to a tall person with a fringe, and he replied that he had. Wheeler said, 'Thank you. Much obliged,' and walked off. William's mother saw Wheeler give her son the penny and the note, and she watched her walking up and down until he returned.

The post-mortem examination on Phoebe Hogg clearly showed she was murdered. In addition to the dreadful injuries to her head and throat, there were defence-wounds to her arms, indicating she had tried to ward off the blows. Phoebe, her daughter, had not been attacked, but had evidently died through exposure or suffocation, through being 'overlaid'. The police steadily built up a case against Wheeler for the murder of Phoebe. The cardigan found draped over Phoebe's face when her body was found was identified by John Pearcey as the one Wheeler wore when they lived together, and which he had seen her wearing on the morning before the murder when he saw her at her door. A nut, found near where Phoebe's body was discovered, was found to be missing from the pram, which was itself found on its side about a mile away. Any doubt that an adult's body could have been pushed in a pram was dispelled thanks to some practical coppering by Detective Inspector Banister, who lay in the pram and was wheeled about in it by a colleague. One wonders what his colleagues had to say about this afterwards.

That December, Mary Eleanor Wheeler stood trial for two murders, which she denied. Justice Denman presided. Mr Forrest Fulton prosecuted; Mr Arthur Hutton appeared for Wheeler. The main thrust of the prosecution case against her was that on at least three occasions, Wheeler had written notes to Phoebe Hogg, one asking her to accompany her to a house at Southend, the others to visit her apartment at 2 Priory Street. Phoebe declined the first two invitations, but seemingly – and strangely, given what she told her sister Martha – accepted the third on 24 October, the day she disappeared. A pram matching the description of Phoebe's was seen in the passage at 2 Priory Street, after which Wheeler was seen pushing a pram containing a heavy weight along the street. Phoebe was found murdered, her body left at the roadside, and Tiggie was found dead two days later. There were other factors: Wheeler's bizarre behaviour at the mortuary; the relationship she had with Frank Hogg and Phoebe.

It was on this last point that the prosecution drew the attention of the jury to three letters, all written by Wheeler and addressed to Frank Hogg, Phoebe's husband. Abridged, they read:

Oct 2, 1888.
My dear F – Do not think of going away, for my heart will break if you do. I won't ask too much, only to see you for five minutes when you can get away; but if you go away how do you think I can live? I would see you married 50 times over. I could bear that better than parting with you for ever, and that is what it would be if you went out of England. My dear loving F, you was [sic] so downhearted today that your words give me much pain, for I have only one true friend I can trust and that is yourself. Don't take that from me. What good would your friendship be with you so far away? My heart throbs with pain thinking about it. I should die. If you love me as you say you do, you will stay. Write or come soon dear. Have I asked too much?
Your loving M.E.

The letter clearly showed that Hogg was contemplating leaving, said Mr Fulton, and the prisoner, being devoted to him, was trying to dissuade him from taking that step. A second letter followed:

18 Oct 1888.
Dearest Frank – I can't bear to see you like you were this evening. Try to be brave, dear, for things will come right in the end. I know things look dark now, but it is always the darkest hour before dawn. You said, 'I don't know what I ask', but I do know. Why should you take your life because you want to have everything your own way? I love you with all my heart and I will love her because she will belong to you. Yes, I will come to see you both if you wish it. So try and be strong. A man should be stronger than a woman.
Your most loving M.E.

This, said Mr Fulton, led to the belief that Hogg was threatening to commit suicide, and also that he was contemplating marriage to Phoebe. There was a third and final letter (undated):

Dear Frank – You ask if I was cross with you for coming for such a little while. If you know how lonely I am you would not ask. I would be more than happy if I could see you at the same time every day. I get so dizzy I don't know what to do with myself. If it was not for your love, dear, I do not know what I should do. I am always afraid you will take that away, then I should give up in despair, for that is the only thing I care for on earth.
With love from your ever loving and affectionate M.E.
P.S. Don't think anyone would know the handwriting.

After outlining the prosecution's case, and before witnesses' testimonies, Mr Fulton told the jury, 'The prisoner struck the deceased woman on the back of the head, causing terrible convulsions, and, finding she had not affected the purpose in a single blow, she repeated it on three occasions and finally cut her throat.'

For Wheeler, Mr Hutton said there was no motive that would have induced her to murder Mrs Hogg; she would gain no benefit from her death. Could the jury rely on the evidence of Frank Hogg? He had never promised marriage. She did not expect marriage. There was nothing to gain there either. Wheeler had been kind to Phoebe; she had nursed her through illness. The crime was committed with 'merciless savagery', but Wheeler was a woman of 'affectionate and kindly disposition'; it was difficult to conclude she could have committed the crime. The jury should pause before they decided it was the prisoner's hand that took Phoebe Hogg's life.

The judge's summing up was long and, it should be said, much weighted against Wheeler. Having regard to the evidence, maybe it was bound to be. It was clear, he said, that between half past three and six o'clock on the afternoon of October

24, Phoebe Hogg died through blows to the head followed by the cutting of her throat, which almost severed the head from the body. It was done in the prisoner's house, which was occupied by the prisoner alone, and she took the body a great distance away and afterwards 'conducted herself so as to indicate guilt'. She had acted throughout the whole matter in such a way the jury could not resist the conviction that she was guilty of murder. Contradicting the defence, he said there was motive: letters written by Wheeler that showed 'strong and ungoverned passion' for the husband which might make her wish to get rid of the woman. After one hour's deliberation the jury returned a guilty verdict. Asked whether she had anything to say, Mary Wheeler replied, 'I am innocent of the charge.'

Post-Trial

Awaiting execution at Newgate Prison, Mary Wheeler requested visits from her mother and sister, and Frank Hogg, her lover. The former arrived on the morning before the execution for a sad farewell in private; the latter didn't turn up, much to her distress. She was also visited by her solicitor, Freke Palmer, to whom Wheeler stated unequivocally, 'I am innocent of the murder.' She asked Palmer to insert the following advertisement into the Madrid newspapers: 'M.E.C.P. Last wish of M.E.W. Have not betrayed'. She told Palmer this was a secret message she was pledged never to reveal. Whatever its precise meaning, she took it with her to her grave. Mary Wheeler was hanged in private at 8 a.m. on 23 December 1890 by James Berry. She was 'quite calm', and walked to the scaffold with very little assistance. To Mr Duffield, the prison chaplain, who accompanied her, she said, 'The sentence is just, but the evidence was false.' This was, perhaps, a confession of sorts, although the precise meaning seems unclear.

As usual at hangings, a crowd gathered outside the prison, in this case about 300 people. Far from protesting against her execution, most of those assembled supported it because of the death of baby Tiggie, and a cheer went up when the black flag was raised. Wheeler was buried within the prison walls, but if her life had ended, the image of her face had not, for Madame Tussaud's created her in wax and purchased the pram for public display.

Author's Verdict

Mary Wheeler hardly had the best start in life. Her father, Thomas Wheeler, was hanged for the murder of a farmer near St Albans, Hertfordshire, in 1880, when she was only 14 years old. Who knows what trauma she suffered in the years that followed, and what her state of mind was when she killed Phoebe Hogg. But did she murder Mrs Hogg, or was she insane, or temporarily insane?

She had motive: jealousy of her victim, who married the man she loved and had his baby. One has only to read her letters to Frank Hogg. He was content to pay secret visits to her home, but not to leave his wife and daughter for her. What was good for Frank was not good for Mary, whose tortured feelings probably led to frustration and hatred for his wife. She invited Phoebe to an empty house in Southend, then wrote notes inviting her to her home. When her former lover, Pearcey, passed on the Thursday morning, he saw the blinds were down. This may have been preparatory to the intended killing of Phoebe, but she did not come that day. Even so, it may prove her intent.

It seems strange that Phoebe, having declined the first two invitations, accepted the third, especially when she remarked to her sister (of the first), 'No one would have thought of looking for me in an empty house.' Clearly she had misgivings about Mary's motives, yet she accepted her invitation on the Friday, when young William Holmes delivered Wheeler's note. Perhaps she intended to tell Mary to keep away from Frank. In any event, when Phoebe entered Wheeler's home she found herself fighting for her life in a frenzied attack – note the defence wounds to her arms and the broken windows. Then, after bashing her head in, Wheeler almost cut her head off. Hatred; total loss of control. And all the while, little baby Tiggie was lying in her pram nearby.

Did she murder Tiggie, whose death seems almost to have been swept to one side at Wheeler's trial? Perhaps, but there is uncertainty, because she died through 'cold or suffocation', unfortunate to be in her pram when the butchered body of her mother was placed upon it to be wheeled off into the night. This does not however lessen for a moment the tragedy of the loss of so innocent a life. It was manslaughter, at least.

Questions remain. Frank Hogg, it seems, was at work when the murder took place. But was he a party to the murder, content to allow Mary to do the dirty work? He too could have had motive. He was a suspect, and rightly so, but there is no evidence to connect him with the murder. And what about Mr Crichton, who called on Mondays? It seems he paid the rent for the privilege. There is no evidence to connect him either, and no apparent motive. Why would he want Phoebe dead?

If, as seems certain, Mary Wheeler's actions were premeditated, she made a poor job of covering up a murder scene. But then her jealousy and hatred of Phoebe may have been so strong that she didn't care about the consequences. The daughter of a murderer, unable to have the man she loved, living in the squalor of Victorian Britain, the rent paid for by a man to whom she was obliged to repay in kind. In truth, she may have lost all rational control. She was determined to entice Phoebe into her lair, and when, finally, she succeeded, she butchered her. Malice aforethought, indeed.

11

A Depth of Wickedness

Amelia Dyer, Bristol, Oxfordshire, Berkshire, Willesden (London), 1896

In March 1896, two advertisments appeared in the *Bristol Times & Mirror*:

> MARRIED couple with no family would adopt healthy child, nice country home. Terms, £10. Harding, care of Ship's Letter Exchange, Stoke's Croft, Bristol.

And, alongside:

> NURSE CHILD. Wanted, respectable woman to take young child at home. State terms to Mrs Scott, 23 Manchester Street, Cheltenham.

Mrs Scott was in fact Evelina Edith Marmon, a single mother who had given birth to a baby girl, Doris, that January, since when she had moved from the small Gloucester village where she lived to Cheltenham. There she found work and lodgings at an hotel run by an elderly widow who was happy to take her and Doris on. Evelina couldn't keep Doris and work for a living, so she decided to find someone who could look after her. Purporting to be a widow, she answered the 'couple's' advertisment. The reply was most encouraging, Mrs Harding writing to Evelina, saying 'we are plain, homely people, who live in our own house out in the country'. She said she would be only 'too glad' to have the baby and would 'take her entirely' for £10, so that she would be no further expense to her family. It would have sounded ideal to Evelina Marmon.

Mrs Harding duly arrived at Evelina's Cheltenham address on 31 March, carrying with her a carpet bag containing baby clothes. Evelina had prepared lots of baby clothes for her to take away. She offered to pay a weekly sum for her keep but Mrs Harding insisted on the £10 one-off payment, assuring her she could visit Doris whenever she wished. Evelina accompanied Mrs Harding as far as Gloucester, where Mrs Harding and Doris, wearing a fawn pelisse – a child's outdoor coat – caught the connecting train to Reading.

One can imagine Evelina's feelings: sad to see her baby go, but pleased she was off to a good home. As for Mrs Harding, she may or may not have gone home to 45 Kensington Road, Reading, that day. If she did, it was only to write a short letter to Evelina, saying she and Doris had arrived safely, and she would write a longer letter soon. In any event, at 9 p.m. that evening she arrived at Paddington station, London, from where she made her way by omnibus to Mayo Road, Willesden. As she got off the bus with Doris, a stranger, Mrs Mary Ann Beattie, seeing her carrying a child and luggage, offered to help, and was presented with the carpet bag. The two women walked along Mayo Road, Mrs Harding to No. 76, where a young woman stood at the door, waiting. Mrs Beattie saw both women and the baby go into the house. Once inside, Mrs Harding took some white tape from a workbasket, wrapped it tightly around Doris's neck and tied a knot in it. Then and there the life of a three-month old baby girl was taken away, before she was wrapped up in a napkin and pushed out of sight.

Mrs Harding's advertisment wasn't the only one published that week. On 15 March it appeared again, this time in the *Weekly Dispatch*. It was seen by Amelia Sargeant, an undertaker's wife. The Sargeants had six children and lived in South Ealing, London. For six months Mrs Sargeant had cared for another child, thirteen-month-old Harry Simmons, having agreed to look after him for 6 shillings a week. His mother had expressed a wish that Harry should be adopted by someone who could bring him up as their own, but with six children of her own Mrs Sargeant couldn't afford it. A one-off fee to have the boy adopted by someone else seemed to be the answer, so Mrs Sargeant answered Mrs Harding's advertisment, receiving a prompt reply. Mrs Harding gave her address as 45 Kensington Road, Reading, and said she would be pleased to have 'a dear little boy'. 'I have no child of my own. He would be well brought up and have a mother's love and care.'

Mrs Sargeant replied, asking to visit the Harding household. Mrs Harding agreed, and on 25 March Mrs Sargeant called at the Reading address. She asked Mrs Harding if she was in the habit of taking in infants. She had taken but two in her life, said Mrs Harding, and they had grown up into adulthood. She couldn't live without children she said, telling Mrs Sargeant that actually her name was Mrs Thomas, but she had not wanted to advertise under her own name. Her husband was a goods guard and was well known in Reading, she explained.

Mrs Sargeant found Mrs Harding's – or Thomas's – home clean and comfortable and agreed she should have the child. She would bring Harry Simmons to Reading, but Mrs Thomas instead arranged to meet her at Paddington station.

On 1 April Mrs Sargeant, accompanied by her husband and young Harry Simmons, met her on the station platform at Paddington and paid her £5, the remaining £5 to be paid on 11 April. Mrs Thomas was accompanied by a woman whom she said was her niece, who had a child called Harold with her. Mrs Thomas took Harry, and Mrs Sargeant sent a parcel of clothes for him when she got home.

Mrs Thomas and her 'niece' went directly to 76 Mayo Road, Willesden, arriving about two o'clock that afternoon. At six o'clock Harold was put to bed. In another room, Mrs Thomas searched the workbasket for white tape. Finding none, she retrieved the lifeless body of Doris Marmon and undid the knot in the tape she had used to strangle her. She then tied the tape around the neck of Harry Simmons. At thirteen months, he may have resisted, but he would have been no match for her as she pulled the tape tight and tied the knot. When she had finished her evil work, she wrapped the lifeless body in a shawl and laid it on the couch in the front room.

The following day, 2 April, the woman who first called herself Mrs Harding, and then Mrs Thomas, but whose name was actually Amelia Dyer, placed the bodies of the two dead children into the carpet bag, along with two bricks. Then, accompanied by the other woman at the house – her daughter, Mary Ann Palmer, known as Polly – and Polly's husband, Arthur, Dyer went to Paddington station, carrying the carpet bag and its grim contents. From Paddington she travelled alone by train to Reading, arriving just after 10 p.m., and made her way directly to the Clappers footbridge over the River Thames, from which she dropped the carpet bag into the dark waters of the river. As she turned to make her way home, she was startled to hear a man say 'Goodnight' to her in the darkness.

Amelia Dyer was born near Bristol in 1838, the youngest of five children to Samuel and Sarah Hobley. The Hobleys were a respectable family, and Amelia was fortunate to receive a good education, leaving school at 14 after which she served an apprenticeship as a corset maker. An education and a trade; she had more going for her than many of her peers. At 24, she took lodgings in Bristol, where she met and married 57-year-old George Thomas, a master carver and guilder. Two years later she began training as a nurse at Bristol Royal Infirmary, but was obliged to give this up when she fell pregnant, giving birth to a daughter, Ellen. She also became acquainted with a midwife called Ellen Dane.

Dane offered services to unmarried pregnant women, and unmarried mothers with babies. The former were often expelled from the family home once their pregnancy showed, so Dane accommodated them for six months or so until the baby was born – for a fee, of course. Unmarried mothers were just as likely to find themselves outcasts, so Dane offered to adopt their babies, either for a weekly fee towards their keep, or for a one-off payment – £10, say – on the understanding that the adoption would be permanent, with no more contact with the mother. The process was known as baby farming.

On the face of it, this 'adoption' looked admirable, the child's mother enjoying a working life in the belief that her baby was cared for, while the baby was given a home. Unfortunately, babies farmed out to the likes of Ellen Dane were neglected, underfed and even drugged to keep them quiet. Eventually they would die. Those 'adopted' for a one-off payment were in grave peril at the hands of an unscrupulous woman who, having pocketed the fee, might murder the child at some stage, or simply farm it out elsewhere. In an unregulated adoption system, many infants died with no questions asked. Today, it may seem difficult to understand why young, single mothers would want to dispose of their babies, but abortion was a crime, and could only be done outside hospital with the risk of fatal consequences for the mother and baby.

In 1869, Amelia Thomas found herself widowed with a young child. Many in her unfortunate position would have struggled to avoid the workhouse. Not she. Instead, she farmed out her daughter, thus enabling her to work as a corset maker or nurse, or baby farmer, the trade she had learned from Ellen Dane. She chose the latter, and advertised for children as 'Mrs Harding', taking single women into her home to have their babies. It seems she may have quit this business about 1870, when Margaret Walters and other women in the baby farming business were hanged or imprisoned. Sensing danger, she went to work at a lunatic asylum.

In 1872, she married William Dyer, an unskilled labourer, and in 1873 the Dyers' first child, Mary Ann, known as Polly, was born. The family lived at Totterdown, Bristol, but disaster struck in 1877 when William lost his job. There was no unemployment benefit, no children's allowance, so Amelia turned to what she knew best. Her advertisments, offering adoption, appeared in the press. Sometimes the word 'Premium' was inserted, which meant a one-off payment was expected, the mother not expecting to see her baby again – as would most likely be the case, once Amelia Dyer had possession of it.

Women came to Dyer's house to give birth, too. When they did there were many occasions when their babies were 'stillborn', dead before they took just one breath. At least that's how their deaths were registered. Then there was the drugging, little mites who should have been crying for nourishment or to have their nappy changed; they wouldn't keep Mrs Dyer awake at night once she'd given them a dose of cordial from the chemists. Several babies at a time would sleep night and day, until, malnourished, they simply faded away.

In 1879, things came 'on top' when Dyer was arrested following the deaths of four infants over a two-week period at her home at Poole's Crescent, Totterdown. One of them was three-month-old May Walters, who died through malnourishment. She was the daughter of a domestic servant, who had farmed her out to Dyer. The registrar refused to register the death and referred it to the coroner. The post-mortem showed baby May to weigh just 6½lb. Dyer reacted by taking an overdose of laudanum, but survived. At the inquests into May's and the other babies' deaths, she escaped a murder or manslaughter verdict through a technicality. Instead, proceedings were taken out under the Infant Life Protection Act, whereby a nurse was not permitted to care for more than one infant under one year old for over twenty-four hours without registering with the police. She was sentenced to six months' imprisonment with hard labour.

When Dyer was freed the following February, she turned her hand to her trade as corset maker. Then she tried running a small general store. When this venture failed, she turned again to taking in babies. The family moved again, this time to Fishponds, Bristol. Babies came and went. It was all too easy for her to relieve mothers of unwanted children and dispose of them, no questions asked. Until, that is, one young mother decided she wanted her baby back.

She was a young governess who was pregnant by the son of her employer. Marriage was out of the question, so she wrote to Dyer, agreeing terms for her to nurse her through her pregnancy and childbirth, thereafter to pay a final sum, £15, to have the baby adopted – by Dyer, of course. So it was; she had the baby and left it with Dyer. But when she returned a few weeks later to ensure it was being cared for and to pay the £15, she was horrified to find the baby Dyer showed her was not hers. She knew, because her baby had a birthmark, but this child did not. What's more, the baby's father was in a position to marry his lover after all, and the couple wanted their baby. Dyer was so worried she moved again, but the couple traced her nonetheless. When they confronted her to demand the return of their baby, Dyer cut her own throat, but her suicide attempt failed and she was sent to an asylum.

On her release in 1892, the Dyers moved back to Totterdown, Dyer taking in women again. They had their babies; some were 'stillborn', some 'adopted out'. By now she was addicted to laudanum and prone to violent mood-swings. She moved again, only to be tracked down once more by the governess and the father of their baby – the couple had married – which was reason again to overdose on laudanum. When the doctor called she attacked him with a poker and was sent to an asylum again. When she was released, the governess and her husband were back at her door, which may have been the reason for yet another suicide attempt, this time in a stream in Ashton Park, Bristol. Then Polly, her daughter, married Arthur Palmer, and she went to live with them at Fishponds.

In December 1894, Dyer was certified again, and sent to an asylum where a note in her file proclaimed there to be 'very little wrong with her'. Released the following March, she went to the workhouse. Here she met an elderly woman, Jane Smith, herself penniless and having to live in the workhouse after the loss of her husband and children. She was persuaded by Dyer that she could help her look after unwanted babies, and that June, the two women went to live together in Fishponds. Once again Dyer advertised and 'adopted' children, telling Granny

Smith, as she was known, the children that disappeared suddenly had gone to new homes with caring families. Then, out of the blue, a man from a newly-formed organisation called the NSPCC called. Dyer was out at the time, so she learned of the visit from Granny. It was time to move again, first to Cardiff, then to Elm Villas, Caversham, with the Palmers.

One of the first children to arrive at Elm Villas was a 9-year-old boy, Willie Thornton, with an old carpet bag as his suitcase. In receipt of favourable payment for him, Dyer was happy to take him on. Later that year (1895) the entire family moved to 26 Piggott's Road, Caversham. Children came and went. At least one died in the house. Shortly after Christmas, the family moved again; Dyer, Granny and Willie Thornton across the county boundary to 45 Kensington Road, Reading, and the Palmers to 76 Mayo Road, Willesden. Dyer now plied her trade as Mrs Stansfield.

Granny would have been blind not to realise there was something amiss, with the constant turnover of children. Many were spirited away mysteriously to a 'good home', leaving behind the nice clothes that had arrived with them which went to pawn, the pawn tickets never redeemed. So, in January 1896, Granny went to the NSPCC and said that Mrs Thomas was taking in children for money. She lived at 45 Kensington Road and had a child now. When the man from the NSPCC called, Dyer – as Mrs Thomas – admitted she was looking after a 6-month-old nurse-child and 9 year old Willie Thornton. Yes, she accepted money for looking after children, who all went to good homes. The baby was taken from her and sent to a local couple for safekeeping, while the NSPCC man told her she could expect periodic visits from now on. A timely warning, but the NSPCC man's visit didn't deter her in the slightest.

That February, Dyer placed an advertisment in the *Western Daily Express* in the name of Mrs Thornley, offering to adopt a child at a 'small premium'. Mary Fry had recently given birth to a daughter, Helena. Keeping her baby was out of the question, but the premium, £10, seemed reasonable, and Helena would have a permanent home. A few days later, 'Mrs Thornley' collected Helena from Miss Fry at Bristol Temple Meads railway station. At 9 p.m. that evening Dyer arrived home with a brown paper parcel about 2ft long, and placed it on the sewing machine. She said nothing about it, and Granny didn't ask. The following morning it had disappeared. About a week later Granny noticed a 'bad smell' emanating from the kitchen cupboard and complained about it. Whatever it was, at 10.30 a.m. on Monday 30 March, she saw Dyer leaving the house with a parcel, saying she was 'going to pawn'.

About 11.30 a.m. that mornng, William Povey was walking by the Thames near Sonning when he saw a woman approaching on the towpath. He noticed she was carrying a brown paper parcel in her right hand, tucked under her cloak. A little while later, she returning by the way she had come, but he didn't see any parcel. Later that morning, Charles Humphreys, a bargeman, noticed a brown paper parcel lying in shallow water. He dragged it from the river into his boat. He was in for a surprise when he began to open it, for when he tore back the paper he found himself looking at a small human foot.

Humphreys reported his find to the police, and the parcel was collected and taken to the mortuary, its contents examined by Dr William Maurice. It contained the body of a baby girl, with white tape wrapped around her neck and tied with a knot. Wrapped around the body were diapers (nappies) and a pelisse. The parcel had been tied with macramé string and had contained a brick to weigh it down in the water. There was no clue as to the child's identity, but a careful examination of the paper wrapped around the body showed some handwriting: *Temple Meads Station, Bristol,* and *Mrs Thomas, 26 Piggott's Road, Lower Caversham, Reading, Oxon. 24-10-95.* An enquiry at the railway station confirmed that the parcel had been delivered the previous October to Mrs Thomas at 26 Piggott's Road, and the railway clerk was able to tell the police that that person had moved to 45 Kensington Road, Reading.

On Friday 3 April, the police were at Dyer's door. When they showed her the brown paper bearing her name and previous address, she said she had thrown it out as rubbish. She admitted her real name was Dyer. When they searched the house they found lots of pawn tickets, letters and baby clothes – and white tape and macramé string, similar to that tied around the baby's neck and the parcel. Dyer was arrested. In the police station she took a pair of scissors from her pocket, but before she could inflict any harm upon herself they were wrested from her by a police sergeant. A few minutes later she slipped a lace from her boot, wrapped it round her neck and tied a knot in it, again to no avail. Genuine attempts at suicide? Or the *modus operandi* of someone when things came 'on top'? Her murderous campaign was over – but no one knew as yet that the day before the police came knocking she had thrown a carpet bag containing the bodies of Doris Marmon and Harry Simmons into the river.

Some of the letters found by the police at Dyer's house gave a clue to the identity of the baby girl recovered from the River Thames. It seemed she might be Helena Fry. Unfortunately, the remains were so badly decomposed the body was unidentifiable. Even so, they charged her with the murder of 'a female child unknown'. When she appeared before the Reading magistrates she declared, 'I do not know anything about it. It's a mystery to me.'

Dyer had lived in Caversham, and now lived in Reading, two communities straddling the river. A search team began to search the Thames. On 8 April Henry Smithwaite dragged what appeared to be rags from the river. As he did so, he saw a brick, then a head, fall out. He had discovered the pathetic remains of a baby boy. Two days later, another body was pulled from the river, another baby boy, with white tape around his neck. Later the same day, four 'draggers' pulled an old carpet bag from the river. When it was taken to the mortuary it was found to contain two infants, one on top of the other. They would be identified as Doris Marmon and Harry Simmons, whom Dyer had strangled at 76 Mayo Road, Willesden. The bag also contained two soot-blackened bricks. Two more infants were pulled from the river on 17 and 23 April, each having been strangled by white tape. The last body was so decomposed it fell to pieces. Inquests were held on all the recovered bodies, but we will focus here on babies Marmon and Simmons.

Evelina Marmon, Doris's mother, recognised her baby at the mortuary. Doris was born on 21 January and had been kept by Miss Marmon until 31 March. Amelia Ann Sargeant, 'greatly distressed', recognised the body of the male child as Harry Simmons. He was about thirteen months old, 'a beautiful child, thoroughly healthy and strong' when she handed him to Mrs Thomas.

Other evidence included the identification of baby clothes, and some of the bricks. Granny Smith identified the one in the first parcel recovered as a brick she used to place her iron on. The soot-blackened bricks used to weigh down the carpet bag were identified by Albert Culham, the Palmers' landlord. Culham had had a fire grate moved in the house, 76 Mayo Road, and had placed some of the loose bricks under a rabbit hutch. They were soot-blackened, like those found in Willie Thornton's carpet bag. Willie identified the carpet bag as his, recognising it by the pattern on it and its condition. Only seven years old, he proved to be a good witness and was commended for the way in which he gave evidence in court.

A man named John Toller testified that he had seen a woman crossing the recreation ground on Thursday night, 2 April, at about 10.50 p.m. He bid her 'goodnight', but she had not replied. He identified Dyer as the woman, saying she had been walking from the direction of the river.

Arthur Palmer, Dyer's son-in-law, was taken into custody, and Dyer's daughter, Mary Ann (Polly) Palmer was also arrested for being an accessory in another child's murder. There is not the room, alas, to include their criminal involvement here. However, what happened to them in terms of their arrests materially affected the case against Dyer.

At the sight of her son-in-law in the dock, and anticipating the same for her daughter, Dyer was very concerned. On 16 April in custody in Reading Gaol, she wrote two letters, which she handed to Mrs Gibbs, the matron. The first, which she requested to be forwarded to Superintendent Tewsley, read (abridged):

Sir,

Will you kindly grant me the favour of presenting this to the magistrates. I must relieve my mind. My days are numbered, but I feel it is an awful thing drawing innocent people into trouble. I know I shall have to answer before my Maker

in Heaven for the awful crimes I have committed, but as God Almighty is my
judge neither my daughter, Mary Ann Palmer, or her husband, Arthur Ernest
Palmer, had anything to do with it. They never knew I contemplated doing
such a wicked thing until it was too late. I am speaking the truth and nothing
but the truth as I hope to be forgiven. I must stand alone before my Maker in
Heaven to give an answer for it all.

The second letter she asked to be forwarded to Arthur Palmer:

My poor dear Arthur,
Oh how my heart aches for you and my dear Polly. I am sending you this to
tell you I have eased my mind and made a full statement. I have told them the
truth, as I hope to be forgiven. God Almighty is my judge. I dare not go into his
presence with a lie. I hope and pray God will forgive me ... I know I have done
this dreadful crime, and I know that I alone have to answer for it ... I hope God
will give you both grace and strength to bear this awful trial. God bless you, my
dear boy.
Your broken-hearted mother.

Broken-hearted, indeed. Amelia Dyer had dispatched without mercy so many
innocents, but when it came to her own kith and kin she was quite prepared to
take sole responsibility.

Dyer appeared before the magistrates on 2 May, charged with the murders of
Helena Fry, Doris Marmon and Harry Simmons. Arthur Palmer appeared with
her, but was discharged. Justice, albeit of a lighter nature, would come for him
later: three months for deserting a 4-year-old girl at Devonport, when he and his
wife were living there under the names of Mr and Mrs Paton. Evidence of Dyer's
letters was given, a 'full confession in court', as the *Berkshire Chronicle* put it. Dyer's
daughter, Polly, was then called to testify. When she stepped into the witness box
Dyer burst into tears.

Mrs Palmer confirmed that on 31 March her mother had come to her house
at 76 Mayo Road, Willesden. She was carrying a baby. She said her mother
told her that the baby belonged to a Mrs Harris, which she was 'holding' for
her. She saw her mother in the sitting room, but she saw nothing more of the
baby. Her mother told her the next day she was going to Paddington station to
'take a little child to nurse'. She accompanied her, meeting Mrs Sargeant and
her husband on the station platform. Her mother introduced her as her niece.
Mrs Palmer had the child Harold with her. Mrs Sargeant handed the child, a
boy, and some money to her mother and an agreement was signed. Back at
Mayo Road, when Mrs Palmer went into the next room to put Harold to bed,
her mother said, 'Don't come in for a few minutes.' When she returned to the
room about a quarter of hour later, her mother was on the sofa, and the little

boy was lying at the head of the couch, covered with a shawl. Her mother said he had gone to sleep. She wouldn't let her near the child, or her husband when he came in.

Mrs Palmer saw the carpet bag under the couch and asked what it was. 'Nothing in particular, but I don't want anyone going into the room,' her mother told her. Later she saw her mother sitting on the couch, but there was no sign of the little boy.

'What have you done with the child?' she asked.

'He's all right. Don't worry,' her mother replied. Her mother went 'out the back' and got a brick, which she placed under the couch. She also had some white tape in a box, and the next time she looked it was gone. Later the parcel and brick had disappeared, and the carpet bag was packed. She accompanied her mother to Paddington, from where her mother went on, alone, to Reading, carrying the bag.

Dyer was committed for trial at the Old Bailey, and remanded in custody to Holloway. Already indicating a defence of insanity, she was transferred into the hospital wing of the prison under the supervision of Dr Scott, the medical officer. The trial took place on 21 May, the murder of Doris Marmon being the one the jury would hear. After Mr Lawrence had outlined the case for the prosecution, Mr Kapadia, defending, called the witnesses he hoped would support a case of insanity.

Dr Logan was the man Dyer had attacked with a poker. She was very violent, he said, and suffered from delusions. She said she heard voices telling her to destroy herself: 'The birds keep saying, "Do it, do it."' However, he saw no objective symptoms of insanity. Dr Fearth, house surgeon at Bristol General Hospital, said Dyer had been admitted in April 1894, having attempted suicide. She was suffering from melancholia, but he could not say she was mad.

'Every person suffering from melancholia is not necessarily mad,' said the judge, to laughter.

She was with 'sound mind' when she was discharged, said Dr Fearth.

Dr Winslow examined Dyer in Holloway, six days before the trial. He concluded she was of unsound mind and suffered from hallucinations. She was not 'shamming insanity.' Voices spoke to her, telling her to take her own life; she could not recollect the crime; she was visited by the spirit of her mother and the boy. She told him, 'The sights and sounds are so horrible I prefer to keep them to myself.' She had visions: she thought she was handling her mother's bones in her coffin; she thought rats were crawling over her.

Dr Scott, the Medical Officer at Holloway, said Dyer had been under his observation since her admission to the prison. He considered she had not been insane during this time. He thought her allegations about memory failure were simulated. Dr Savage had observed her in Holloway for one hour, concluding she was 'not mentally unsound'. He had been told Dyer's mother was insane, but he knew she had not been. Finally, one of Dyer's brothers – 'a bent man with white hair and a beard' – testified. He was asked, 'Was your mother ever insane?'

He replied, emphatically, 'Never!'

'Was there ever a case of insanity in your family?'

'No.'

In his closing address, Mr Kapadia urged the jury to bear in mind that 'thrice had this woman been confined in asylum'. It was one of the peculiarities of homicidal mania that its victims desired to destroy those they loved best. Dyer's actions were inconsistent with sanity, he said, because she had made no attempts to destroy the traces of the deeds committed. The closing statement on behalf of the Crown was short, concluding with, 'They might as well abolish the crime of murder as accept the theory set up by the defence.' The jury took five minutes to find Dyer guilty. Her face 'assumed a ghastly hue', and two male prison wardens held her arms to support her.

Passing sentence, Justice Hawkins told her, 'You adopted a cunningly devised plan to get into your possession money, by pretending falsely that you would be a mother to the poor little babies whom you destroyed. You knew the money you received would not be sufficient to sustain life for any lengthened period of time. You never intended that life should be sustained at all. You practised wicked treachery towards the mother of one of these babes, and perpetrated as barbarous a crime as one can conceive. Under the same pretence you got another little child whom you slaughtered on the very same evening, and you sank their little bodies to the bottom of the river. You have carried on this wicked and cruel trade for many a long day.' He then sentenced her to death. Dyer had nothing to say. Instead, she rose to her feet and with the help of two warders slowly walked down the steps at the back of the dock, and was taken to the condemned cell at Newgate Gaol.

The charge of 'accessory before the fact' against her daughter, Mary Ann Palmer, still remained.

Post-Trial

Although condemned to death, the involvement of Amelia Dyer in the court proceedings concerning this grim case was, it seemed, not yet over. 'A sensation was caused in Reading by a singular development in the child murder case,' reported the *Berkshire Chronicle*. Sensation indeed, for the solicitor for Dyer's daughter, Mary Ann Palmer, Mr Woods, went to the Lord Chief Justice and obtained from him a Crown subpoena directing Dyer, 'without excuse or pretence', to appear as a witness at the Berkshire Assizes on 16 June at her daughter's trial on the charge of accessory. Woods then went to Newgate Gaol and served the subpoena on a representative of the governor.

To say this was unusual would be an understatement. A woman condemned to die was being asked to attend court as a witness, some days after the proposed date of execution, which would thus have to be delayed. Did anyone believe that her testimony, if given, could be treated as reliable, and would it be right to delay sentence in any case? The Home Secretary didn't think so. Instead, in a statement in the House of Commons, he declared the subpoena 'inoperative', and said the law must take its course. Mrs Dyer was 'legally dead' from the moment of her condemnation; it was undesirable that the closing days in her life should be disturbed by 'unnecessary distractions' when the interests of society required that the law should be carried out.

Just before nine o'clock on Wednesday 10 June 1896, James Billington entered Dyer's cell and pinioned her arms before she was led, scarcely able to walk, to the scaffold. She had nothing to say: no expression of sorrow or of regret; no message for her victims' mothers or her own family. It seems she died quickly. The black flag, hoisted to proclaim sentence had been carried out, might just have readily been seen as flying in tribute to her poor victims. A few days later, when her daughter, Polly, appeared at the assizes, no evidence was offered against her and she walked free.

Author's Verdict

Amelia Dyer, able to earn a living as a corset maker or a nurse, chose another trade: the murder of children for money. She sought out young, pregnant women who, facing the prospect of being thrown into the workhouse or losing their employment, had little option but to part with their babies, but they did so believing they would be provided for. Instead they were handing them to a pathological killer. Her defence lawyer said her activities were inconsistent with sanity 'because she made no attempt to destroy the traces of the deeds committed.' Yes, she did! She wrapped the lifeless bodies of her victims in brown paper and dropped the weighted parcels into the Thames. She changed her name and her address many times over. Greed, not insanity, was the reason for her actions.

Babies are innocent. Babies are dependent. They stare in wonder at this strange new world they are a part of. As long as they can look back into the faces of those they know and trust – mum, dad, grandparents – they know they are OK. Doris Marmon and Harry Simmons would have done the same, until they found themselves looking back into the face of this stranger, But they would have trusted her too, even as she was taking the white tape from the work basket. She had no pity, no human feeling at all – until it came to protecting her daughter, when her maternal instincts were commendable indeed.

She was cold, she was heartless. She took Doris Marmon from her mother and, having travelled to her daughter's house at Willseden, she sought out a length of tape, wrapped it around Doris's neck, and strangled her. She took Harry Simmons to the same place and did the same thing. On each occasion her daughter, Polly, was in the house. Since she was a child she had seen babies come and go, moved to many different addresses with her mother. Could anyone really believe she didn't know what was going on? What did she think happened to the babies her mother brought to her house, and what did she think was in the carpet bag? She was fortunate to walk away unpunished.

How many children did Amelia Dyer murder? She was in the baby farming 'business' for over twenty-five years, except when things were looking dicey or when she was locked up. Babies came and went with amazing regularity. Some were born and died then and there, in her home. Others died through neglect. Those like Doris Marmon and Harry Simmons and Helena Fry and countless others were 'adopted' and murdered. We cannot know how many; it may be hundreds. Dyer died quickly at the hands of the hangman. Many will believe it was more than she deserved.

12

'A Motive So Utterly Inadequate'

Mary Ann Ansell, Hertfordshire, 1899

As a resident of the Metropolitan Asylum for Imbeciles, Leavesden, near Watford, 26 year old Caroline Ansell would have known few of life's luxuries, and certainly would not have expected to be a regular recipient of mail, not even from her own family. And yet, in the early months of 1899, the postman called several times.

It was a rule at the asylum that all parcels addressed to patients, or inmates as they were unfortunately called, had to be opened by staff, whilst letters could simply be handed, unopened, to their intended recipient. Nurse Alice Felmingham, in charge of Ward 7, had had care of Caroline since the previous December, so it would have been routine for her to intercept her mail.

The first, a small parcel sent anonymously in February, contained some tea and sugar. Nurse Felmingham opened the parcel, and whilst she may have been surprised at its contents, hardly necessary for a resident at the asylum, she passed it on to Caroline. The following day Caroline made some tea, courtesy of her unknown benefactor, and at once complained of it tasting bitter. 'You've made it too strong,' she was told, and the tea was discarded. The sugar seemed to be moist, and that was discarded too.

Caroline's next dispatch was a letter. After she had read it, Nurse Felmingman saw her in tears. The letter, Caroline explained, had been sent to her by her cousin, Harriet Parish. It read (verbatim):

> Dear Carrie, I now send these few lines to tell you that your father and mother is dead. They died last week and I am very sorry for you, and the dear little ones that are left.

On this sad and unexpected news, Caroline wrote in reply to Ms Parish, asking for her parents' funeral cards and some black ribbon so that she could be 'in mourning'. The response was a letter from her father, telling her that he and her mother were both alive and well, and expressing indignation at a report to the contrary. Then, on Thursday 9 March, Caroline received another parcel.

Nurse Felmingham opened the parcel and found it to contain a piece of cake, 'presenting the appearance of a flat jam sandwich, with the substance constituting the middle layer being very yellow'. This, like the first parcel, had been sent anonymously. She gave it to Caroline, who threw the wrapper away. At teatime the following day (Friday) Caroline treated herself to some of her cake – about half of it, in fact. Two other patients had some too. One, Kate Maloney, tried some, but spat it out, saying it tasted bitter.

On Saturday morning Nurse Felmingham saw that Caroline was sick and that the whites of her eyes had turned yellow. By 1.15 p.m., at lunch, she looked even worse. She was given a 'black draught', then some toast, which she threw up immediately. The women who had eaten some of the cake were also sick, vomiting and complaining of internal pain. Another patient, Mary Smithers, ate some of the cake on Saturday, and she too fell ill. On Sunday morning Caroline felt a 'little better' and went to church as usual. She ate beef for lunch, but was sick again. The other women had started to recover, except for Mary Smithers. On Monday, Nurse Felmingham was off duty, but on Tuesday morning she saw Caroline's lips had turned black and her eyes looked 'peculiar'. She called Dr Blair who sent her to the infirmary at once.

Throughout that day Caroline remained conscious, but could not speak. She died at eight o'clock that evening. Dr Blair put the cause of death down to peritonitis. On Wednesday, Mary Smithers was sent to the infirmary with the same symptoms, but fortunately recovered.

Caroline Ansell was one of five children of James and Sarah Ansell, who lived in Tankerton Street, off Gray's Inn Road, London. At the resulting inquest into her death, Sarah Ansell said that neither she nor her husband had sent Caroline anything through the post. Harriet Parish said she had not written to Caroline for two years, and had certainly not written the letter telling her of the 'deaths' of her parents, nor was that letter in her handwriting.

On Thursday 16 March, Caroline's mother came to the asylum, accompanied by Mary Ann, Caroline's younger sister. Dr Blair said he suspected Caroline's death had something to do with the cake. They said they knew nothing about any cake. 'Well, I suspect it very much and I recommend a post-mortem examination,' said Dr Blair. Mrs Ansell said she would consult her husband about it, whilst Mary Ann was more concerned about acquiring a death certificate. She saw Edward Farmer, the porter, and asked him if a death certificate could be obtained at the asylum. It could not, he told her. She asked him where she could obtain one. Farmer, regarding her as 'unhinged' at the death of her sister, kindly wrote a letter for her, addressed to the registrar.

Mrs Ansell and Mary Ann then returned to London, where Mary Ann said to her father, 'Father, if I were you I would not let them have a post-mortem examination.'

'Very well, you write him a letter,' he replied, meaning Dr Blair. Mary Ann wrote a letter at his dictation (Mr Ansell being illiterate) which read,

For why do you want a post-mortem examination on the body after being in your care four years? We decline to give you authority.

Dr Blair, who was also treating the still-sick Mary Smithers, had voiced his suspicions to the coroner, who overruled the Ansells and ordered the post-mortem examination to take place. It was carried out by Dr Alfred Cox, who said there were 'signs' which led him to believe that death had occurred from acute irritant poisoning. The inquest into Caroline's death was adjourned until 10 April, by which time a significant development took place: the arrest of Caroline's sister, Mary Ann, on suspicion of murder.

Superintendent Wood, in charge of the police investigation, had much to tell the resumed inquest. First, that he had taken the viscera – the tongue, vocal organs, part of the gullet, kidneys, liver, gall bladder, spleen, the stomach and other internal organs – to an 'eminent expert', Home Office Pathologist, Dr Thomas Stevenson, at Guy's Hospital, London. Dr Stevenson's conclusion was that the condition of the organs was characteristic of phosphorus poisoning, which produced fatty degeneration of the liver, kidneys and heart within two or three days of its administration. In fact, his search for traces of phosphorus was negative, but phosphorus is rarely detected if a patient survives for three or four days after it has been administered, as Caroline had. She may have recovered if she had had immediate help, but there was no cause to think she had been poisoned.

Superintendent Wood had also handed letters (including the one purporting to be from Ms Parish), and a Christmas card Caroline had received, to a handwriting expert, Mr Gurrin. The words on the Christmas card indicated it had been sent by Mary Ann, and was in her handwriting. He also handed Mr Gurrin the brown paper wrapping, which Caroline had thrown away, but which was found in the 'female side of the asylum' by police. The wrapping had a London postmark. Superintendent Wood told the court how, on 7 April, he had obtained a warrant and that very day had arrested Mary Ann at the address of her employers, Mr and Mrs Maloney, in Great Coram Street, London, where she had worked in service for three and a half years. When Superintendent Wood charged her with murdering her sister, Mary Ann replied, 'I know nothing whatever about it. I am as innocent a girl as ever was born.'

Mary Ann had a piece of blue paper in her pocket, which, she explained, contained 'questions she was going to put at the inquest'. Its contents (verbatim) were read out to the court:

Why was we not sent for to see my sister before she was near death, so as we could have a word with her in time? Who it was that had been sending the

parcels to her? When the nurse that was supposed to examine the cake found it
was heavy why did she not make a further examination on it, and when one of
the inmates was seen to spit it out why was the others allowed to finish eating
it? When friends are sent to come and see the inmate, either in life or death, is
it a rule that when a attendant takes you to the place where the body is to be
viewed to shut the door in your face? When Caroline was placed under the care
of a doctor and nurse and put in the infirmary, what she put in there for? Was
it for sickness of poison? Why did they not send word to her parents in good
time? If it had been done this trouble would not have happened.

What had led the police to suspect Mary Ann of sending her sister bitter tea, and
cake laced with poison, and why would she do such a thing? Damning evidence
of motive and method was uncovered.

John Cooper, an insurance salesman employed by the Royal London Friendly
Society, caused 'quite a sensation' when he testified at the inquest. It had been
his practice, he said, to call at the address of Mr and Mrs Maloney, Mary Ann's
employers, at Great Coram Street, to collect insurance premiums, which were
often paid on their behalf by their maidservant, Mary Ann. Being a good salesman,
he had, from time to time, invited Mary Ann to insure herself. She had declined,
but on 6 September 1898, after paying the usual premiums on her employers'
behalf, she said she would like to insure her sister Caroline's life. They were fond of
each other, she said, and if anything ever happened to her she would like to 'bury
her respectably'. She told Cooper that Caroline lived in Watford, and was a general
servant at the Leavesden Asylum. She knew if she had said Caroline was a 'lunatic'
the company would not have insured her. The premiums, Cooper told her, were
3 pence a week for £22 10 shillings in the event of Caroline's death, when she, Mary
Ann, would be entitled to the money. (In fact, if Caroline died within six months
Mary Ann would be entitled to only £11 5 shillings, one half of the sum insured.)
The paperwork was completed, and the policy sent to Mary Ann that October.

On 17 March 1899, just three days after Caroline's death, Cooper received the
following letter from Mary Ann:

> Dear Mr Cooper,
> I send these few lines to ask your advice. What I should do about my sister's
> insurance, as she died on Tuesday, and can you come and see me tomorrow as
> early as possible. If you can call I would be very thankful . . .

Cooper replied, telling Mary Ann to take the insurance policy and death
certificate to a branch office and she would be paid – but no death certificate had
been issued. Then, on 22 March, Cooper called to see Mary Ann, and told her he
had discovered her late sister had been an inmate at the asylum, and therefore the
insurance was null and void. He also told her that if she gave him her policy and

insurance payments book he would refund her premiums. She was unable to do so, she said, because she had mislaid them. A bizarre but relevant exchange then took place, between Cooper and an inquisitive juror.

'Is it possible to insure another person without his or her knowledge?' the juror asked.

'Yes,' Cooper replied, 'in the case of a relative. Queen Victoria is insured by hundreds of people and never knows it.'

If Mary Ann had motive – monetary gain – she had to employ a method to kill Caroline in such a way so as not to arouse suspicion about her untimely death. She would poison her. But how could she acquire poison?

Emily Noakes worked in her father's 'oil and colour' shop near to the Maloneys' house, where Mary Ann was maidservant. Mary Ann, a regular customer, had come into the shop and asked for some phosphor paste, as the Maloneys had 'a great many rats'. Noakes had sold her four or five bottles since 1 January. But Mrs Maloney had never sent Mary Ann to buy rat poison. There were sometimes rats in the house, but she, Mrs Maloney, set traps for them herself. Mrs Maloney said that Mary Ann slept in the lower part of the house, where she had the opportunity to use the cooking range.

Henry Gurrin, the handwriting expert, had examined the documents he had been given by Superintendent Wood. The handwriting on the letter purported to have been sent by Harriet Parish, he said, was the same as that on the blue paper taken from Mary Ann on her arrest and on the brown wrapper – although it had been disguised – and the Christmas card, which Mary Ann agreed she had sent to her sister. The implication was that Mary Ann was responsible for all the handwriting. Bottles of poison, the handwriting, sending letters and parcels to her sister, taking out insurance on her sister's life, her sister dying within six months; small wonder the inquest jury declared 'that the deceased died from the effects of phosphorus poison contained in the cake sent by Mary Ann Ansell in order to obtain the insurance money on the policy held by her'.

At the Hertford Assizes that June, Mary Ann, aged 21, was tried for the murder of Caroline. Justice Mathew presided. In a 'firm and loud' voice she pleaded, 'Not guilty, my lord.' Mr Rawlinson, for the prosecution, opened by telling the court that Caroline Ansell had received a letter and, previously, a Christmas card and two parcels, one containing tea and sugar, received on 22 February, the other, containing a cake, on Thursday 9 March 1899, and that she had eaten some of the cake the following day and had died the following Tuesday. The cake had been laced with phosphorus. One by one, the witnesses stepped forward to present the prosecution case.

Nurse Alice Felmingham recounted her evidence, previously given at the inquest, of Caroline receiving letters and parcels and the Christmas card, and of her sickness and the sickness of other patients after they had eaten the cake. Mr Rawlinson drew particular attention to the letter purported to have been written to Caroline by Harriet Parish, telling Caroline her parents were dead. 'What was the purpose of such a letter?' the jury might have wondered. He provided the answer readily enough. By the rules of the asylum, if a patient became seriously ill, notice would be sent to the parents, and further notice sent if the patient died. Mary Ann, who sent the letter, knew that if Caroline died, the authorities would write to her parents and an enquiry might be set up – the last thing Mary Ann would want. She wanted the authorities to believe that it was no use sending a report of Caroline's death to her parents, that they should send it to her next of kin – none other than herself.

Mr Rawlinson told the jury how phosphorus poisoning 'acted differently' to other poisons. When phosphorus is first taken it produces sickness and nausea, and irritation internally. The patient seems to get over it in twenty-four hours, and afterwards gets well except for slight discomfort. This state of health lasts for two to three days. But what is really happening is that the poison is acting on the kidneys and liver, causing enlargement of the latter and 'fatty degeneration' of both, accompanied by jaundice and acute pain, after which there is little hope. Caroline was doomed from the moment she consumed half of the cake, despite seeming to get better for a short time.

Testifying in her own defence, Mary Ann flatly denied writing the letter purported to have been sent to Caroline by their cousin, Harriet Parish. She denied sending the parcels too, and that the handwriting on the brown paper recovered was hers. She agreed buying four of five bottles of phosphor paste from Emily Noakes, saying she was frightened of rats and that her employer, Mrs Maloney, had taken no notice of her complaints. Her wages were adequate, she said, and she was never in great want of anything, including insurance money. Asked why she had insured her sister's life, she said she did so because the agent, Mr Cooper, pressed her to. She agreed she was engaged to be married at the time of her sister's death, but the 'young man' was not earning sufficient for them to get a home together. Their engagement was postponed until he could earn more money. Asked if she was fond of Caroline, she said, 'two sisters who were better friends never lived'.

Mr Clarke-Hall, defending, told the jury the whole weight of the case hung on motive. The sum of £11 5 shillings was 'inconceivably inadequate', he said, even in her 'humble station in life', to enable a man and woman to live comfortably after marriage. Would she have gone to a shop where she was perfectly well known and bought enough poison to kill three adults? It was natural for a servant, who was 'kept in the kitchen', to want to destroy rats there. As to the cake, it was true that there were opportunities for Mary Ann to have made it. Great stress had been made on the yellowness of it, but phosphor paste is whiter than flour. Yellow atrophy was a known disease, more likely to attack unmarried women. It was impossible to distinguish the symptoms between yellow acute atrophy from those of phosphorus poisoning. Was it not possible the former had caused Caroline's death?

Did Mary Ann send the cake? The jury had to be satisfied she wrote the address on the wrapper, otherwise the connecting link in the chain of circumstantial evidence was missing. The handwriting on the wrapper was in a 'laboured hand', with a great similarity to the writing of girls of that particular class. Certain differences were apparent in the writing; Mr Gurrin, the handwriting expert, had said the writing on the wrapper was in a disguised hand, and on the wrapper 'Asylum' had been spelt correctly and in another case incorrectly. The seeds of doubt: that was what Clarke-Hall was trying to sew in the minds of the jury.

The judge had the last word. Drawing attention to Mary Ann's purchase of phosphor paste to kill rats, as she maintained, it had not been bought on her employer's instruction but was her own decision. She had not charged the cost to her employer. As for the tea and sugar, there was no proof that it had been sent by Mary Ann – nor, indeed, had it been proved that the sugar contained poison. He hinted that the handwriting on the wrapper, the letter written to Cooper, the insurance man, the Christmas card – which Mary Ann admitted sending – and the blue paper with the prepared questions, in her hand, was all made by the same person, 'but the jury must judge that for themselves'. Dr Stevenson, he said, was one of the 'greatest analysts of the day' and had concluded the case was one of phosphorus poisoning. The defence had suggested the 'poor woman' had died of yellow atrophy of the liver, but that would have caused shrinkage of the liver, which had been found to be of normal size. If Mary Ann was guilty, said his lordship, the jury should have no sympathy with her because, for the sake of a few pounds, she had been willing to sacrifice the life of her poor sister. The jury retired to consider their verdict, emerging after over seven hours to declare Mary Ann guilty as charged.

The judge, 'assuming the black cap', sentenced Mary Ann to death, telling her, 'You deliberately took the life of your sister, an afflicted woman who had never been a burden to you and who had the utmost claim upon your affection and compassion. You were moved to perpetrate this terrible crime for the sake of the small sum of money you would receive on the policy of insurance effective upon her life. Never in my experience has so terrible a crime been committed for a motive so utterly inadequate.' Mary Ann, apparently unmoved, turned to go down the steps, then screamed out hysterically. Her mother, who was present, also screamed and called out. The court emptied rapidly and the judge resumed with a civil action, a claim about alleged detention of goods near Potters Bar.

Post-Trial

Many people campaigned for a reprieve, sympathy for Mary Ann's plight based on the widespread belief that she was insane. As the *Hertfordshire Advertiser and Times* reported, 'The prisoner's relatives were tainted with insanity: her father's mother was subject to fits; her sister, Caroline, whom she murdered, was insane; her younger sister, Martha, is a confirmed imbecile; Mary Ann, as a child, was known as "silly old Ansell".' Her defence engaged Dr Forbes Winslow to report on her mental condition, but he was not permitted to see her. He nevertheless stated that, in his opinion, Mary Ann was a mental degenerate and not responsible for her actions, basing his conclusions on hereditary insanity, and behaviour during the trial. The authorities had seen fit to have Mary Ann 'examined' by their own people, but not by a specialist on behalf of her defence.

Even the foreman of the jury protested: 'We had no idea she would really be hanged'. Another juror pointed out Mary Ann's family's history had not been presented at her trial, and if it had been their verdict would have been such that she would not have hanged. Mr W. Johnson, of London, presented a petition of 1,000 signatures for the exercise of the Royal prerogative of mercy. Mrs Ansell said Mary Ann had been 'silly' from the time she went to school, and Mr Ansell said he had never heard Mary Ann 'breathe a word of malice' against Caroline.

When they visited their daughter in prison, she asked, 'Can you forgive me, father?'

'Certainly I can,' he replied. 'If I don't forgive you, how can I expect to be forgiven myself?'

Another petition was drawn up, signed by a long list of Members of Parliament. But the Home Secretary could not see how he could make an exception to the rule. Mary Ann's fiancé was not named and did not give evidence. He told reporters she had tried to pressurise him into marriage, setting a date for the wedding, even though he said they couldn't afford it. They would have to wait until they had saved enough money, he said.

The 'day of doom' arrived, 19 July 1899. The hangman was James Billington. By 7 a.m. a crowd gathered on the railway bridge near St Albans Gaol, about 3,000 in all. If they were hoping for a last minute reprieve, they would have been disappointed to hear the grim tolling of the bell in St Peter's Church, signalling the imminent execution. Also disappointed were the newspaper reporters. Hitherto, they had been permitted to watch and report on proceedings. Not this time.

The scaffold was situated behind the prison gates, barely thirty yards from the condemned cell. The 'sad procession' made its way to the 'engine of death', where it took but a few moments for Billington to draw a cloth cap over Mary Ann's head, tighten the strap around her dress and place the noose about her neck. At 8 a.m. he pulled the lever. Outside the prison walls, the crowd was silent, all eyes on the flagpole. At 8.02 a.m. the black flag was hoisted. For a moment, it remained furled, as though reluctant to be the bearer of sad news, then slowly it spread and fluttered in the breeze. St Albans Gaol closed in 1924; many years later, the gatehouse became a familiar sight on television when it appeared as Slade Prison in the opening credits of the sitcom, *Porridge*.

Author's Verdict

Mary Ann Ansell killed her sister by apparently baking a cake, lacing it with poison and posting it to her, after writing to her first, telling her their parents were dead so that she, Mary Ann, would receive notification of her death and no one would be suspicious. Afterwards, she persuaded her illiterate father that a post-mortem wasn't a good idea and wrote to the authorities on his behalf to say so. A heartless crime, committed for financial gain. But did she plan this venture alone – or is there a missing ingredient? The man she would marry, for example, who, strangely, remains in the background, and who, let it be said, would have had just as much to gain by the death of Caroline as Mary Ann. He said she tried to 'pressurise' him into marriage, but he told her they had to save enough money first. Perhaps, but it would have been interesting to learn what he had to say if he had testified on oath.

Mary Ann killed her sister; but did she murder her? The doctors who passed judgement on her sanity or otherwise were those appointed by the Home Office, but an expert engaged on her behalf was not permitted to see her. Why? Did they believe Dr Forbes Winslow might disagree with their appointed experts and, if so, would the Home Secretary have then been obliged to commute the sentence? Mary Ann's parents suffered great personal tragedies: of their four daughters, one was killed in an accident, one was murdered and a third was hanged. Having regard to this, and the possibility, likelihood even, that insanity was an ingredient, or that maybe 'silly old Ansell' was acting under the coercion of another, perhaps she should have been given the benefit of the doubt and spared the noose.

13

The Worst of Human Passions

Emily Swann, West Riding, Yorkshire, 1903

Emily Swann was 42 years old, a married woman with eleven children. She lived at George Square, Wombwell, with her husband William, a glass blower, and their family. One fateful Saturday, 6 June 1903, neither William nor Emily was at home: William was at work, whilst Emily was drinking with her friend Mary Ann Ward, a widow, at the latter's house on the opposite side of the Square.

Emily's visits to Mary Ann's were now on a daily basis, due to the presence of Mary Ann's lodger, 29-year-old John Gallagher. Gallagher, a labourer at the local pit, had previously lodged with the Swanns, but had been thrown out by William Swann when Swann found out that Gallagher and Emily had been sleeping together when he was at work. The situation came to a head on 11 May, when Swann found his wife with Gallagher in the kitchen, and his wife struck him on the head with a poker. When Swann retaliated Gallagher attacked him, and with his wife's help gave him a thrashing. It was hardly unreasonable for Swann to order Gallagher out of the house, but the pair were still found on occasion in the Swann household by William. On 4 June, Swann, presumably losing his patience, threw a tin mug at his wife, upon which Gallagher threatened to throw him out of his own house. The next day witnesses heard Gallagher threaten to 'kill Swann before morning'.

Which brings us back to the afternoon of that fateful Saturday, when Misses Swann and Ward were drinking in the latter's house. They were not alone. Also present that afternoon were Gallagher, whom we may assume was also drinking, Mary Ann's son Edward and his friend Walt Wigglesworth − neither of whom were drinking − as well as Martha Ward, Mary Ann's daughter-in-law, and 13-year-old Rose, Mary Ann's daughter.

John Gallagher, who had been served notice of dismissal by his employers, told everyone, including Mrs Swann, that he would be moving back to his native Middlesbrough. This would not have pleased Emily, who clearly was enjoying her sexual liaison with the younger man. In any event, that afternoon Gallagher sent Mary Ann's daughter, Rose, to the local pawnshop to redeem a coat and waistcoat he had pledged the previous week. When Rose brought the garments to the house she placed them onto the table, whereupon Mrs Swann snatched them up and took them directly across the square to her own house, a gesture probably intended to somehow prevent Gallagher leaving. Gallagher followed her, so that once again the pair were ensconced in the Swann household.

Which is where, returning from an honest day's work, William Swann found them, his wife in the kitchen, Gallagher coming down the stairs. It would have been understandable for Swann to have deduced that once again his wife had been having 'improper relations' behind his back, but on this occasion there was no violence between himself and Gallagher, possibly because the latter persuaded him he was only collecting his belongings before departing for good. Whatever was said, Gallagher left the house and returned to Mrs Ward's.

A short while later Mrs Swann, now wearing a shawl, also returned to Mrs Ward's house. On entering she removed the shawl and declared, 'See what our Bill has done!' She was referring to a newly-acquired black eye. On seeing it, Gallagher jumped to his feet and said, 'I will go and give him something for himself. I will kick his ribs off.' With that he went at once to the Swanns' house, followed by Mrs Swann. What then occurred, the press of the day described with missing expletives and we must use our imagination to fill in the blanks. Mrs Swann, according to Walt Wigglesworth and others, said, 'I hope he will kill the -----.' Mrs Swann got into the house first, as witnessed by John Dunn, a neighbour who lived opposite and saw Gallagher shaking the door of the house until it flew open, shouting, 'I will coffin the ----- before morning.' Dunn heard the sounds of a struggle, with Mrs Swann shouting, 'Give it to the -----, Johnny,' and after about ten minutes Gallagher emerged from the house and returned to Mrs Ward's, declaring, 'I have broken the -----'s four ribs and I will break him four more.'

Gallagher had some more beer before going outside again, when John Dunn heard him shout, 'I will murder the ----- before morning. If he can't kick a ----- man he shan't kick a ----- woman.' He went back into the Swanns' house and Dunn again heard the sounds of a struggle, with Mrs Swann calling, 'Give it to him, Johnny.' This went on for about ten minutes, then Dunn saw the pair emerge at the door holding hands, after which Gallagher returned to Mrs Ward's, and Mrs Swann went back into her own house. When Gallagher returned yet again to the Swanns' he could not get in, for Mrs Swann had locked the door.

Shortly afterwards Mrs Swann went to Mrs Ward's and asked her to come with her to her house. At first Mrs Ward would not go, but then she agreed and went with her son Edward, and Walt Wigglesworth. Inside they saw William Swann lying on the kitchen floor with his head against the cupboard. A poker lay on the floor, nearby. The threesome – Mrs Ward, Edward and Wigglesworth – returned to Ward's house. On being told what they had seen, Gallagher laughed and danced on the floor, saying, 'I am not guilty. I have not ----- well done it.' He then went with Mrs Ward to the Royal Oak public house where they drank whisky, after which he, Gallagher, disappeared. The time was about 7 p.m.

An hour later Dr Foley went to the house and declared William Swann to be dead. Later again the police were called. It was soon evident that they needed to speak to John Gallagher, and his description was circulated, both to other forces and throughout the media:

> John Gallagher, 29 years of age, 5ft 7½in, fresh complexion with dark brown hair and moustache. Tattoos on both arms: cross flags on the right upper arm, girls holding flowers on each forearm. Last seen wearing a blue cloth jacket and vest, brown cloth trousers, grey cloth cap, red and green spotted tie. He was discharged from the West Yorkshire Regiment for misconduct.

The focus of the police was on Gallagher, not Mrs Swann.

The inquest into William Swann's death was opened at the Horse Shoe Hotel, Wombwell, on 9 June. The coroner was Mr Dossey Wightman. The *Mexboro' and Swinton Times* reported that 'Local opinion was not at all favourable to the widow of the deceased, many expressing their belief there was not much difference between her and Gallagher'. Mrs Swann, who was obliged to attend, was all in black, save for a broad white bandage across her right eye. She was thus easily recognisable to the sizeable crowd, but there were 'no strong marks of disapproval' as she walked to the scene of the inquest.

After telling the court of how her husband had given her the black eye, Mrs Swann said she had told Gallagher it was no concern of his, and that she had witnessed his attack on her husband in their house. He struck him many times, she said, and when she tried to pick her husband up Gallagher struck her on the chin. Gallagher, she said, then started hitting her husband with an armchair, calling him a '----- bastard,' before going out of the house. She tried to help her husband and give him some water before going to Mrs Ward's, where she told Gallagher, 'You have killed him.' She had not seen him since. She said her 6-year-old son had been present when Gallagher had beaten her husband to death.

Dr George Atkins had made a post-mortem examination. There were several external bruises to the right temple, cheekbone, neck and upper chest. The brain was congested with blood and the base of the skull was 'filled with a lot of blood'. Cause of death was effusion of blood into the brain, caused 'probably by violence'. The breastbone, fourth, fifth, sixth and seventh ribs on the right side were fractured. There were nearly twenty bruises in all, showing great violence.

After hearing the testimonies of those who were present at Mrs Ward's on the day, the coroner told the jury they might not consider the evidence of Misses Swann and Ward as reliable due to them being drunk at the time. They duly brought in a verdict of wilful murder against John Gallagher and 'wished to call attention to the fact that if Gallagher had heard the remark of Mrs Swann – "I hope he punches him to death" – whether she should not be considered to some extent guilty'. The coroner remarked that although that was not a question for the jury to deal with, 'it was a proper question for all that'. Afterwards, a crowd, 'grown to larger dimensions than ever', awaited the appearance of Mrs Swann, who had to run the gauntlet of a hostile demonstration accompanied by booing.

The following day, thousands of people attended the funeral of William Swann, who was regarded as having been a hard-working, popular man. Feelings against Mrs Swann ran high, and the police would not allow her to proceed to the cemetery. For her the future looked uncertain. For John Gallagher, who had fled, his fate was already sealed.

The police spared no effort in tracing Gallagher. His flight from justice was traced through Sheffield and Bradford, and when the police at Middlesbrough got wind of his apparent intention to visit his family there they called at his sister's house, only to find their quarry had fled into the town centre. Finally they tracked him down to another house, where he was arrested. On the journey to Barnsley, Gallagher talked about anything save the matter in hand, the murder of William Swann. He was wearing the same clothes and had lived the life of a tramp when on the run. News of his capture was relayed by a telegram, which was displayed in 'Mrs Lodge's window'. On the evening of 4 August, the day her husband was buried, Emily Swann was arrested.

Appearing before the magistrates, Gallagher appeared nervous, whilst Mrs Swann turned her head towards friends and relatives and even managed a smile. The prosecution duly went through the evidence, of events before and including 6 June. In particular the fact that Gallagher had gone to the Swann household and beaten William Swann not once but twice that evening, and that he went a third time but was unable to get in. An additional witness, Charles Swift, said that on the night previous to the murder, between eight and nine o'clock, he heard Gallagher whistling and then saw Mrs Swann at her door, and later the same evening he heard a quarrel in the Swann household accompanied by 'a smashing of pots'. Then, when passing Swift's house, Gallagher had remarked, 'I have given him a black eye and I'll righten him in the morning.' John Gallagher was not only a man to mete out punishment, but fastidious in his announcements to boot.

John Dunn, as well as testifying about events of the evening of 6 June, was explicit about what happened the previous evening. Between 8.30 and 9 p.m. he saw William Swann arrive home from work. Gallagher was in the Swanns' kitchen, and when Swann walked through the door, Mrs Swann struck him with a poker. Gallagher then punched and kicked him, whilst Mrs Swann exclaimed, 'Kick the ----- to death. Kick the ----- swine. Kick him out of the way and I will help thee.' Dunn had seen Gallagher visiting the Swann house after he was no longer lodging there, 'at three in the mornings and once at four.' Lavinia Ward said a week before the murder she heard Gallagher say he would kill him (Swann) before he went away, and on the evening of the murder itself he had come to her house and said he had given him two black eyes and would kill him. She had heard Mrs Swann express the wish that Gallagher would 'Punch Swann's ----- ----- in', adding that she would stand by and see him do it. John Taylor, another neighbour, said on 25 May there was a fight in the Swanns' house between Swann and Gallagher, when he heard Mrs Swann say, 'Go on, give him it. Punch the ----- to death.'

Police Sergeant Minting said that when he went to the scene of the crime on 6 June he saw the deceased man lying on the floor, and a poker nearby. He asked Misses Swann and Ward, who were both still in the house, what had happened but could get no satisfactory account. All Mrs Swann said to him was, 'He isn't dead, is he? He can't be dead!' When Detective George Hudson of the Middlesbrough force arrested Gallagher, he replied, 'I might as well speak the truth. I never used the poker, but the woman did.' Remanded to the Leeds Assizes, neither had anything to say, although Mrs Swann 'threw several kisses to her friends and relatives' as she left the courtroom.

The pair stood trial at the Leeds Assizes that October. Justice Darling presided, with Mr Tindall Atkinson prosecuting, and Mr Michael Innes and Mr H. Newell representing Gallagher and Emily Swann respectively. Both accused pleaded 'Not guilty'. Swann wept bitterly in the dock; Gallagher showed no emotion. There was no doubt, said Mr Atkinson, that William Swann met his death under circumstances of the greatest brutality. There was no doubt either that when Gallagher lodged with the Swanns he became 'unduly intimate' with Swann's wife, and that he had gone there after he had ceased to be a lodger. He mentioned the threats to Mr Swann and the events of Saturday 6 June. Particularly damning was that Gallagher, after assaulting Mr Swann in his home, had returned soon afterwards to attack him again. The injuries spoke for themselves.

One by one the witnesses stepped forward, just as they had at the inquest and the magistrates' court. These included a young man called Albert Harper, who said he had been sitting on Mrs Ward's doorstep when he heard Mrs Swann say, when Gallagher was going to her house, 'I hope he kills the -----. I hope he kicks him to death.' And then, when Gallagher was going to the house a second time, he heard him declare, 'I will finish him out before I go to Bradford.' When asked by the judge whether he had been drinking that day he replied, 'Never had a drop, sir.'

Mr Atkinson said that after Mrs Swann had gone to Mrs Ward's house with her black eye, if the case rested there and Swann had died from the injuries received on the first occasion, it might be said that the charge could be reduced to manslaughter. But, back in Mrs Ward's house, Gallagher had time to reflect and had gone back to Swann's house, saying he would 'murder him before morning'. Mrs Swann had used words of incitement, and there was no other conclusion for the jury except that Gallagher went back on the second occasion to finish off the bloody work he had done on the first, and that Emily Swann had encouraged him.

Defending Gallagher, Mr Innes said that William Swann died in his own house 'in consequence of acts in which Gallagher took a considerable part'. But what was the state of Gallagher's mind? According to the law, in a crime of murder there must be in the mind of the person who did the act a capacity for realising that he took responsibility for what he did. But if the evidence exhibited such circumstances of passion, excitement and confusion of mind the case might not be one of murder. The point the jury had to decide was whether this crime was one of deliberation or passion. There was not the slightest doubt that Gallagher and Mrs Swann had contracted 'illicit relations', but a man should not be hanged because he had committed adultery.

There had been violent language used, said Mr Innes, but the jury must bear in mind that among a particular class in Yorkshire common language was violent, especially in colliery districts like Wombwell. It was common to hear people say, 'I'll break his neck,' or 'I'll knock his head off,' without any intention of doing anything of the sort. When Mrs Swann was hurt she went to Gallagher as her natural avenger and protector. 'Besotted with drink and inflamed with miserable, misdirected love for the woman, he went to the house and administered the chastisement he intended.' He went back a second time, but it was difficult to estimate the exact amount of irritation in a man's mind at a given moment. 'There was not a man or woman who would not have applauded what he did,' said counsel. When Gallagher was told Swann was dead, he danced on the floor. Could the jury conceive a fact that spoke more directly to them of imbecility, of a wild, confused levity of mind than this? There was no suggestion of the use of a knife or other weapon, except a poker and possibly a boot. Did that not mean the crime was not premeditated? Would the jury say he committed the crime deliberately, wantonly and with calculation? Or would they say he committed the act in a moment of passion? There was only one verdict, that of manslaughter, which he claimed 'with all sincerity'.

Mr Newell, for Mrs Swann, admitted that as the mother of eleven children her conduct had been reprehensible, wicked and sinful. It had not been stated that a single blow or act of violence had been committed by her; the case against her was that she had incited Gallagher to do the deed, and it therefore rested on the language that she used. He supported his learned friend in saying that intemperate language was commonly used in the district, and the best of them used language 'ridiculous for its extravagance'. How many times did people say they had caught their 'death of cold' when they meant nothing so serious? They heard threats every day without implying an intention to carry them out. When Gallagher started to thrash William Swann, his wife said, 'I hope he will kill the ------.' But did they think for a moment she hoped her husband would be killed?

Mrs Swann had shouted to Gallagher, encouraging him to assault her husband. But when Gallagher came back a third time to the house the door was locked, a fact of great significance, because the only person who could have locked the door was Mrs Swann. When the police came that terrible night all she could say was, 'He can't be dead!' She meant her husband should get a good thumping, that's all. Incitement to murder was not proved, and he invited the jury to bear in mind that where there was doubt, the prisoner should have the benefit.

The judge said William Swann was killed in the presence of the two prisoners by injuries inflicted by either or both of them. 'If a man struck a blow making another man angry, and before his blood had time to cool the man retaliated, that might justify a conviction for manslaughter.' But the threats uttered could not be treated as 'mere empty idle sayings' when the prisoners said what they hoped would occur did occur. They were not empty words. Gallagher had said, as he went to the Swanns' house for the second time, 'I'll finish him before I go to Bradford'. This showed a determined intention, to go back and finish the job that had been half begun.

Mrs Swann's defence, said his lordship, was that Gallagher 'did it', and she had nothing to do with it except to stand by. 'But,' he added, 'one did not commit murder only with one's hand; if one person instigated another to commit murder, he or she was also guilty.' Clearly, he meant the jury should consider whether Mrs Swann's words amounted to incitement or whether she took any part in the attack on her husband or not. If so, she would be guilty of murder. It took the jury half an hour to convict both prisoners of murder. Mrs Swann's response, when asked if she had anything to say, was, 'I am not afraid to meet death because I am innocent, and will go to God.'

Wearing the customary black cap, his lordship said they had used language that meant that either of them would take William Swann's life, having on two occasions used brutal violence towards him. Having beaten him, having wounded him, having gone away with time for their blood to cool, they came back and between them they killed him. There was one piece of evidence, he said, that was not given but which he would now refer to. When Gallagher was taken into custody he had said 'she hit the man with the poker'. This was not strictly evidence against her (it was uncorroborated), but his lordship was convinced that this statement was in part true. He then passed the only sentence the law allowed for the crime of murder. As he spoke, Mrs Swann listened with her eyes half closed and then, turning to leave the dock, she half smiled and blew a kiss to someone she recognised in the gallery. Gallagher walked briskly down to the cells after her.

Post-Trial

Condemned to death, John Gallagher and Emily Swann awaited their fate in Armley Gaol, Leeds. Gallagher was fully resigned to the inevitable, making no effort to win a reprieve. He received but one visit, that of his sister. The interview was described as 'painful'. For them both, presumably.

Mrs Swann's demeanour was altogether different, as she waited in vain for the Royal Prerogative of Mercy to be exercised in her favour. She blamed Gallagher for everything, saying that if she was a bad woman it was what other people had made her. She suffered frequent outbursts of hysteria and had to be watched night and day by the prison matrons. She had frequent visits from her family, though not, sadly, her 81-year-old mother, who could 'not undergo the ordeal', or her youngest child, who was not allowed to see her but was given a sixpenny piece in sympathy to 'passify it'. Otherwise her family was allowed to visit her, albeit on the opposite side of a barred partition.

If Swann could not see her mother, she could at least write to her, and she did. In a letter, dated 24 December, she wrote (through another party, since she was illiterate):

> Do not mind, dear mother, what people say about me; if they had their sins written on their foreheads it would take a big Salvation Army bonnet to cover them ... Love my children while you live, for my sake.

On the eve of their executions, Gallagher admitted his guilt to Father Vos. Mrs Swann too made a verbal confession, and was then of 'a much calmer frame of mind'. At 9 a.m. the following day, 29 December, John Gallagher and Emily Swann were led from separate cells to be hanged together by John Billington Junior and Tom Pierrepoint.

As they approached the scaffold, Mrs Swann said, calmly, 'Good morning, John.'

'Good morning, love,' replied Gallagher.

They stood together as Billington secured the ropes and drew the white caps over their faces. Then the bolt was drawn, and just as two persons had committed the ultimate crime together, so they died together, she instantaneously, Gallagher 'in a second or two'. Outside, the usual crowd dispersed, 'two feeble tolls' of the prison bell announcing that sentence had been carried out, the hoisting of the customary black flag having been abolished. They were buried in quicklime within the prison walls.

Author's Verdict

Oh, how they tried. The men in wigs who would defend the indefensible. It was their duty, after all. Michael Innes's task was impossible; he was trying to defend the indefensible. Describing Gallagher's feelings as 'inflamed with miserable, misdirected love', and inviting the jury to consider his actions as a 'crime of passion', he even added, 'There was not a man or woman who would not have applauded what he did.' Justice Darling described his speech as 'eloquent'. How did he manage to keep a straight face? Gallagher's only hope was a conviction for manslaughter, which he might have secured, along with his life, if he had attacked William Swann once. But having gone to his house and attacked him, and then with time to reflect, gone again to finish the job, which he did with equal brutality, he committed murder. He was probably drunk, his judgement thus impaired; but drunkenness is no excuse.

Emily Swann was heard by several people to incite Gallagher to beat her husband, and on more than one occasion. Both defence lawyers described such language as 'common, especially in colliery districts'. Perhaps so, but seeing her husband being beaten before her eyes and calling out, 'Punch the ----- to death' and the like could have meant only one thing: that she wanted Gallagher to do just that. The judge's remark that, in his view, Gallagher's assertion that Mrs Swann had used the poker was 'in part true', was pure speculation. Neither he nor anyone else could ever know who did or did not use the poker, or even if it was used at all.

The Swanns had eleven children. Some were adult and presumably had left home, but there would be other, younger ones. One wonders where they were when the incidents in the Swann household were taking place. It is noted here, but was not much commented upon at the time, that the Swanns' 6-year-old son not only witnessed the brutal attack on his father, but also his mother urging on his assailant. What images did that little boy carry with him for the rest of his life? The murder of his father wasn't the only crime his mother and her violent lover committed.

14

A Passage Full of Crime

Edith Jessie Thompson, Essex, 1922

It's around midnight, Tuesday, 3 October 1922. Percy and Edith Thompson are walking home to Kensington Gardens, Ilford, having been to the theatre in London. They are minutes from their front door. As they walk along the pavement, a man emerges from the darkness and pushes Mrs Thompson to the ground. Her head strikes the pavement and she is momentarily dazed. Her husband grapples with the stranger, but it is not an even contest as the man draws a knife and stabs him repeatedly, one thrust penetrating into the mouth, another severing the carotid artery.

As Percy Thompson slumps to the ground, his wife screams, 'Oh don't. Oh don't.' She sees the fleeing attacker as he passes beneath a streetlight. He is wearing a grey trilby hat and blue overcoat. She sees blood coming from her husband's mouth. She runs into the road and encounters two neighbours, Mr Clevely and Miss Pittard. Mrs Thompson screams, 'Oh my God, help me. My husband is ill, he is bleeding on the pavement.' All three run toward the doctor's surgery. Mrs Thompson rings the doctor's doorbell before rushing back to her husband. Miss Pittard tells the doctor there is a 'severe case of illness' along the street, and hurries after Mrs Thompson. She asks her what happened. Mrs Thompson replies, 'I don't know. Somebody flew past and when I turned to speak to him blood was pouring out of his mouth.' Eight minutes later Dr Maudsley arrives on the scene and declares Percy Thompson dead.

Later, Edith Thompson will tell her husband's brother, Richard, 'Percy had a seizure, coming from the station. He complained of neuritis in his leg and he was rubbing it as he walked and before I knew what happened he fell against me.' What she didn't say was that her husband had been attacked, and that she had seen his attacker and knew perfectly well that he was 21-year-old Frederick Bywaters, who was acquainted with both she and her husband and with whom she had been having a relationship for fifteen months.

Edith Thompson, aged 28, was the eldest of the five children of William and Ethel Graydon. The family had lived in Dalston, London, but in 1898 moved to Manor Park. In 1911 she found employment at Carlton & Prior, a wholesale milliners in the city. Percy Thompson was 33, and had worked as a clerk for a London shipping agent. He met Edith in 1909, when he was nineteen, she only fourteen. He told her father he wanted to do the 'proper thing'; he would continue to see Edith but wouldn't get her 'into trouble'.

In 1902, a Mr and Mrs Bywaters moved to Rectory Road, just around the corner from the Graydons, and in June that year Mrs Bywaters gave birth to their second child, Frederick Edward Francis. It was not surprising when, in later years, young Freddy numbered Edith's brothers among his friends, as they lived so close and attended the same school. Meanwhile, Percy Thompson courted the young Edith, waiting for the day she would be old enough to marry him. Marry him she did, in January 1916. That year, 13-year-old Frederick Bywaters left school. Two years later he joined the merchant navy, when P&O took him on as a laundry steward, and in 1919, after the death of his father, the Bywater family moved to Upper Norwood. In 1920 the Thompsons moved to Kensington Gardens, Ilford.

In April 1920, fate took a hand when 19-year-old Bywaters came knocking on the Graydons' door, saying his ship would be laid up in Tilbury for refitting, and staying with the Graydons, as a paying lodger, would be more convenient than having to travel to and from his mother's. That May he moved in, and was introduced to Edith Thompson who routinely called at her parents' on her way home from work on Friday evenings. Bywaters was a man of the world now, probably full of confidence and aware of his attraction to women. Not that anything other than polite discourse took place between he and Mrs Thompson. Far from it; when Percy was introduced to Bywaters he expressed the opinion that Freddy was 'a smart, interesting boy'. For the next seven weeks Bywaters would dine with his hosts, the Graydons, and the Thompsons when they called on Fridays.

In June 1921, the Thompsons decided to holiday on the Isle of Wight. They invited the Bywaters and Avis, Edith's sister. If they were trying to match-make Freddy and Avis, things didn't go according to plan, for Bywaters' attention instead focused on Edith, whom he kissed when they were on a charabanc trip on the island. When they returned home, the Thompsons decided, probably at Edith's behest, that Bywaters could stay with them as a paying guest. On 27 June, Freddy's birthday, with Percy Thompson at work and Edith off work for the day, she gave Freddy breakfast in bed. She also gave him herself.

Thereafter the threesome lived under the same roof, and all the while the dashing young lodger was having an affair with his host's wife. From July until mid-October, Bywaters was away again, at sea. In a letter to him Edith wrote, 'We've said we'll always be pals. Shall we say we'll always be lovers, even though secret ones?'

It couldn't last, of course. After a month or so, Percy Thompson began to notice Bywaters' fawning attention towards his wife. Once, when Percy struck Edith during an argument, Bywaters stood between them. Percy told him to leave the house, which he did. But he and Edith continued to see each other until he departed on his next voyage, on the passenger liner, *Morea*. If he was out of the sight of Edith, he was not out of her mind. During the time he was at sea, she wrote to him many times, about the work of novelists and her sexual revulsion for her husband. She also wrote several times about the possibility of killing her husband.

What did Bywaters have that her husband did not? Percy was dour, steady, unexciting perhaps; Bywaters was young, dashing, and the dangers of their relationship possibly brought some kind of thrill for them both. For Edith, Freddy was the escape from her dreary existence with her husband. What she was to Bywaters we cannot know; although still very young, he was now a man of the world, and for all Edith knew, he had a girl in every port.

One night in February 1922, Percy was in bed with Edith when he woke and told her a friend had given him a prescription for insomnia. He had taken the draught and now felt sick. She realised his insomnia and apparent illness could be commented on by both of them, to friends, say, and if he were to die of an 'overdose', no one would believe it wasn't 'accidental'. She said as much to Bywaters in a letter.

The same month the *Daily Sketch* reported on the case of the Revd Horace Bolding, who was found dead on 4 January. His wife, Ada, a nurse, had been having an affair with an older man, Dr Preston Wallis. Wallis, whose wife had left him, employed 28-year-old Ada, who moved into his house as his nurse and probably his mistress. Dr Wallis sold his house to the Boldings, but remained in it as a paying guest and to look after the surgery. Bolding then died of hyoscine poisoning. Suicide seemed unlikely, but his wife and the good doctor were cleared of suspicion of murder. Edith Thompson could not have failed to see the similarities in the situation involving her husband and Bywaters, and that of the Boldings and Dr Wallis. In any event, she posted the newspaper cutting to Bywaters. Was it merely 'out of interest' – by chance, Dr Wallis had been her physician – or was she trying to tell him something, like how easy it would be to get rid of Percy by poisoning him?

The *Daily Sketch* also covered the story of Freda Kempton, a dancer, who had been found dead in her Paddington flat in 'mysterious circumstances'. The police suspected she had died as a result of cocaine and cyanide of potassium. Edith sent the article to Bywaters. 'The Kempton cutting may be interesting if it's to be the same method', she wrote. In another letter she added a note, saying, 'Don't keep this piece,' which related to her putting quinine into her husband's tea. He said the tea tasted bitter. Edith wrote, 'Too bad about the taste, I'm going to try the glass again. I've got an electric light globe this time.' She'd been dropping particles of glass into his tea too – or had she? Was it simply a fantasy – a throwaway remark intended to make her lover laugh? In another letter she wrote, 'I used the lightbulb three times but the third time he found a piece, so I've given up until you come home.' Much was made at Edith Thompson's trial of *Bella Donna*, a book by Robert Hitchens. In it Hitchens writes, 'It must be ever remembered that digitalin is a cumulative poison, and the same dose, harmless if taken once, frequently repeated becomes deadly.' 'Is this any use?' Edith had written to Bywaters.

Bywaters' final voyage on *Morea* lasted from 9 June until 23 September, during which time Edith wrote twenty-four letters to him. In one of his letters to her, Bywaters wrote that he was jealous of her husband. Her reply contained a sentence that showed she did, perhaps, truly wish the death of her husband, and that she was inciting Bywaters to bring it about. She wrote, 'He has the right by law to all that you have the right to by nature and love … be jealous, so much that you will do something desperate'. *Do something desperate.* What did she mean?

On 2 October, Edith wrote to Bywaters, urging him to find her 'a job abroad', saying she would 'go tomorrow'. She ended the letter with the sentence, 'Don't forget what we talked about in the tearoom, I'll risk and try if you will …' She was probably referring to whatever they said in a conversation they had had the previous Friday afternoon. The prosecution at her trial would suggest that 'risk' and 'try' meant an attempt to poison her husband.

On the fateful night, 3/4 October, Percy and Edith went to the Criterion Theatre in Piccadilly. Bywaters was at the Graydons' that evening. Later, when the Thompsons were walking home to Kensington Gardens, Ilford, he was waiting. What isn't known is whether Edith knew what was going to happen. But happen it did, a cold-blooded and ruthless attack on a man walking home with his deceitful wife, and when Bywaters fled the scene, Edith Thompson saw him clearly enough.

When the two policemen saw the knife wounds in the mortuary they knew Percy Thompson had been attacked. Sergeants Mew and Grimes went to the scene to search for a murder weapon. They didn't find one. When they asked Edith if she could account for the cuts on her husband's neck, she replied, 'No, we were walking along and my husband said "Oh!" and I said "Bear up," thinking he'd had one of his attacks. He fell on me and walked a little farther; he then fell against the wall and then to the ground.' One wonders at the arrogance of a woman who, having just witnessed her husband's brutal murder, would yet protect his killer with such outright lies. Meanwhile, Bywaters arrived home at 3 a.m. His mother heard him enter the house and called out, 'Is that you?'

'Yes mum,' he answered.

At 11 a.m. the following day, another policeman was asking Edith Thompson what happened. He was Inspector Francis Hall, to whom she gave a similar account of the incident as before. Hall told her the matter was now a murder investigation, and she was taken to Ilford police station.

Looking for a motive, the police thought 'another man' was a possibility. It wasn't long before they had his name. Richard, Percy's brother, told them that the 'sailor' who had lodged with the Thompsons was 'overly familiar' with his brother's wife. Detective Inspector Wensley asked Mrs Graydon and her daughter Avis directly, 'Who is Freddy Bywaters?' Mrs Graydon told him that Bywaters was at their house on the night of the murder, but left about eleven o'clock. Anyone with a 'copper's nose' would have known then who their man was. The police were soon watching Bywaters' address, the *Morea* in Tilbury docks, the shipping office and the Graydons' house, not to mention the railway stations.

Bywaters spent the next day shopping with his mother, knowing that the day after he would be sailing for distant shores on board the *Morea*. At 6.15 p.m. he called at the Graydons'.

Edith's father showed him a copy of the *Evening News*. 'This is a terrible thing if it is true,' he said.

'It is only too true,' Mr Graydon told him, adding that Edith was at Ilford police station. Minutes later the police were knocking on the door.

Told he was being detained, Bywaters said, 'I know nothing about it.' He made a statement, admitting meeting Edith on 'several occasions'. On the evening of the murder, he said, he left the Graydons' about 11 p.m. He went to East Ham station, booked a ticket to Victoria, arrived there at 12.20 a.m., then walked home to Upper Norwood, arriving about 3 a.m. The first he knew of Percy Thompson's death was in a newspaper. He never carried a knife and had never owned one. Mrs Thompson had written to him 'two or three times'. 'I might have received one letter from her at home. The others I received on board ship. I have destroyed them.' The police found two of her letters in his bedroom.

Edith, too, made a statement:

We proceeded along Belgrave Road ... my husband fell against me and called out 'Oo-er.' He was staggering. He was bleeding. I cannot remember whether I saw anyone else there or not. I know Freddy Bywaters. We have been in the habit of corresponding. His letters to me and mine to him were couched in affectionate terms. I am not in possession of his letters. I have destroyed them all ...

Although Edith and Bywaters were both in Ilford police station, neither was told that the other was there. They would soon know. As Inspector Hall led her from the mess room, a door swung open and there, just 3ft away, was Freddie. As they bundled him away, she exclaimed, 'Oh God, what can I do? Why did he do it? I didn't want him to do it.' She then amended her statement, saying:

A man rushed out from the gardens and pushed me away from my husband. I was dazed … I saw my husband scuffling with a man. Freddy Bywaters was running away. He was wearing a blue overcoat and a grey hat. I knew it was him although I did not see his face.

Inspector Hall showed Bywaters Edith's statement, and asked him if there was anything he wished to add to his. He then made a further statement:

Mrs Thompson was not aware of my movements on Tuesday night. I waited for Mrs Thompson and her husband. When near Endsleigh Gardens I pushed her to one side. I said to him, 'You have got to separate from your wife.' He said, 'No.' We struggled. I took my knife from my pocket and we fought and he got the worst of it. I ran away. The reason I fought with Thompson was because he never acted like a man to his wife. He always seemed several degrees lower than a snake. I loved her and I couldn't go on seeing her leading that life. I did not intend to kill him. I only meant to injure him. I have had the knife some time. It was a sheath knife. I threw it down a drain.

This, then, was the confession of Frederick Bywaters, to killing a man who had allowed him to stay in his home, whose wife he had been seeing behind his back and whom he attacked with a knife as he walked home on the streets of Ilford. Until Edith and Bywaters saw one another in the police station, the police were dealing with two liars. Police tactics – allowing them to unexpectedly see one another – led some way to the truth. But what part, if any, did Edith Thompson play in the murder of her husband? There was insufficient evidence at this stage to prove she played any, but she and Bywaters were both charged with murder nonetheless. Four days later the police recovered the knife from a drain in Seymour Gardens. Then, on 12 October, they found the damning evidence they said incriminated Edith Thompson: the letters and newspaper cuttings she had sent to Bywaters, found in his box aboard the *Morea*, all of them since 21 November the previous year, save the two they had already recovered.

When Bywaters and Mrs Thomson appeared before the magistrates, Mr Stern, in her defence, said, 'She told lies, but that does not make her guilty.' Quite so, but the content of some of the letters – bitter taste in tea, pieces of glass – made it seem that Edith Thompson was implicated in some way in her husband's murder. Glass and poison; it was only a matter of time before the police exhumed Percy Thompson's body. A further post-mortem examination was made by the pathologist, Sir Bernard Spilsbury, who found no indication of poisoning or attempts to poison, and he detected no glass in the intestines. This hardly proves none was taken, but neither was there proof that Edith Thompson caused any poison or glass to be administered.

The pair stood trial at the Old Bailey that December. To say that the case had caught the public imagination would be an understatement. Unemployed men stood from 4 a.m. for a place in the courtroom, then sold their tickets for as much as £1 to those prepared to pay. The charge against both prisoners was murder. An attempt by the defence to have the pair tried separately was thrown out.

Opening the case, the Solicitor-General, T.W. Inskip, covered all the background of the Thompsons and Bywaters, including Bywaters' affair with Edith. He then turned to the letters Edith had written to Bywaters, and the newspaper cuttings she had sent to him, quoting from some of them. From one letter he read: 'It is the man who has no right who generally covets the woman ... but darling, you will have the right soon, won't you?' From another: 'You must do something this time'. A newspaper cutting read: 'referring to the poisoning of a curate by hyoscine'. Another cutting: 'Poisoned Chocolates for University Chief – ground glass in box'. Another's headline ran: 'Beautiful Dancer Drugged ...', an account of the poisoning of a woman by cocaine, who was suspected of having cyanide of potassium administered to her.

In a letter dated 1 April 1922, Edith Thompson wrote:

He [her husband] put great stress on the tea tasting bitter, as if something had been put into it. I think whatever else I try it in again, he will recognise it and be more suspicious, and if the quantity is still not successful it will injure another chance.

In the same letter, she continued: 'I am going to try the glass again, when it is safe'. On 24 April: 'I used the light bulb three times. The third time he found a piece, so I have given it up till you come home'. Her letters, said Inskip, showed 'she preyed on the mind of this young man by her suggestions that, although it was his hand that struck the blow, it was her mind that conceived the crime.'

In another letter she wrote:

I was buoyed up by the hope of the light bulb, and I used a lot, big pieces ... Would not the stuff make some small pills, coated with soap and dipped into liquorice, like Beecham's?

Later she quoted from the novel, *Bella Donna*: 'Digitalin is a cumulative poison and the same dose, harmless if taken once, frequently repeated becomes deadly. Is it any use?' Although the book was a novel, said Inskip, she was planting the idea in Bywaters' mind. Another letter, dated 4 July, read: 'Have you studied bi-chloride of mercury?' 'It is clear throughout this correspondence that she was urging Bywaters to commit murder,' said Inskip.

Inskip said that on 23 September, Bywaters' ship docked at Tilbury, and they met two days later. On the Sunday or Monday just before the murder she again wrote to him: 'Don't forget what we talked about in the tearoom. I will still try if you will. We have only three and three quarter years left, darling'. The last sentence alluded to an apparent agreement that they would commit suicide together in five years if Edith were not free by then. The question the jury would have to consider was whether she incited Bywaters to commit the murder. If they were satisfied that she had, and that incited by her 'controlling hand' he committed the murder, she would be as guilty as him.

Bywaters said there was never an agreement between them that they should poison her husband, and when asked if there had ever been any agreement to use violence against him, he replied, 'No, the greatest violence was separation.' Asked whether, having read her letters, he thought she had given poison to her husband, he replied, 'It never entered my head at all. She had been reading books.' On the question of divorce and separation, he said, 'She had spoken to him about a separation but he would never agree to it.'

'In one letter she wrote, "Darling, you must do something". What did that refer to?' Bywaters was asked.

'I hardly know.'

'What was it she wanted you to do?'

'Take her away.' She had wanted him to take her abroad; she had mentioned Bombay, Australia, Marseilles.

'When she wrote, "There must be no failure this time", what did that mean?'

'Failure to get a separation, failure to take her abroad.'

'She wrote about "electric light globes".'

'I thought she was trying to put herself in the same place as the character in *Bella Donna*. It was mere melodrama.'

'Had there been any agreement that anything violent should be done to her husband?'

'No. Nothing at all.'

He said he bought the knife in 1921, and took it with him on voyages. He carried it in an inside pocket of his overcoat, and it was there on the night of 3 October. He saw Mrs Thompson for lunch that day. He knew she and her husband were going to the theatre that evening. 'I was thinking about Mrs Thompson, of how unhappy she was. This was the trend of my thoughts on the way to East Ham station. I thought, "I don't want to go home, I feel too miserable. I want to see Mrs Thompson to see if I can help her." I turned and walked in the direction of Ilford. I thought if I could see them I might be able to make things better. I intended to see Thompson, to come to an amicable arrangement for a separation or a divorce.' Until that moment he had no intention of going to Ilford that night. 'It came across me all of a sudden.'

He saw the Thompsons walking along Belgrave Road. 'I overtook them and pushed Mrs Thompson with my right hand. With my left hand I held Thompson, getting him by the back of his coat, and pushed him on the street, swinging him round. I said to him, "Why don't you get a divorce or a separation?"'

'He said, "I am not going to give it to you."'

'I said, "You take a delight in making Edith's life hell."'

'He said, "I have got her. I will keep her. I will shoot you." As he said that he punched me in the chest and I drew my knife and put it in his arm.'

'Why did you draw your knife?'

'Because I thought I was going to be shot.'

From the moment of his arrest right through to giving his evidence, this was the first time Bywaters mentioned anything about him thinking Percy Thompson had a gun.

When asked if he had any recollection as to how the wounds on the back of Thompson's neck were given, he replied, 'All I can say is, I had the knife in my left hand and they got there somehow.' After that he ran away. 'I didn't realise Thompson was dead. When I left him he was standing up.'

Inskip asked him about his relationship with Mrs Thompson. Quoting the passage, 'Don't forget what we talked about in the tearoom, I will still risk and try if you will', he asked Bywaters what he thought the risk was. Bywaters replied, 'The risk of being knocked about when she was asking for separation or divorce.' He carried the knife, he said, because it was handy for him at sea and useful at home.

There were variations in the two statements he made to the police.

'You made falsehoods?'

'Yes, because I wanted to help Mrs Thompson. My one idea was to shield her.'

He said it was not his intention to injure Thompson; he meant to stop Thompson killing him. 'I didn't know I was stabbing him. I tried to stop him from shooting me.' He did not actually see a gun.

Edith Thompson was next to testify. She didn't have to. In fact, Curtis-Bennett, her defence counsel, was mortified when she insisted on stepping into the witness box, and she did so against his advice. The main prosecution case was based on her letters and cuttings, of which Curtis-Bennett had 'an answer to every incriminating passage'. But she, it seemed, wanted to 'save the boy'. Answering questions in a low voice, she denied she had ever tried to injure her husband, or poison him, or given him ground glass. She admitted to the suicide pact – 'I said it was far easier to be dead' – and sending the letters and cuttings.

In one letter, she explained, 'drastic measures' meant leaving England with Bywaters. Of the 'tea tasting bitter' incident, she said this was imaginary. Of 'using the light bulb three times, but the third time he found a piece', there was 'no truth in it whatsoever.'

'Referring to the novel, *Bella Donna*, why did you write and ask Bywaters if digitalin was any use?'

'I wanted him to think I would try to help him, to keep him.'

'What did you discuss in the tearoom?'

'My freedom.'

'Had you ever had any desire for Bywaters to injure your husband?'

'None whatever.'

Of the night of 3/4 October, she said: 'When we got to Endsleigh Gardens a man rushed out. I don't remember anything except being knocked aside. When I came to my senses I saw my husband some distance down the road. He seemed to be scuffling with someone. I went to him and he fell against me and said, "Oo-er." I helped him along beside the wall on to the pavement. I thought he was hurt. I went for a doctor.' She saw blood coming from his mouth. Here she burst into tears, and went on, 'He [the doctor] said, "He is dead." '

'Had Bywaters ever suggested he would stab your husband?'

'Never.'

'Why did you tell the police you had not seen anyone?'

'I was very agitated and did not want to say anything against Mr Bywaters. I wanted to shield him.'

'Had you the remotest idea that any attack was to be made on your husband that night?'

'None whatever.'

She implied Bywaters suggested she should poison her husband. Justice Shearman interrupted, saying, 'Give him something in his food to make him ill?'

'That is what I surmised,' said Mrs Thompson, 'that I should give him something so that if he had a heart attack he would not be able to resist it.'

'Bywaters had suggested he would bring you something, with a view to poisoning your husband possibly?' asked Inskip.

'That was not the idea.'

'To hurt him?'

'To make him ill.'

'You urged Bywaters to send it instead of bringing it?'

'That is so. I did that to let him think I would do anything he suggested in order to prolong his affection. I wanted him to think I was eager to help him in any way he suggested.'

'Did the suggestion come from Bywaters, to give him something?'

'Yes.'

'You welcomed this suggestion?'

'I did not.'

'You are suggesting that it was Bywaters' suggestion, and you were humouring him and did not do it?' The judge asked Inskip. Inskip replied that he was.

'You were acting to Bywaters that you wished to destroy your husband's life?' Inskip asked Mrs Thompson.

'I was.'

The judge then asked her: 'Did I take you down rightly as saying "I wanted him to think I was willing to take my husband's life?"'

'I wanted him to think I was willing to do what he suggested.'

The questioning led to what they talked about in the tearoom.

'We talked about me getting a position abroad.'

Mr Whiteley, for Bywaters, said there was no dispute, that Percy Thompson had met his death owing to a blow inflicted by Bywaters. But the poignant tragedy of the case, as far as Bywaters was concerned, was that there, sitting next to him in the dock, was one dearer to him than his own life. The jury may have noticed that he, Mr Whiteley, had asked no questions of Mrs Thompson. He was entitled to. Why did he not? Because Bywaters's instructions were that 'neither by word nor deed in conducting his case should a word be said by us that would in any way hamper the defence of Mrs Thompson'.

According to Whiteley, the most important question for the jury was to decide whether there was any agreement between Mrs Thompson and Frederick Bywaters to murder Percy Thompson that night. This was not a court of morals; whatever view they might take of their adulterous relationship was irrelevant. Her letters did not suggest Bywaters was lending himself to any suggestion that her husband should be injured or poisoned. He was trying to break away from the 'entanglement', but Mrs Thompson was determined he should not break away. The letters should be read from the point of view of the recipient, not the writer. Bywaters was not party to her intentions.

On the night of 3/4 October, Bywaters, on an 'irresistible impulse', walked to Belgrave Road. His objective was to meet Percy Thompson to 'make arrangements' with him, not to kill him. Thompson struck him in the chest and said, 'I will shoot you,' at the same time putting his right hand into his pocket. It did not matter that he did not carry a revolver. What mattered was that Bywaters believed he did. In self-defence he took out his knife and stabbed him. The verdict must be 'Not guilty'.

For Edith Thompson, Curtis-Bennett said that if she knew what was going to happen that night, and she took her husband to a spot where he was murdered, she was guilty. But the jury would see that the whole of the evidence was to the contrary. The prosecution case was founded on nothing but letters and guesswork. They had found no trace or poison or broken glass. Mrs Thompson told lies to keep her lover, Frederick Bywaters. Bywaters said she lived in melodrama, a life of make-believe. He urged the jury not to consider the charge against her until they were satisfied Bywaters was guilty, a decision, he said, which 'would never come to them.'

It was indisputable, said Inskip, that Percy Thompson was killed by Bywaters, who went to the spot he chose around midnight, a 'most unsuitable hour' to engage in a discussion about separation. Bywaters had said for the first time in court that he thought Thompson was about to produce a gun, something that did not appear in either of his statements. Such a defence, if true, would have been produced long before he stood in the witness box. Four or five deep blows had been inflicted with the knife, one 14ft from where the attack began. In the case of Mrs Thompson, he said that if she and Bywaters agreed to kill Thompson, and he killed in pursuance of that agreement, it was murder against them both.

The judge said the prosecution implied Bywaters carried the knife that night to lie in wait for Percy Thompson. 'One wound came in behind the neck and out into his mouth. Another was driven with such force it ran to the spine. A third, which the doctor thought might have been inflicted from behind, cut the gullet and the artery, rendering death inevitable.' He said the jury would have a simple task arriving at their decision. He asked the jury to consider whether the killing of Percy Thompson was arranged between the woman and the man. If a woman said to a man, 'I want this man murdered. Promise me you will do it,' and she believed he would keep his promise, and murdered him, she was also guilty of murder.

A lack of evidence made the letters important. 'For months they had been corresponding, for months the woman had been writing to the man, inciting him. If you find him guilty of murder, was this woman an active party to it? Her story is that she knew nothing about it. You will not convict her unless you are satisfied she agreed that Bywaters should murder her husband, and that he did it by arrangement with her.'

If ever a jury retired with a difficult case to consider, it was that of Edith Thompson; not Bywaters, whose conduct spoke for itself. After two and a quarter hours they returned to the courtroom. Bywaters walked firmly to his place in the dock, but Edith Thompson was in such a state of distress she had to be half-carried. The jury's verdicts were: on Frederick Bywaters, 'Guilty'; Edith Thompson, 'Guilty'. Asked if he had anything to say before sentence, Bywaters replied, 'The verdict of the jury is wrong. Edith Thompson is not guilty. I am not an assassin.' Edith Thompson, when the same question was put to her, groaned but made no reply. The black cap was placed upon the judge's head, whereupon he passed sentence of death on them both. Mrs Thompson threw up her arms and exclaimed, 'Oh God, I am not guilty', upon which she collapsed and was carried from the dock.

Post-Trial

It took just five minutes to reject the appeals, Lord Hewart remarking that the case was 'a squalid and indecent one of lust and adultery'. Bywaters wrote to the Home Secretary:

> Edith Thompson and I are innocent. Mrs Thompson never had any intention to poison her husband or kill him. Those letters were the outpouring of an hysterical woman's mind, to relieve the tension and strain caused by the agony she was suffering … there was no plan or agreement between Mrs Thompson and I to murder her husband.

The Home Secretary was unmoved.

When Thompson was told the news, she broke down, screaming, 'I never did it!' Sobbing in despair, she was pinioned to her bed and injected with morphia. The next four days would be a living hell as, in drugged sedation, she awaited death, her only comforters the wardresses – strangers all, but who, let it be said, would share her sadness, her pain. A million people signed a petition, asking for them to be spared; even Bywaters, for whom condemnation had turned to admiration for his loyalty to Thompson.

Bywaters' fate was sealed, but his distraught mother had not given up. Writing to the king, she put the blame squarely on Edith Thompson: 'Like many boys of his age he fell under the spell of a woman many years older than himself'. She was highlighting what had been considered her son's best defence: the 'older woman' – the very route his defence team would have chosen had Bywaters permitted them.

Shortly before 9 a.m. on 9 January 1923, John Ellis, the hangman, looked through the inspection hole of Thompson's cell. He saw a woman whom he described as 'bright and cheerful', laughing at the jokes of the two wardresses who were trying to keep her mind off what was coming. But as he, his assistant, the governor and the chaplain stood in silence, waiting for the final minutes to pass, they heard a low moan emanating from the cell. It sent a shuddering chill down the spine of every person who heard it. They then witnessed a scene that would never fade from memory.

Edith Thompson was in a state of utter collapse. As the chaplain uttered consoling words, the wardresses did their best to help, even though they were close to breaking down themselves. As Ellis pinioned her hands behind her back, she drifted into unconsciousness and slumped back into her chair. Her legs were strapped, and she was carried to the scaffold, where Ellis put the white cap over her head, then the noose. Somehow they held her upright, her feet resting on the trapdoors, her head lolling forward on her chest. She was oblivious to what was happening when Ellis pulled the lever.

As Edith Thompson was hanged, she suffered a massive haemorrhage; or, as the rumours had it, her 'insides fell out'. This fuelled a belief that she might have been pregnant. It is a relevant point, since if pregnant her execution would have been 'stayed' until after the birth of her baby, after which she would almost certainly have been spared. It is doubtful that she was pregnant, for had she been she would surely have said so. At the same time, half a mile away, Frederick Bywaters faced his execution with great fortitude. Whatever the truth in this tragic affair, he did his best to save Edith Thompson. Now he could do no more. At 9 a.m. he shook hands with the hangman, William Willis, and made his way to the scaffold without hesitation. It was reported that he 'died like a gentleman'. Edith Thompson and Frederick Bywaters were buried in the grounds of the prisons in which they were executed, Holloway and Pentonville respectively. Thompson's remains were re-interred in Brookwood Cemetery, Surrey, in 1971, together with three other women, to facilitate the rebuilding of Holloway Prison.

Author's Verdict

Frederick Bywaters murdered Percy Thompson and was justly convicted. Had it not been for the interest in his co-accused, Edith Thompson – writers, the media, the public – it is doubtful if anyone would have cared particularly. To steal up on a man at night, armed with a knife and cut him down as Bywaters did, for whatever reason, is wholly indefensible. 'I didn't intend to kill him,' he said. Maybe he didn't. But every man must be responsible for his actions. His account of Thompson possessing a gun was risible. If true, he would surely have mentioned it at the outset. 'You will have a simple task at arriving at your decision,' the judge told the jury.

The one witness to the crime, the victim's wife, instead of readily identifying the killer, instead told lies, first at the scene, then to her brother-in-law, then the police and finally, at her trial, when she declared, 'I don't remember anything except being knocked aside.' She only admitted knowing who her husband's killer was when she saw him in the police station.

Edith Thompson's letters to Bywaters were the backbone of the prosecution's case. They contained references to her apparent desire to bring about the death of her husband. Her defence maintained they were no more than the product of her imagination, that even if she wanted her husband dead she would never have done any of these things. Bywaters himself said he didn't believe any of it. In any event, there was no evidence that Thompson tried to poison her husband, and no glass was found in his body. The judge's opinion of their liaison was clear enough by the words he scribbled on his notepad: 'Great love – nonsense. Great disgust'. The prisoners' conduct – their adultery – in times of strict moral standards, was as much on trial as the murder of Percy Thompson.

Did Edith Thompson know Bywaters would turn up that night and kill her husband? If she did not, then one could argue that no matter how many letters she wrote, and no matter what she wrote in them, they had no bearing on the crime and Bywaters alone was guilty. But then we have 'common purpose', where two people who seek the death of a third are both guilty no matter who actually takes the victim's life. So, when she implored Bywaters to 'do something desperate', did she mean 'where you like, when you like, however you like', and did murder on the streets of Ilford fit the criteria? Her conduct immediately after the crime – those lies – suggests this may be the case. Or did 'do something desperate' mean to find her a job abroad? No one can be certain about her intentions, or what she meant.

If no one can be certain, then the case against Thompson was not proved 'beyond reasonable doubt', as the law requires. No matter she committed adultery, no matter what she wrote, no matter that she lied after the deed, no matter that her infidelity was frowned upon in those days of different social standards. She should not have been convicted and therefore she should not have hanged. As to the Home Secretary having the option of commuting her sentence to one of life imprisonment, it is not difficult to see his problem. They were both found guilty. If Bywaters had to hang, how could he spare Thompson? He had to spare them both, or neither. To commute Thompson's sentence on the grounds of gender would not have been fair.

15

A Deflection of Blame

Susan Newell, Lanarkshire, 1923

Thomas Dickson of Airdrie was on his way to Glasgow market. That morning, Thursday 21 June, he was working for a local fruit merchant. Driving a lorry, he left Airdrie about 8 a.m., passed through Coatbridge and when approaching Baillieston he saw two women and a child by the side of the road. On sight of his approach one of the women shouted out, 'Are you going to Glasgow?' He stopped, and said he was. He was then asked if he would give 'this woman and child a lift', to which he said he would always help anyone in need.

Stepping down from the lorry, Dickson saw the woman had with her a 'go-cart' (or 'go-chair'), which was laden with a bundle, covered with a bed mat, and which he helped to lift up on to the lorry. The woman and child, a little girl, sat inside the cab. The woman said she was going to Glasgow to look for rooms, and asked to be dropped off 'any place at all'. Dickson considered Duke Street to be suitable. As he helped her lift the go-cart from the lorry she said, 'Just steady the handles and I will get it off myself.' He noticed she was anxious to ensure the cover over the bundle was not disturbed. He tried to help her to steady the bundle, but she knocked his hand away, saying, 'Go on with your lorry. I will manage it myself.' Dickson drove off, probably satisfied that he had helped someone in need.

Events had not gone unnoticed. Mrs Helen Elliot, who was looking out from her kitchen window, had seen the go-cart and the large bundle it contained. She also saw something Thomas Dickson didn't see: as the woman was picking the bundle up to place it on to the cart, Mrs Elliot saw her get hold of a 'little foot' and push it back under the cover. If that wasn't surprising enough, she then saw a head 'topple over', and hang out from the bundle. The woman tried to tie it in with an old rag, but her efforts to avoid detection were futile, for the alert Mrs Elliot was already on the way downstairs to her sister Mary's, and together they went outside to the entrance to a close, where they saw the woman trying to cover the bundle with a brown coat.

Mrs Elliot told two other women what she had seen and hurried after the woman with the little girl and the suspicious bundle on the go-cart. She and her sister saw her pass through a gateway leading to a coup (an open space). As they followed, the woman saw them, hoisted the bundle on to her back and told the little girl to push the go-cart.

Robert Foote, a retired soldier, saw the woman trying to climb a six-foot wall into another close. The woman saw him and tried to escape by climbing some railings alongside a playground. Foote ran out into the street and beckoned to Police Constable McGennett, who had been told of events. As the woman tried to run away McGennett stopped her, and asked her where the bundle was. She led him to the back of a staircase leading from the close to an upper storey of the building. The constable uncovered the bundle and found himself looking at the lifeless body of a young boy. When asked what she had to say, the woman replied, 'It was not me who did it. It was my husband.' Her husband had struck her, she said, and the little boy was in the house at the time. When she had told her husband she was going to lodge a complaint of assault, he lifted the little boy onto the bed and choked him.

PC McGennett arrested the woman, and took her and the little girl to the police station, together with the body of the little boy. The woman was Susan Newell, 28 years, and the little girl was her 6-year-old daughter, Janet. Mrs Newell reiterated that she had had a row with her husband, and when the little boy screamed her husband seized him and lifted him onto the bed and choked him 'till he was black in the face'.

For three weeks Susan Newell had lived in lodgings with her husband, John Newell, at 2 Newlands Street, Whifflet, Coatbridge. They occupied an upstairs room and their landlady, Mrs Annie Young, occupied the kitchen. Mrs Bell also had a room in the building. The Newells were 'always rowing'. They rowed on the evening of Sunday 17 June, after which Mrs Young, who was an invalid, decided enough was enough. She wanted them out, and asked Mrs Morgan, a neighbour, to tell the Newells to quit.

The following Tuesday, PC Thomas Gilchrist was on duty in Ross Street, Coatbridge, when Mrs Newell spoke to him about lodging a charge of assault against her husband. He directed her to Whifflet police office. On Wednesday morning, she told him her children were being neglected by her husband and asked him where the Cruelty to Children inspector was, adding that her husband had been paid 30 shillings at work and she had not seen him since. That same morning Mrs Bell was in Mrs Young's kitchen when Mrs Newell knocked on the door, and said she might have her husband arrested for thrashing Janet.

At 5.10 p.m. Robert Johnston, a tube worker, came home to 23 Whifflet Street from work. His 13-year-old son John was not at home, but that was no cause for alarm, and Johnston and his wife Margaret went out to the local cattle show. By 9.15, however, the Johnstons were surprised when young John had still not come home. Mary, John's sister, said he would be at the Garden Picture House.

John Johnston, 'an engaging little fellow', had returned home from school that afternoon, Wednesday 20 June, but after tea had gone out to help another boy, James McGhee, to sell newspapers. James had the job of newspaper boy, but got John to help him, paying him a penny in each shilling earned. That evening he met John about six o'clock in Dundyvan Road outside the Co-op and gave him nine newspapers to sell. When Christina Main saw John about 6.30 p.m., walking towards Newlands Street, he had some newspapers under his arm. He was seen again at 7 p.m. by another school chum, Alex Cook, who spoke to him.

At 6.30 p.m., when Mrs Morgan knocked on the Newells' door to tell them Mrs Young wanted them to go, it was opened by Mrs Newell. She told her Mrs Young wanted she and her husband out by Saturday. Mrs Newell went directly to see Mrs Young and asked if they could stay until Monday, which was agreed. That evening the three women, Mrs Brown, Mrs Morgan and Mrs Young, were in the latter's kitchen when they heard someone go upstairs. 'It's the paper boy,' said Mrs Young. They heard him enter Mrs Newell's room, then they heard 'three dumps', or thuds. Mrs Morgan remarked that it would be 'Mrs Newell packing'. Shortly after, Mrs Newell knocked on the door and asked if Mrs Young had a box, but she did not. At that time Janet McLeod, Mrs Newell's daughter, was playing in the street with 8-year-old Agnes Grant.

At eleven o'clock Robert Johnston went to the Whifflet police office and reported his son missing. The last person to see him was Alex Cook; the next was PC McGennett in the Glasgow stairwell, many miles away. John Johnston's body was identified by his heartbroken father and grandmother. He had been murdered. This was revealed by a post-mortem examination on Friday evening, by Professor John Glaister, who gave cause of death as throttling, and dislocation of the spinal column of the neck. The throttling was due to compression of the windpipe by hand. There were also marks on the scalp produced by the 'forcible application' of a blunt instrument by more than one blow, and there were marks of burning on the head, probably caused by falling onto a gas ring.

Learning of the death of John Johnston, the Chief Constable, William McDonald, went with Detective Sergeant Charles Lockhart to the room the Newells rented, gaining access with a neighbour's key. They found the room in 'disorder', with the gaslight still burning at the end of the mantelpiece. The go-cart, it turned out, belonged to Mrs Young. There was no doubt this was the place where John Johnston died, and Susan Newell, now in custody, had placed the blame fair and square at her husband's door.

Interviewed by Lieutenant Fordyce, Mrs Newell said the previous night she and her husband had quarrelled. A boy whose name she did not know was in the house at the time, and when her husband was about to strike her, the boy screamed. Her husband seized him, threw him onto the bed and choked him till he was black in the face. While that was being done, she said, she fainted, and when she recovered her husband was gone and the boy was dead. She took up the body, rolled it in a bed mat and laid it on a couch where it lay all night. Her daughter came in later and was put to bed. That was about nine o'clock. The following morning she got her daughter up, gave her breakfast, lifted the bundle into the go-cart and made her way to Glasgow.

Mrs Newell's daughter, 6-year-old Janet, was interviewed by Woman Constables Blair and Duncan. In a statement, Janet said she had seen 'a boy' in the house but could not say where he had to go. When she was urged to 'tell the truth', she grabbed WPC Duncan's hand and said, 'My daddy choked him with his hands and he died.' Her mother had been standing at the foot of the bed, and had told him to stop, and he had hit her, Janet, with a poker.

Dr Greenhill, the police surgeon, examined Mrs Newell, forming the opinion that 'there were no signs of insanity'. She was cool, subdued, and answered questions freely and intelligently. He considered the burn to the boy's face had been caused after he died. The police had the account of events from mother and daughter, albeit not quite the same. Clearly they had to trace the prime suspect, John Newell, of whom nothing had been seen and whose whereabouts were unknown.

In fact, on the Thursday, the day his wife was arrested pushing a dead boy in a go-cart, John Newell was in Haddington, near Edinburgh where, the following day, he saw a report in the *Scotsman*, in which he read about the murder of John Johnston at 2 Newlands Street, Whifflet, and that his wife was in custody. Newell's actions were hardly those of a fugitive: he went straight to Haddington police station and told the police who he was. He was arrested and brought back to Coatbridge. When cautioned, he replied, 'I know nothing whatever about it. I was not in Coatbridge from Tuesday night till Wednesday night.' At Coatbridge police station, he gave a comprehensive account of his movements, including on Wednesday evening, when John Johnston was murdered.

The last occasion he had been at home, he said, was at 11.15 a.m. on Tuesday, after which he attended his brother's funeral and collected 30 shillings from work. At 7.30 p.m., in the company of another brother, David, he was assaulted by his wife in the street – she head-butted him twice in the face – then went to his father's house, briefly, but stayed at the Parkhead Model Lodging House that night. He came into Coatbridge again about 11.30 a.m. on Wednesday morning, bought some liver and went back to the lodging house to cook it, before going into Glasgow and buying a clay pipe and other things at a paper shop; then he went to a pub. After that he returned to Coatbridge where, at 10.30 p.m., he visited his sister, Mrs Shanks, at Buchanan Street, spending an hour there before going to the police office, where he learned there was a warrant in force for his arrest for deserting his wife (although he wasn't arrested). He stayed at Lamont

House all night, until about six o'clock the next morning (Thursday), returning to his father's house in Summerlee before going to another lodging house at Airdrie for breakfast. He then got a lift on a lorry to Leith, and from there walked to Haddington, spending Thursday night in another lodging house. His intention was to leave his wife and go to England, but on Friday, he read the *Scotsman* newspaper, which gave an account of the murder and went straight to the police.

Newell stated he was not in the house, 2 Newlands Street, at any time on Wednesday. The police checked out his alibi, tracing and speaking to witnesses who all verified his story. He was indeed at all those places at the times he indicated. Nevertheless, he was in the Coatbridge area – he visited the police station and his sister that evening. So, his alibi was not quite cast-iron. In any event, he was charged with murder and sent for trial, along with his wife.

The trial of John and Susan Newell opened in the High Court of Judiciary, Glasgow, that September, the *Coatbridge Express* reporting that public interest was so intense that people seeking admission to the courtroom began to assemble at 7.30 a.m. 'Men with mufflers and women with shawls formed the larger part of the crowd'. When Susan Newell arrived in a police van there was much booing. She raised her collar and hurried into the building.

Lord Alness presided, with Lord Kinross appearing for the prosecution; Messrs Gentles and Crawford defended Susan and John Newell respectively. They both pleaded 'Not guilty' to the murder of John Johnston, and both entered special pleas. Not surprisingly, John Newell's special plea was his alibi, stating that on 20 June he was not present at 2 Newlands Street, where the murder took place. Susan Newell's special plea was one of insanity on the date of the crime. Before the trial got under way the jury had to be sworn. This proved to be far from straightforward, as ten of the nominees were women, and as each came forward she was challenged by Mr Gentles and informed that 'her services would not be required'. Accordingly an all-male jury sat to hear the case.

Special pleas of alibi and insanity notwithstanding, the trial got under way. In a harrowing scene, Margaret Johnston, the murdered boy's mother, giving evidence, collapsed in the witness box on sight of her son's clothing and the go-cart. All the witnesses testified, including Mrs Young, Mrs Brown and Mrs Morgan, the three women who were so close to the crime that night. Then followed the 'sensational' evidence of Susan Newell's 6-year-old daughter, Janet, who had earlier told police, 'My daddy choked him with his hands and he died.' In the packed courtroom, under the gaze of the legal men and in the presence of her mother, she had a different story to tell.

After recovering from her 'first excitement', Janet said she recalled the boy going upstairs 'to her house' while she was playing outside. She did not see him come down again. Later her mammy took her to Dufffy's public house. She had a jug with her and went into the pub, leaving Janet outside. She came out with beer in the jug, and was also carrying whisky and wine. Lord Kinross then asked Janet a series of questions:

'Where did you go when you got home?'

'Into the room.'

'Did you see anything?'

'A little wee boy dead on the couch.'

'How did you know he was dead?'

'I went over to look.'

'What did your mother say?'

'Keep quiet.'

'Did your mother do anything?'

'She drank the beer.'

'What did she do?'

'She took my father's drawers and put them over his face. His nose was bleeding. She got a poker to get the floor up to try to get the wee boy in, and we tried to get a box from Mrs Young.'

'The same night, where did you sleep?'

'In the house.'

Janet said she did not see her stepfather that day. She saw him on the Tuesday when he went to a funeral and he did not come back. Lord Kinross's questioning resumed:

'There were two ladies who spoke to you on this happening. Did you tell them the same as you told us today?'

'No. I forget what I told them.'

'Do you remember telling them it was your daddy who choked the boy?'

'Yes.'

'Why did you tell them that?'

'Mammy told me.'

'That is what she told you to say?'

'Yes.'

On Mrs Newell's alleged insanity, Dr Greenhill said it was his opinion there was no sign of it. She had answered his questions 'freely and intelligently'. Professor Glaister had reported with regard to the question of insanity on behalf of the Procurator Fiscal. He did not think she was of 'unsound mind'.

Mr Gentle asked, 'Are women, suddenly subjected to a great trial, more easily affected than men?'

'Yes, particularly if hard pressed.'

'You have heard evidence that this woman was deserted by her husband, left with no money and about to be turned into the street. Is that the kind of thing that might affect her mental balance?'

'It might make her desperate, owing to the cruelty of the situation.'

The judge enquired, 'Is there anything in the evidence to suggest that at the time of this crime the woman was suffering from frenzy or insanity?'

'I have heard nothing here nor from her that that existed,' replied Professor Glaister.

Mr Gentle again: 'I suppose it is possible for a person to be perfectly sane on 13 September (the date of Professor Glaister's report) who was insane on 20 June?'

'That is so.'

'Have you ever heard of temporary insanity, sudden frenzies, in which a person may have completely lost self control?'

'Yes, in some cases.'

'What class of society did Mrs Newell come from?'

'Practically of the tinker class.'

'Not a high type mentally or intellectually?'

'No, nor a high moral type.'

Witnesses supporting John Newell's alibi placed him in Glasgow and Coatbridge, as he maintained. Lord Kinross then withdrew the charge against him. There was absolute silence in the courtroom, finally broken when his lordship told the jury, 'The Advocate Depute has withdrawn the case against the male prisoner. I feel bound to say he has used wise discretion. It is now your duty to return a formal verdict as against the prisoner John Newell.'

This was done, whereupon Lord Alness told Newell he was discharged.

'Thank you, my lord,' said Newell, who, without a glance at his wife, stepped down, and left by a private exit, his liberty – and his life – assured.

Susan Newell now stood alone.

Mr Gentle outlined the legal position on the point of 'abnormal condition of mind', which would reduce murder to culpable homicide. He said that when he first read the story he thought the woman, 'if she did it,' must have been mad. There was no evidence of premeditation, nor of malice against the boy. There was no motive shown that could have affected a rational mind. What could the act have to help her in any conceivable way? She must have been mad at the time, he said, his view supported by 'bringing the body in a go-cart with her daughter on top of the bundle into the teeming streets of Glasgow.'

His lordship reiterated the facts, from the time John Johnston left his house to deliver newspapers about 6 p.m. on the Wednesday, to the arrest of Susan Newell in Glasgow, the following day, pushing his lifeless body in the go-cart. Was she the assailant? The boy entered the room alive and he left it dead. Three thuds were heard by the women next door; Mrs Newell and the boy were the sole occupants of the room. Was she insane *at the time*? 'There must be alienation of reason such as misleads judgement, so that the person does not know the nature and the quality of the act he is doing ... or that he does not know that what he is doing is wrong.' Eccentricity, aberration of mind, weak-mindedness, did not amount to insanity. The evidence was that she was 'cool, collected, intelligent and balanced' in all that she said. Dr Garry had found no trace of insanity, and there was 'nothing to suggest at the time of the crime this woman was other than sane'. He said that a man who struck a blow, not with the intention of killing, but to commit serious injury, whose victim died from the attack, that was murder. The jury had a choice of several verdicts: that Mrs Newell was insane at the time, in which case she must be acquitted; that the case was 'not proven' (a verdict under Scottish law); culpable homicide; or guilty of murder. It took the jury thirty-seven minutes to decide on the latter.

His lordship addressed Susan Newell. 'I decern and adjudge you, Susan Newell, to be carried to the prison of Glasgow, therein to be detained until 10 October, and on that date, within the walls of the prison, and by the hands of the executioner, to be hanged by the neck on a gibbet till you be dead and your body thereafter to be buried within the walls of the prison, and your whole moveable goods are decerned to be escheat and forfeit to His Majesty's use.' Mrs Newell calmly, and without showing emotion, stepped lightly down the steps, escorted by a wardress and three policemen.

Post-Trial

Susan Newell was due to hang on Monday 10 October, but her solicitor and counsel applied to the Secretary for Scotland, Lord Novar, for a reprieve. Their application went unanswered over the weekend, which must have been agonising for her. On Monday morning a telegram was at last received from the Home Office: 'The Secretary regrets that he is unable to discover sufficient grounds to justify him in advising interference with the due course of the law'. When the Lord Provost and the Town Clerk went to the prison to break the news to Newell, she fainted, 'and would have fallen through the floor had the doctor and matron not caught hold of her'. As she was led away from the condemned cell, she called out loudly for her daughter.

John Ellis, who had hanged Edith Thompson at Holloway in January, awaited his client at the scaffold. As he tied Newell's hands behind her back and slipped the white cap over her head, she protested, exclaiming, 'Do not put that thing on me.' Scarcely were the words out of her mouth when Ellis pulled the lever. Ellis was an efficient hangman, and Newell died instantly. He described her as 'exceedingly brave'. Outside, in Cathedral Square, a crowd of 200, mainly women, kept silent vigil. Susan Newell met her fate in Duke Street Prison, not far from the place she was arrested, pushing John Johnston's body in the go-cart. Her daughter, Janet, was brought up in a convent.

Author's Verdict

John and Susan Newell were both indicted for this crime, but John Newell walked from the court, his alibi believed by the judge, prosecution and, ultimately, the jury. However, although witnesses confirmed his movements, he was not able to prove comprehensively that he did not visit 2 Newlands Street, the home he shared with his wife, that evening, and he was in Coatbridge around the material time. Nevertheless, it seems unlikely that he was involved in the murder. Would he so readily have gone to the police at Haddington if he had been, when he was already well on the way to England, where he sought to get away from his wife and start a new life? Then we have the testimony of his stepdaughter, who lied at her mother's behest when questioned by the police, but had another story to tell when she stood in the witness box, an innocent who was surely telling the truth when questioned, however gently, by the men in wigs.

Why did Susan Newell kill the boy? For the money in his pocket, however little the amount? She did visit a pub afterwards and buy beer and spirits. Because she just couldn't take any more stress after her strained, possibly brutal, relationship with her husband? Or was she insane? The doctors didn't think so; neither did the judge. Some of the points concerning her sanity or otherwise were nonsense: she was 'practically of the tinker class', 'not a high type mentally or intellectually'. As for the assertion that 'women, suddenly subjected to a great trial, are more easily affected then men', to which Professor Glaister replied, 'Yes, if hard pressed,' this is risible. Barristers could have talked all day about insanity, the jury would have been no wiser.

Susan Newell was probably suffering from the consequences of the disastrous relationship with her husband. He had drawn his pay and fled, leaving her alone with her daughter, facing eviction from their home. There would be no single mother's allowance, no re-housing by the council, not then. She may have been at her lowest ebb when John Johnston called with her newspaper, and succumbed to some sort of angry response; not against the boy, but her husband, life itself, who can say? Her conduct afterwards was wicked, blaming her husband for something he didn't do, and telling her daughter to lie. She would have seen her husband hang for the crime. Today, she would probably be convicted of manslaughter on the grounds of diminished responsibility, a legal term which would have embraced the circumstances in which she found herself. The verdict here is that her conviction, given the law at the time, was right, but that the Home Secretary should have commuted her sentence to one of life imprisonment.

John Johnston was the son of a respectable, hard working family, a member of the juvenile lodge of the Good Templars and the Boys' Brigade. On the day of his funeral the shops closed, as did his school, and a large crowd marched in procession, led by the band of the Salvation Army, to Airdrie Cross. From here, they carried on in silence to New Monklands Churchyard, where his little body was interned. His headstone carried the simple but moving message: 'In Memory of John Johnston, from his playmates.'

16

An Eternal Triangle

Charlotte Bryant, Dorset, 1935

'Nice looking with raven-black hair, flashing green eyes and full breasts', Charlotte McHugh was born in Londonderry about 1904. Ill-educated and illiterate, she grew up in difficult times, when Ireland was struggling for independence from British rule. When she was old enough she turned to prostitution, and welcomed as her clients British soldiers who were serving in the Province. They were the ones with money, after all. But Charlotte was unhappy. Most of the young soldiers only wanted her for sexual favours and would disappear until they wanted her again. But one soldier didn't disappear. Frederick Bryant was in his early twenties, a military policeman in the Dorset Regiment and veteran of the First World War. As for her, she regarded him as her ticket to a better life in England, and when he was discharged from the army he took her to the promised land. In 1925 they were married at Wells, Somerset, and Fred found employment as a cowman at Over Compton, near Yeovil.

The Bryants lived in a tied cottage in the village for the next thirteen years, during which time she bore five children. Charlotte, who became bored with village life, drank heavily and, with no income – Fred made little as a cowman, despite working twelve hours a day – she found life in England little different to the one she had left behind in Ireland, and so turned once again to selling her body. The locals knew her as 'Killarney Kate' a name that suited as she was from 'over the water'. She was regarded here as a drunkard and a slut, but Fred, who knew about his wife's activities, told a neighbour that he didn't care. It seems he took the pragmatic view: 'Four pounds a week is better than thirty shillings.'

Charlotte may have accepted that, for her, things would never change. But change they did, in December 1933, when a man calling himself Bill Moss came into her life. Moss, whose real name was Leonard Edward Parsons, was a dealer in 'horses, linoleum and other things', and came from Bridgwater. He was in lodging at Babylon Hill, near Sherborne, when he became 'friendly' with the Bryants, so much so that Fred asked him to stay. This may have been to please Charlotte, who, after so many other men, had fallen for a man she said was 'better than all the rest put together'. It seems that when Fred went to work with his cows, Moss took his place in the matrimonial bed.

This situation couldn't last. In 1934, when Fred's employer found about out about the goings on in the cottage, Fred was sacked and he and his wife – and Moss – were evicted. The Bryants moved to Coombe, near Sherborne, where Fred again found employment as a cowman. Moss went with them, and life went on as before. From time to time Moss would visit his common law wife, Priscilla, who lived with their four children. Then he would return to the Bryants, where he was more than happy to drink in the local pub with Fred and sleep with Fred's wife. Once again, however, things couldn't last.

It seems on several occasions in 1935, Charlotte asked Moss if he would marry her, telling him she would be 'a widow soon'. He was so put off with the idea he left the house that October. Charlotte went with him, to Dorchester, where they stayed in rented rooms for a couple of nights, but she soon returned to Fred. Moss then sent her a telegram, asking her to meet him at Bradford Hollow. She came with Fred and a policeman – to keep the peace, presumably – and Fred invited Moss back to the Bryant household, which he visited nightly. Only this time it was to see Fred. Or so he said.

In May 1935, Fred took ill after eating the dinner his wife had cooked for him. The doctor diagnosed gastro-enteritis. In August he was ill again, and recovered; he was ill again on 11 December, and once more recovered. Then, on 21 December, he fell ill again, and this time there would be no recovery. The doctor wanted him to go to hospital, but he refused. So, that night, a friend of Charlotte, Mrs Lucy Ostler who had come to live at Coombe that October, stayed in the house to help look after him. Mrs Ostler was a widow with six children, and Charlotte had become friends with her. Her staying over may have been to the chagrin of Fred, perhaps suspecting that his wife, after so many relationships with men, might now be in a relationship with a woman.

That night, when Mrs Bryant went to bed, Mrs Ostler remained downstairs by the fire. About three o'clock in the morning, she heard Charlotte say to her husband, 'Will you have the Oxo, Fred? I have just put hot water in it.'

He replied, 'Yes.'

Soon after, Mrs Ostler heard him vomiting. The next morning, Charlotte and Mrs Ostler went upstairs to find him in a 'very bad state', and unable to get up. He was taken to Sherborne Hospital, suffering 'excruciating cramps' in the stomach, and died at 2.45 p.m. Frederick Bryant had been a healthy, fit man, and the doctor at the hospital refused to issue a death certificate. A post-mortem examination revealed cause of death to be as a result of acute arsenical poisoning.

Charlotte Bryant and her five children were placed in the care of the Poor Law Institution at Sturminster Newton, and the police went to the house to investigate. They searched, but found no arsenic. They questioned the neighbours, asked pharmacists if anyone had sold arsenic to 'a woman', meaning Mrs Bryant presumably.

Mrs Ostler told the police about a green-coloured tin she had seen in a cupboard. 'Don't touch it,' she said Charlotte had told her, adding, 'I must get rid of this. I have done nothing. Parsons (Bill Moss) often brings things home.' Charlotte would not say what the tin contained, but told her not to say anything anyway. A few days later Mrs Ostler was cleaning under the copper (boiler) when she saw the tin. 'It was burnt and charred. I threw it into the yard because the ashes were to go on to the compost. It's probably still there.'

The police searched the yard and found the tin. Written on it were the words, 'Weed Killer. Poison'. It was sent for analysis to University College, London, where scientists found it had contained traces of arsenious oxide. Meanwhile, Mrs Ostler had more information, saying she had been looking at a newspaper when Charlotte asked her what she was reading.

'I am reading about a poisoning case,' said Mrs Ostler.

'What was the case?' asked Charlotte.

'A case of arsenic poisoning.'

Charlotte asked what she would give anyone if she wanted to get rid of them.

'I would not think of doing anything like that,' said Mrs Ostler.

On another occasion, when the two women were talking, Charlotte had said, 'I don't like Fred. I hate him.'

Following this, Superintendent Cherrett went to the Poor Law Institution where he formally charged Mrs Bryant with the murder of her husband. She replied, 'I have never got any poison from anywhere, and that people do know. I don't see how they can say I poisoned my husband.' She was arrested, and appeared before the Sherborne magistrates on 10 February 1936, when she was remanded in custody. The police had arrested the apparent culprit, but had they considered someone else might have poisoned Frederick Bryant's food? Lucy Ostler, for example. Or Bill Moss. As it was, rather than being suspects, they would appear as witnesses for the prosecution.

At the committal proceedings in March, Dr Roche Lynch gave evidence about the examination of Frederick Bryant's organs. They were in a remarkable degree of preservation, despite Bryant dying on 22 December. This was consistent with acute arsenical poisoning. The amount of arsenic in the body, except hair and nails, was 4.09 grains, in the form of arsenious oxide, so Bryant must have received a dose two or three times that amount. The history of illnesses in May, August and December was consistent with arsenical poisoning too, he said. It frequently happened that the recipient of arsenic recovered from one or more doses, only to die of another dose.

Bottles containing tea and milk were examined. Dr Lynch said that each contained ten grains of weed killer – seven grains of white arsenic. In spite of a water-soluble dye in the weed killer, he suggested it could not be detected in tea or milk. Ashes from the Bryants' kitchen grate contained 41.5 parts arsenic per one million, and ashes and earth from the garden 92 parts per one million. The last dose of arsenic administered to Bryant might have been administered at least six to eight hours before death. Twelve to thirty-six hours was more likely.

Charlotte Bryant stood trial for her life at the Dorset Assizes that May, charged with murdering her husband. She pleaded 'Not guilty'. For the Crown, the Solicitor-General, Sir Terence O'Connor, said that 'on a certain day at a certain place this woman bought some arsenic; she took the arsenic home, put it into her husband's tea, milk, or whatever it might be, and he consumed it, and of that consumption he died.' Quite how he could prove she bought arsenic isn't known, since this was never established. Nevertheless, he said, on at least four occasions in 1935 Frederick Bryant was the victim of the administration of 'very large quantities of arsenic'. How he could prove this either is doubtful, since arsenic was proved to be in his body on the last occasion only, when he died. 'I am afraid what dramatic writers call the eternal triangle is not absent from this case,' said Sir Terence, adding, 'she was a woman with the strongest motives for destroying her husband in order that the marriage might end.'

Sir Terence said Bill Moss, whom we should now regard by his proper name, Leonard Parsons, had lodged with the Bryants. She was his mistress for 'a considerable time'. Mrs Bryant had said that her youngest child was that of Parsons. In November 1935, Parsons 'took himself off' and Mrs Bryant never saw him again.

Sir Terence turned to the 'four illnesses'. On 14 May 1935, while Mrs Bryant was away with Parsons, Mr Bryant was found on the stairs very ill, after he had eaten his midday meal, alone. He was suffering from cramp in the calves, 'the symptoms of arsenic poisoning.'

One Sunday in August Parsons had heard Mr Bryant say to his wife, 'What's this?'

'Weed killer,' she replied.

On 6 August a doctor diagnosed Bryant as having gastro-enteritis. He was ill again on 11 December. Sir Terence reiterated events of 21 December, when Mrs Ostler stayed and Mr Bryant took ill and was taken to hospital. There had been 'exhaustive enquiries' by the police to try and establish whether she had bought any arsenic from chemists in the neighbourhood, and it was 'fair to say' there was no evidence that she had. 'One of the weaker links in the chain of evidence,' he said.

Ethel Staunton, who lived next door, said that in May, Mr Bryant was ill, 'groaning and shuddering', in great pain and holding his stomach. Bernard Staunton, her husband, likewise said that when he was working with Mr Bryant on 11 December he seemed to be in great pain and was holding his stomach. Lucy Ostler said that after Frederick Bryant died, Mrs Bryant asked her what an inquest was. When she told her, Mrs Bryant said, 'If they can't find anything they can't put a rope round me.' When Mrs Bryant said she hated her husband, Mrs Ostler said, if so, why didn't she go away with Parsons, as she had done before, and not bear her husband malice? Mrs Bryant said she did not want to leave the children.

J.D. Casswell, defending, addressed Mrs Ostler, who confirmed that her husband had died some years ago, and there were rumours that the police were 'digging around his grave'.

'The police were questioning you, were they not?'

'Yes.'

'Did it occur to you that you were alone with this man (Bryant) just about an hour before he was taken ill?'

'Yes.'

'Did you think afterwards that the police suspected you?'

'No.'

'You did not think, when somebody is poisoned, and there were only two grown-ups in the house at the time, people are apt to be suspicious of one or the other or both?'

'Yes.'

'I suggest you were frightened; you were afraid of what might happen to you when you made your statement [about the tin] to the police.'

'I was, in a way.'

'Didn't you invent the whole story about that tin?'

'No.'

Leonard Parsons said he met Mrs Bryant at the end of 1933, when he called himself Bill Moss. He became friendly with both she and Mr Bryant, and sometimes stayed at their house. When asked whether intimacy had taken place between him and Mrs Bryant, he replied, 'Oh yes, it began at the end of 1933, and continued through 1934 and 1935.' At the latter part of 1935 he and Mrs Bryant had been away together, to Dorchester, Weymouth, Plymouth and Yeovil.

'Did Mrs Bryant ever make a suggestion to you about marriage?'

'Yes, she said she thought she would soon be a widow and I would marry her. That was in the summer of last year.'

'When was the last time she made that suggestion?'

'About August.'

'Have you ever had in your possession any weed killer?'

'No.'

'Have you ever taken any weed killer into the Bryants' house?'

'Never.'

Parsons admitted he had lived for eleven years with a woman and then left her. She had four children by him. He contributed towards their upkeep as much as possible. He agreed Mrs Bryant came to Dorchester with him, and stayed two days. When she went home he sent her a telegram asking her to see him. She came with her husband and a policeman. Fred knew he had been with his wife but they did not quarrel. In fact, he invited him back to the house again, after which he went nightly to see him. He decided to leave the house because trade was bad and he could hardly make a living there. He had not seen Mrs Bryant since.

'Had anyone suggested to you that Mr Bryant was killed with weed killer?'

'No.'

Casswell held up a blue-coloured bottle, and suggested on one occasion he had poured some of the contents onto a stone in front of Mrs Bryant and two of her children, Lily and Ernie, and the contents 'fizzled'. Parsons denied doing such a thing. It was suggested he told Mrs Bryant that if he poured the contents down her throat, that is what would happen inside her. He denied this too.

Sir Terence had more questions for Parsons:

'Was there a time when you wanted to give some treatment to a mare?'

'Yes, in 1935.'

'What kind of medicine did you get?'

'I wanted to get some arsenic.'

'Where?'

'At Sherborne, at a chemist's.'

'Were you able to get any?'

'No.'

'Why?'

'Because I was not known.'

'Did you take any steps as regards the police?'

'I did. I went to the "super" and asked him if I could have a little bit.'

'Did he help you get it?'

'No.'

'Was there any other occasion when you tried to buy arsenic?'

'No.'

Edward Tuck, an insurance agent, said Mrs Bryant told him, 'I would like to insure my old man.' He called at the house on 20 December, where he saw Mrs Bryant, Mrs Ostler and several children. He also saw Mr Bryant, who looked 'a very sick man'. Mrs Bryant said he had been ill for about a year with gastritis. Mr Tuck did not want to do business as far as Mr Bryant was concerned, but 'some insurances were effected for the children'. Mrs Bryant took money from a box. He saw silver and £1 notes. 'There was no shortage of money in the house,' said Tuck. On 23 December – the day after Mr Bryant's death – he met Mrs Bryant and Mrs Ostler near the house. Mrs Bryant had a bundle with her and said she had just got back from the hospital. The bundle contained her late husband's clothing. She said, 'Well, he has gone. I have been a good wife to him; nobody can say I have not, and nobody can say I have poisoned him'. He said, 'She put the emphasis on the "I" – "Nobody can say *I* poisoned him."' This was before the cause of death was known.

Chief Inspector Alexander Bell, who took Mrs Bryant's statement, said Mrs Bryant had said, 'I am going to speak the truth'. Her statement (abridged) read:

I know Leonard Parsons, known as Bill Moss. He told my husband he did not like his lodgings and my husband asked him to stay with us. I got very angry and Moss went away on the Saturday evening. I did not tell Fred I went away with him. I took my two children Lily and Billy. We went to Dorchester. Moss got single tickets for us back. Fred was pleased to see me. When I slept with Moss I did not allow him to have anything to do with me.

Three days later Moss sent me a telegram asking to meet him. I gave the telegram to my husband. We all went to Bradford Hollow. There was a bit of a flare up but my husband did not strike Moss. My husband had Moss back at the house the same night. He stayed with us nearly all the time. After we went to live at Coombe Farm Moss came to live with us. My husband and Moss used to go everywhere together. There was never any question about me going away with Moss again. I do not like the man. There has been talk about Moss being the father of my baby. That is not true. I have never carried on with him in a bad way. I have not seen him since he left us on October 15. I do not know what caused my husband's death. My husband was not insured.

Whether a former prostitute who sold her body, first to soldiers, then to locals in England, was telling the truth when she said she had never 'carried on with a man who was better than all the rest put together', who was living under the same roof as her, a man she followed with her children when he left, is to be doubted.

Dr Lynch said he had 'no doubt whatsoever' that Frederick Bryant died from acute arsenical poisoning. Arsenic was in every organ he examined. He estimated the body contained 4.09 grains of arsenic. The finding of arsenic in the fingernails – 33 parts per million – supported his view that the attack in August was due to acute arsenical poisoning. He could not say about the attack in May.

It was time for Mr Casswell to defend Charlotte Bryant. Against what evidence, precisely, you might ask? 'There is plenty of suspicion,' he said, 'but it falls short of the proof needed for a conviction.' Referring to the previous illnesses, on each occasion a doctor was called by Mrs Bryant, 'the very man of whom she would have the most fear.' The doctor was called on 21 December. 'Was that the work of a guilty mind? It was the opposite.'

There was no evidence that Mrs Bryant had purchased arsenic. Traces of arsenic in minute quantities may have come from coal and been brought into the house on other people's boots. He admitted Mrs Bryant was 'immoral', but going away for two or three days with another man didn't make her guilty of murder. Mr Bryant didn't seem to mind; he knew his wife was going out with Parsons; there was no reason for her to kill her husband to get Parsons. She had a home, and a husband. Would she have left that to associate with a man the police were after for failing to maintain his children? It was not she who was chasing Parsons, it was he who was chasing her.

Charlotte Bryant said she was on good terms with her husband: 'There was never a breath wrong with my husband and I until Leonard Parsons came along.' She said it was always Parsons who wanted her to go away with him. When questioned by Sir Terence, she denied discussing anything about poisoning with Mrs Ostler. She denied ever poisoning her husband's food. She denied ever seeing a tin marked 'weed killer'.

Two of Mrs Bryant's children were called in her defence. Lily, aged 10, said she had never seen the tin. She had seen Parsons pour the contents of a blue bottle 'on to the stone outside' and say to her mother, 'If you don't look out I will ram that down your throat'. 'It fizzled all up,' she said.

Ernest, aged 11, said that on the day his father died he was with his mother and Mrs Ostler when there was a conversation about a chemist's shop. It was Mrs Ostler who was speaking about it, not his mother.

Were these two testimonies contrived to support Mrs Bryant? There will always be that suspicion.

Justice MacKinnon told the jury there were two questions for them to consider. One, did Frederick Bryant die of arsenical poisoning? And two, if he did, was the poison administered by his wife? 'There can be no doubt to the first, but there remains the doubtful question – infinitely more doubtful – whether the arsenic was administered by the accused.' It was physically possible that he took the arsenic himself, he said, but unless he was insane it was almost impossible. 'No human being, having gone through the agony of one attack, would face it again.' It was possible the arsenic might have got into something he ate. 'It was a dirty house, but if the illnesses were due to arsenic, it is inconceivable an accident could happen a second, still less a third time.' If it was not himself, it must be somebody else. 'You can dismiss the possibility of the children as not worth thinking about.' He went on, 'Parsons was there, but not in December. Mrs Ostler was there in December, but she was not there in August or May.'

He turned to the scrapings, recovered from the tin containing ashes. Dr Roche said coal ashes normally contained 48 to 50 parts of a million of arsenic. The ashes from the copper fire had 149 parts of a million, and the scrapings from the tin contained 58,000 parts of a million of arsenic. This indicated the likelihood that arsenic was present in greater quantity in these two sources. One finds it difficult to consider how the weight of proof against Mrs Bryant is strengthened by these figures. In any event, this was the evidence the all-male jury had to consider, which they did for an hour before returning a guilty verdict. When the clerk asked if Charlotte Bryant had anything to say about 'why sentence of death should not be passed', she replied, 'I am not guilty.' When the judge passed sentence she broke down and almost collapsed, and was carried from the court by two wardresses; from thence she was taken to Exeter Gaol for execution.

Post-Trial

Bryant's appeal against conviction was heard in June. She was represented by J.G. Trapnell. One might think she had strong grounds for acquittal, given the evidence, or lack of it, at her trial. Trapnell said the jury should have been warned by the trial judge that Dr Lynch had said the symptoms at Frederick Bryant's earlier illnesses were only *consistent* with arsenical poisoning; there was no evidence that arsenic was actually found. Thus, he said, the summing up by Justice MacKinnon was defective, as it contained nothing of 'a cautionary nature'. He also proposed to call new evidence, that of Professor William Bone of the Imperial College of Science.

First, though, he made reference to the tin that contained traces of arsenic, said to have been burnt in the fire copper after Mr Bryant's death, and the charred remains found on the rubbish heap. He argued that there was no conclusive evidence that the ashes analysed came from the fire copper. This would be important, especially having regard to Mrs Ostler's evidence: 'Don't touch it, I must get rid of this,' Mrs Bryant had allegedly told her. As far as calling Professor Bone was concerned, the Lord Chief Justice, Lord Hewart, had this to say on a matter which affected the life of a mother accused of murder: 'The court is of the opinion that there is no occasion for the further evidence (of Professor Bone). We set our faces like a flint against it. It would be intolerable if the court were to listen to the afterthoughts of a scientific gentleman in a capital case.' One would have thought it intolerable if the court *didn't* listen in a capital case.

The prosecution had said Mrs Bryant had given her husband doses of arsenic in May and August 1935, and there was evidence that she hated her husband, provided by the testimony of Mrs Ostler, who said Mrs Bryant had asked what one gave to someone one wanted to be rid of. The summing up by Justice MacKinnon was 'scrupulously fair', said his lordship. He dismissed the appeal. But Bryant repeatedly asserted her innocence, and wrote to the king, begging for mercy. It is doubtful whether His Majesty read her letter. At 8 a.m. on 15 July 1935, Charlotte Bryant was taken from her cell and hanged by Tom Pierrepoint. A Catholic priest who had attended Mrs Bryant in her last moments said she never confessed to the murder of her husband.

Author's Verdict

Who poisoned Frederick Bryant? Charlotte, his wife? Leonard Parsons? Lucy Ostler? Someone else?

There was no evidence that Charlotte Bryant had any arsenic, despite the unsubstantiated statement of counsel: 'On a certain day at a certain place this woman went and bought some arsenic.' Her husband's life was not insured; she had nothing to gain financially by his death. Much of the evidence against her was provided by others who were themselves suspects, or at least should have been. They would have been only too pleased to have the police use them as witnesses. On the other hand, there were indications that Mrs Bryant was the culprit. 'Nobody can say *I* poisoned him,' she said, before the cause of her husband's death was announced. And maybe she did want to get rid of him to secure Parsons' affections. Or Ostler's affections.

There had been rumours the police were 'digging around Mrs Ostler's husband's grave'. Clearly, they considered she might herself be a poisoner. If her husband had been poisoned, wouldn't the emphasis have shifted somewhat? As it is, we do not know. Was Ostler having a lesbian relationship with Mrs Bryant? If she was, wouldn't Frederick Bryant have been in *her* way, and wouldn't *she* have had a motive? Parsons, or Moss if you will, admitted trying to acquire arsenic for his sick mare. Did he succeed, and did he murder Fred? And what was that business with the blue bottle and its fizzy contents?

The trial judge made two interesting comments. The first: 'You can dismiss the possibility of the children as not worth thinking about.' Until he said that, did anyone consider a child as the murderer? Or simply someone who had administered arsenic as a prank? Then, ruling out Parsons and Ostler, 'Parsons was there, but not in December. Mrs Ostler was there in December, but she was not there in August or May.' In other words, that left Mrs Bryant as the only suspect. Isn't it the case that everyone – the public, the police, the lawyers, the judge, and even the Lord Chief Justice himself, regarded Charlotte Bryant as the immoral mother who slotted nicely into the picture as the person who administered arsenic into her husband's food or drink – the arsenic no one could prove she had. Maybe she *was* guilty. But the case against her was never proved.

17

Driven by Suffering

Ruth Ellis, Hampstead, London, 1955

Easter Sunday in South Hill Park, a quiet street in Hampstead. A small, blonde woman lurks in the shadows outside the Magdala Tavern. The pub is busy over the Bank Holiday weekend, but the woman stands alone and unseen. She knows the man she is waiting for is inside. His van is parked outside, facing down the street, driver's door by the pavement. She waits. It is just a matter of time.

Just after nine o'clock he emerges, accompanied by a friend. She steps from the shadows. 'David!' she calls out. He ignores her. Or maybe he didn't hear. 'David!' she calls again. He turns and sees her, seemingly unsurprised at her unexpected presence, her voice heralding the onslaught of another 'domestic', or so he thinks. She'd been trying to contact him all weekend, after all. But if her presence isn't a surprise, what she's holding in her hand is – a .38 Smith and Wesson revolver, pointing straight at him.

He turns and runs, trying to get to the other side of the van. She fires twice, gunshots ripping through the quiet of the Hampstead suburb. He staggers against the side of the van, blood oozing from his wounds, smearing onto the panels of the van. He calls to his friend, 'Clive!' But Clive can't help him; no one can. She steps forward and fires again and again, even as he lies on the ground. Finally, she raises the gun to her own temple and squeezes the trigger. Nothing happens. She lowers the gun and pulls the trigger again. This time it fires. The bullet ricochets off the pavement and strikes the hand of a woman passing by.

Hearing gunfire, people spill out of the pub. One of them is Alan Thompson, who calmly confronts the gunwoman.

'Will you call the police?' she asks him, quietly.

'I *am* the police,' he says, and arrests her.

An ambulance screams to the scene and conveys the victim to New End Hospital, but he is pronounced dead on arrival. The injured woman is Gladys Kensington Yule. Her husband commandeers a passing taxi and she, too, is taken to hospital. The blonde woman is Ruth Ellis, aged 25. She is taken to the police station, where she tells Superintendent Crawford, 'I am guilty. I am rather confused.' The man she has killed was her lover, 25-year-old David Moffat Drummond Blakely.

Ruth Ellis was born Ruth Neilsen in Rhyl, North Wales, on 9 October 1926, one of six children of Arthur Neilsen, a musician, and Elisaberta, a refugee who fled Belgium during the First World War. Neilsen was her father's stage name, which he changed from Hornby. He plied his trade on the cross-Atlantic liners of the day, but when work dried up the family moved to Hampshire, then to Southwark, London. When Ruth was fifteen she worked as a machinist, but through ill health took up dancing as a therapy and then obtained work as a photographer's assistant. In 1944 she gave birth to a baby boy, the son of a married Canadian soldier whose surname was Clare. Clare went home and Ruth's baby, Andrea – or Andy – was born that September. Ruth's sister, Muriel, looked after the child, so that Ruth could go out to work.

At the age of nineteen Ruth found work as a model at the Court Club, near Marble Arch; then, in 1950, she met George Ellis who, at 41, was a good deal older than she, but would have offered security thanks to his salary as a dentist. They were married and went to live in Southampton, where, the following year Ruth gave birth to a daughter, Georgina. By then her marriage to George Ellis was on the rocks, thanks to his alcoholism and the physical abuse she suffered at his hands. She returned to London with her two children and went to work at Carroll's Club, which was the Court Club with a new name.

If the club's name was new, so too was the clientele, which included racing car drivers, young men with money to splash out. It was here that Ruth met two men who would reshape her life, with tragic circumstances. David Blakely and Desmond Cussen were both attracted to her, and both would share her bed on and off for nearly two years. On her twenty-seventh birthday, the club's owner, a vice boss, made Ruth manageress at the Little Club, Knightsbridge, with a two-bedroom flat above as part of the deal.

David Blakely had had a privileged upbringing. He was educated at boarding school and served his National Service as an officer. On discharge he became a management trainee at the Hyde Park Hotel. He was privileged, but not a lot of use, since he couldn't hold down the job. Not that this would have bothered him when he inherited £7,000 on the death of his father in 1952. His stepfather kindly provided him with a flat and a job at Penn, Buckinghamshire, where he lived part of the time and had a fiancée, Linda Dawson; the other part he spent at Ruth's flat in London. Blakely had two passions: Ruth, and his own racing car, which he raced at home and abroad.

No doubt Ruth and Blakely enjoyed a thriving sexual relationship, and their mutual feelings may have amounted to true love for one another. But each was jealous of the other, and each in turn suffered: he through her activities at the club – entertaining 'clients', she through his constant womanising. Alcohol, too, played a part, so much so that Blakely's presence drove customers away and led to Ruth being sacked. A young woman with a son to support – Georgina was adopted – she wanted security, and she got it. Not through Blakely; it was the 'other man', Desmond Cussen, who took Ruth under his wing when she and Andy went to live at his flat.

Cussen was 32, a former RAF pilot and now a company director. He had long coveted Ruth, offering to pay for Andy's education, as well as acting as her chauffeur. Yet, even now, Blakely and Ruth continued to see one another, even in Cussen's flat with his consent. It seems Cussen would do anything for Ruth. In 1954, when Blakely broke off his engagement, Ruth thought it was for her, but she discovered he was still sleeping around. Their relationship continued thus until January 1954, when Ruth and Cussen took a flat as Mr and Mrs Ellis, in Egerton Gardens, Kensington – which the besotted Cussen kindly paid for while Blakely visited. It was here, during one of their rows, that Blakely beat her up, which included punching her in the stomach, and Ruth, who was pregnant, suffered a miscarriage. Then he sent flowers. It was the typical 'domestic violence' scenario, two people who loved and loathed, who could not live together and could not live apart. Meanwhile, Cussen was on hand for whatever sexual favours he could enjoy with Ruth.

In February 1955, with Cussen away at the time, Ruth and Blakely had a major row in the flat. Blakely called two of his friends, Ant Findlater and Clive Gunnell, and told them Ruth had tried to stab him. He had a black eye – and so did Ruth. The three men drove off in Gunnell's car, and Ruth then had Cussen, who had returned, driving her around trying to find Blakely. They turned up at Penn, where it seems Cussen might have beaten David up. But the latter fled to London, later the same day sending flowers to Ruth with a note: 'Sorry, darling. I love you.'

Things came to a head that fateful Easter weekend, with fatal consequences, for Ruth and David Blakely at least. Desmond Cussen, when the dust finally settled, lost the woman he loved, but he did at least retain his liberty.

Ant and Carole Findlater had been friends of Blakely for years, having met through the business of racing cars. The Findlaters lived in Tanza Road, Hampstead, a few minutes' walk from the Magdala Tavern. On the morning of 8 April, Good Friday, Blakely left Ruth at the flat in Egerton Gardens, having promised to take her for drinks at the Findlaters' that same evening. We must assume he had no intention of keeping to that arrangement, for that day he told the Findlaters he wanted to get away from her, and the Findlaters offered to let him stay in their flat for the rest of the weekend.

By 9.30 p.m. on Good Friday, when Ruth still hadn't heard from Blakely, she telephoned the Findlaters. She spoke to their nanny who told her no one was at home. She called again and this time spoke to Ant, who told her David was not there. She kept calling, and eventually the phone was taken off the hook. By now Ruth would have been angry, hurt, possibly hysterical and probably drunk. In any event, she called Cussen who agreed to drive her to Tanza Road, where she repeatedly rang the doorbell without reply. She then went into the street and broke the windows of Blakely's van. The police were called – this was at two o' clock on the Saturday morning – and by the time they arrived, Blakely and the Findlaters were in the street, remonstrating with Ruth. The action of the police was typical of the time: a conciliatory approach and a prayer that when they left things would calm down – as they did. But they had to be called again when Ruth started hitting the van windows once more. Finally she was persuaded to desist by Cussen, who drove her away before the police arrived a second time.

That Saturday Ruth made lunch for herself and Andy, after which Cussen took her back to Tanza Road where he dropped her off. At 4.30 p.m. she saw Blakely, the Findlaters and their nanny emerge from the flat and drive off. Cussen picked her up, and later drove her yet again to Tanza Road where the Findlaters were now hosting a party – with Blakely no doubt present and very much enjoying himself, drinking and womanising, in Ruth's mind at least. So Cussen took her home. Sunday she spent with Cussen, and that evening, at about 8.45 p.m., Blakely and Clive Gunnell drove the short distance to the Magdala Tavern for a quick drink and to buy some booze and cigarettes to take back to the flat. Blakely left his van outside, where Ruth would have had no problem finding it, having got there, she would say at her trial, by taxi. It was then only a matter of waiting ...

On 10 April, after her arrest, Ruth Ellis made a voluntary statement, in which, in her own words, or at least the words she would have used with some prompting by detectives, she gave her own account of events. Abridged, it read:

> David did not come home on Saturday. I intended to find him and shoot him. About eight o'clock this evening I put my son to bed and put the gun in my bag. A man had given it to me about three years ago as security for money. I took a taxi to Tanza Road and as I arrived David's car drove away from Findlaters' premises. I dismissed the taxi and walked down the road to the nearest pub, where I noticed David's car outside. I waited till he came out with a friend I knew as Clive. David went to his car. I was a little way from it. He turned and saw me and then turned away from me. I took the gun from my bag and shot him. He turned and ran a few steps round the car. I thought I had missed him so I fired again. He was still running and so I fired a third shot. I do not remember firing any more but I must have done.

Ruth Ellis was charged with the murder of David Blakely and appeared at the Old Bailey in June. Justice Havers presided. The trial would last only a day and a half. For the prosecution, Christmas Humphries said that in 1954 and 1955 Ellis had had 'simultaneous love affairs with David Blakely and a man named Cussens.' It seemed Blakely was trying to 'break off the connection' and Mrs Ellis was angry at the thought that he was leaving her, even though she had another lover. 'She therefore took a gun which she knew to be loaded and put it into her pocket. She said in her statement, "I intended to find David and shoot him." She found him and shot him dead by emptying the revolver at him. Four bullets went into his body, one hit a bystander and a sixth went we know not where.'

Ellis's counsel, Melford Stevenson, told the jury of ten men and two women, 'There is no question here but that this young woman shot this man. But we ask you return a verdict of manslaughter not of murder.' He said that jealousy worked upon her state of mind to such an extent as to cause provocation. 'Ruth Ellis's story is a long and painful one,' he said. 'She found herself in an emotional prison from which there seemed no escape.'

Desmond Cussen was obliged to testify. He admitted that Ellis was his lover 'for a short time'. 'I was terribly fond of her,' he said, understating the truth. He had seen bruises on her 'on several occasions.' He had sometimes helped to disguise her bruises with makeup.

Clive Gunnell gave his account of the shooting. 'I went round to the passenger seat of the van. The door was locked so I had to wait for David. While I was waiting I heard two bangs and a shout of "Clive!" I went round to the back and saw David lying on the floor and Ruth Ellis was firing the gun into his back.' A firearms expert said one of the shots had been discharged from a distance of under three inches.

There was no disputing that Ruth Ellis shot Blakely; no issues of identification or motive. She was seen to shoot him and was found at the scene holding the murder weapon. She admitted shooting him; she offered no excuse. The strategy of her defence was clear: they had to seek a verdict of manslaughter.

Melford Stevenson said: 'One of the ingredients in the offence [of murder] is what we call malice. The law provides that if a person, finding themselves in a position in which this unhappy young woman now is, has been subject of such emotional disturbance operating upon her mind she is for the time being unseated in her judgement, it is open to you to say the offence is not murder but manslaughter.

'This story leaves no doubt that David Blakely was a most unpleasant person. The fact stands out like a beacon, that this young man became an absolute necessity to her. However brutally he behaved, however much he spent on entertainments of his own, however much he consorted with other people, he ultimately came back to her and she always forgave him. She found herself in something like an emotional prison, guarded by him, from which there seemed no escape. She was driven by the suffering she had endured at his hands to do what she did. Her judgment for a time was unseated, her understanding was gone, and malice, an essential ingredient of murder, was absent.'

Testifying, Ellis gave a full and frank account of her marriage and divorce from George Ellis, the relationship she had with Blakely and Cussen, the rows, the abuse, the endless break-ups and reconciliation. 'He only hit me with his fists or hands and I bruise very easily,' she explained, as though mitigating on his behalf that he didn't do worse. She explained her actions over the Easter weekend, including her repeated visits to Tanza Road. 'Like a typically jealous woman I thought there was something going on I should know about.'

Prosecuting counsel had but one question in his cross-examination. 'When you fired that revolver at close range into the body of David Blakely, what did you intend to do?'

Ellis replied, 'It is obvious when I shot him I intended to kill him.'

Duncan Whittaker, a consultant psychologist, examined Ellis in Holloway. He found her sane, and said he was 'impressed by her equanimity'. She was in a situation and could not find a way out. Of her feelings on the day she shot Blakely he said at that time she both hated and loved him. 'If only he had spoken to her on the telephone her emotional tensions would have been released and the incident would not have occurred.'

The following morning, when the hearing resumed, Justice Havers said he had decided, 'after careful consideration to the defence's legal submissions', that there was insufficient material to support a verdict of manslaughter on the grounds of provocation. Melford Stevenson, for Ellis, said if that was the case it would not be appropriate for him to say anything more to the jury, since to do would be impossible without asking them to disregard his lordship's ruling. The judge then addressed the jury, saying, 'This is not a court of morals, this is a criminal court. You should not allow your judgement to be swayed or your minds to be prejudiced against the accused because she committed adultery, or because she was having two persons at different times as lovers. But I am bound to tell you there does not seem to be anything in her evidence which establishes any defence to the charge of murder. It is not a defence to prove she was a jealous woman.'

He went on, 'What is meant by malice is this: it means the formation of an intention to kill or do grievous bodily harm. Premeditation is unnecessary, but there must be intent. She said she was upset and wanted to kill Blakely. She had a revolver and went to Hampstead and shot him. "When I fired the revolver at close range I intended to kill him."'

He concluded, 'If you are satisfied she deliberately fired those shots at Blakely, and as a result he died, it is not open to you to find a verdict of not guilty. If you are in reasonable doubt whether at the time she intended to kill him, you can find her guilty of manslaughter.' (This would not be manslaughter on the grounds of provocation, as outlined above.) After just twenty-three minutes, the jury returned a guilty verdict for murder. His lordship, now wearing the black cap, sentenced her to death, saying, 'The jury's verdict was the only verdict possible.'

Ellis replied, simply, 'Thank you.'

Post-Trial

Although she refused to appeal against conviction, Ruth Ellis's legal team did so on her behalf, writing to the Home Secretary, Gwilym Lloyd George. Despite this, and pressure from the press and public, including a petition of 50,000 names and a personal plea from her father – 'I ask you as a distraught father to show her mercy' – there was no reprieve. On the eve of the execution, a crowd of 500 chanted Ellis's name outside Holloway Prison. Some people banged on the prison gates, demanding to see her, to pray with her. The following morning, William Connor, known better as Cassandra, the *Daily Mirror* columnist, wrote movingly of events:

> It's a fine day for hay-making. A fine day for fishing. A fine day for lolling in the sunshine. And if you feel that way, and I mourn to say that millions of you do, it's a fine day for a hanging. If you read this before nine o'clock this morning, the last dreadful obscene preparations for hanging Ruth Ellis will be moving to their fierce and sickening climax. The public hangman and his assistant will have slipped into the prison. They will have spied on her to form an 'impression' of her physique. A bag of sand will have been filled to the same weight as the condemned woman and will have been left hanging overnight to stretch the rope. The hands that place the hood over her head will not be our hands, but the guilt will belong to us as much as to the wretched executioner …

That Wednesday morning, 13 July, 1,000 people gathered outside Holloway Prison. Shortly before 9 a.m. Ruth Ellis was taken from her cell and hanged by Albert Pierrepoint, and buried within the prison walls, the last woman to be lawfully executed in Britain.

David Blakely was buried at Holy Trinity Church at Penn, Buckinghamshire. The inscription on his headstone, faded now, reads, 'He was great of heart, comely and courageous.' In 1971, Ruth Ellis's remains were disinterred and buried in St Mary's churchyard, Amersham, in the same county, not far away from the man she loved and murdered, her headstone bearing the name, Ruth Hornby, her father's original name. Her resting place is unidentifiable now; her son, Andrea, destroyed the headstone in 1982, shortly before he committed suicide.

In 2002 lawyers lodged an appeal on the grounds that Ellis had suffered from post-miscarriage depression, that her defence team was negligent and that she had been persuaded to commit the crime by Desmond Cussen. The appeal was heard in September 2003, when the court was asked to overturn the murder conviction for one of manslaughter on the grounds of provocation. It was also claimed that Ellis had suffered from 'battered woman syndrome' and that the judge's interpretation of the law was incorrect. The verdict, delivered in December, was that she had been 'properly convicted', that for provocation to succeed it had to be proved she was subjected to immediate violence. The court confirmed that, had the crime been committed today, the jury would have been asked to consider the defence of diminished responsibility, an option not open to the jury then.

Author's Verdict

At her trial Ruth Ellis pleaded not guilty to murder, then admitted the crime: 'It is obvious when I shot him I intended to kill him.' A defence of 'provocation' was hardly appropriate. Provocation implies instant, or almost instant, reaction to some act; it was hardly an 'instant reaction' to acquire a gun, track down her victim then shoot him at close range. She was driven by jealousy, stress and loss of control – not provocation in the sense that it was instant. Under the law of the day she was rightly convicted, and the death penalty was the only sentence the judge could pass.

But another option was open to the Home Secretary, who could have commuted her sentence to life imprisonment, and it is the verdict here that he should have. Her counsel was right in saying, 'Her judgment for a time was unseated', for hadn't she suffered through a long and protracted relationship with a selfish and violent individual, a man who beat her and displayed no loyalty to her, who failed to provide a sound, stable and loving existence? True, in some respects, they were as bad as each other: each was unfaithful; each of them drank excessively; neither possessed the desire or willpower to go their separate ways. This sad case typifies so-called domestic violence, where it seems to anyone outside the relationship that the easy thing for the couple to do is part, but to those inside it is somehow impossible. It also highlights the need for police officers, called to 'domestic' incidents, to deal with violent, often drunk, aggressors, and refrain from a conciliatory approach, a tactic now hopefully obsolete.

On 12 July, the day before she was due to hang, Ellis imparted certain information to her legal team on condition they would not use it to try and save her. She said that over the weekend of the murder she had been drinking with a man she would not name, and that it was from him she had acquired the gun. This man, she said, took her to Epping Forest and showed her how to use it. He, not a taxi as she had stated, was the means of conveying her to Hampstead to seek out and kill David Blakely. Can there be any doubt that the 'man' was Desmond Cussen, who, if it was, played some part in the crime, as an accessory at least? The information was passed to the Home Office but, being uncorroborated, it was not pursued.

Many murder cases have been covered in these pages, and we have seen those convicted pay the ultimate price for their crimes. By 1955, however, many people convicted of murder had their sentences commuted. Why not Ruth Ellis? Because she used a firearm, probably, and because she also shot a passer-by, albeit inadvertently, a factor the Home Secretary would have taken into account. Otherwise there doesn't seem any logic in exercising the death penalty in Ellis's case when others were spared. In 1958, Mary Wilson, of Felling, was convicted of murdering two husbands and probably murdered four, all by poisoning, but was not hanged. One final thought: if the circumstances in this case had been reversed – if Blakely had shot Ruth Ellis and been sentenced to hang – would there have been as much coverage in the media, and would so many have protested?

Bibliography

NEWSPAPERS & PERIODICALS

Airdrie and Coatbridge Advertiser
Barnsley Chronicle
Barnsley Independent
Bedfordshire Mercury and Huntingdon Express
Berkshire Chronicle
The Blether
Boston Guardian
Bristol Express and Devonshire News
Chard and Illminster News
Coatbridge Express
Daily Mirror
Dumfries and Galloway Standard and Advertiser
Durham County Advertiser
East Somerset Telegraph
Evening Standard (London)
Gallovidian
Glasgow Herald
Hertfordshire Advertiser and Times
Lincoln, Rutland and Stamford Mercury
Mexboro' and Swinton Times
Newcastle Daily Chronicle
Reading Observer
Somerset County Gazette
The Times
Watford Observer
Yorkshire Times and Express

BOOKS

Appleton, Arthur, *Mary Ann Cotton: Her Story and Trial* (Michael Joseph, 1973)

Ellis, John, *Diary of a Hangman* (True Crime Library, 1996)

Rattle, Alison and Vale, Allison, *Amelia Dyer: Angel Maker* (Andre Deutsch Ltd, 2007)

Weis, René, *Criminal Justice* (Penguin Books Ltd, 2001)